JOHN PAUL HANNA is an attorney and a partner in the firm of Thoits, Lehman & Hanna, Palo Alto, California. He is the author of *Teenagers and the Law* and editor and author of *Youth and the Law*. In 1967 the California Jaycees named him one of the "Five Outstanding Young Men" of the year; he was also designated "Man of the Year" by the City of Palo Alto. Mr. Hanna has served as chairman of the Youth and the Law Committee for the Northern Santa Clara County Community Council and, for three years, as chairman of the Continuing Education of the Bar for the Palo Alto Bar Association. He is a member of the Real Property Section of the American Bar Association and the California State Bar Association.

THE COMPLETE LAYMAN'S GUIDE TO THE LAW

John Paul Hanna

PRENTICE-HALL, INC., ENGLEWOOD CLIFFS, NEW JERSEY

Library of Congress Cataloging in Publication Data

Hanna, John Paul.
   The complete layman's guide to the law.

   1. Law—United States—Popular works.   I. Title.
KF387.H28   340'.0973   74-7490
ISBN 0-13-161232-8

PRENTICE-HALL INTERNATIONAL, INC. *(London)*
PRENTICE-HALL OF AUSTRALIA PTY., LTD. *(Sydney)*
PRENTICE-HALL OF CANADA, LTD. *(Toronto)*
PRENTICE -HALL OF INDIA PRIVATE LIMITED *(New Delhi)*
PRENTICE-HALL OF JAPAN, INC. *(Tokyo)*

Foreword

Most people make their way through the intricate web of laws crisscrossing their everyday life by simply applying their common sense and general knowledge. They deal with the law in a perfectly competent manner without considering themselves trained in the law. This is as it should be. If laws could not be dealt with on a practical basis, either they could not be enforced or society would grind to a halt.

Nevertheless, a more sophisticated awareness of our legal system is becoming increasingly important to the average citizen. Before he can use the law to order his affairs or settle his disputes, a person must have some idea of his legal rights and duties. Common sense may enable him to take care of some matters himself or may in other cases convince him to see a lawyer. But if all common sense and general knowledge of the law leave a person in doubt, a legal reference book written for the layman may well be useful in helping him decide what to do. It is always well to consult a lawyer in order to be certain. Neither common sense nor this book can adequately prepare the reader to handle legal problems on his own; for the reader to assume otherwise would only prove the aphorism: a little knowledge is a dangerous thing.

Beyond handling his personal legal problems, every citizen needs to know something about current law to fulfill his political responsibilities. Much of the legal structure described in this book is under continuing scrutiny by state legislatures and by Congress. Controversial changes in these laws are often proposed. Voters—participants in the political process—cannot very well understand or evaluate proposed changes unless they know something about the existing law.

There is need for the layman to become more acquainted with the functions of the courts. The court is his first bulwark of defense for legal rights. The more people know about them, the more inclined they are to support the judicial process. Because we have lost sight of the importance of the courts, I hope that this volume will cause people to become more interested in the courts and to take an active part in bringing about a more effective administration of justice—a job not only for lawyers and judges but for the public as well.

The honorable

TOM C. CLARK

Associate Justice of the
United States Supreme Court (Ret.)

Preface

The law is everybody's concern. Ignorance of the law is no excuse, but we all can't go to law school. Howard Hughes can afford a full-time lawyer, but not many others can. Legal advice is expensive. Joe Citizen needs a handy reference guide to help him know and understand the legal system. This book doesn't give legal advice, but it can point you in the right direction when you need guidance.

One word of caution: no book can give you up-to-date correct answers to all legal questions. There are too many laws and they change too fast. There is no substitute for a good lawyer. This book will help you to know when to seek a lawyer, how to find him, and how to get the most out of him. It will also help you settle some legal affairs without a lawyer. Either way, the time invested in reading it will be well spent. The table of contents, index, and general format are designed to make it easy to use as a reference. Put it next to your dictionary and encyclopedia.

JOHN PAUL HANNA

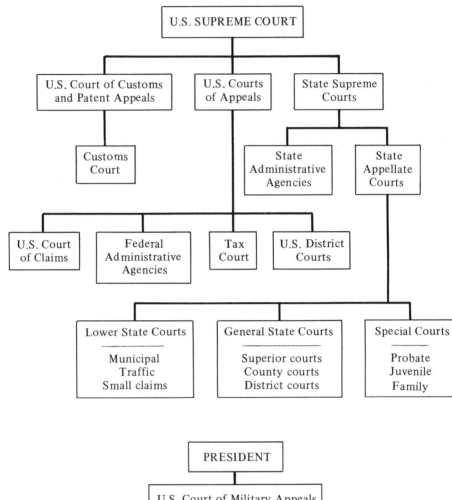

Outline of Contents

Contents

IV. CONTRACTS

V. LAWSUITS

VII. BUSINESS AND LABOR LAWS

VIII. CRIMINAL LAW AND PROCEDURE

IX. CIVIL WRONGS (TORTS)

X. REAL PROPERTY

XI. CONSTITUTIONAL LAW

XII. MOTOR VEHICLES

XIII. CIVIL RIGHTS

XIV. MISCELLANEOUS LAWS

I. Basic Legal System

A. WHERE DO LAWS COME FROM?

There are three major legal systems in the modern world: civil law, common law, and socialist law. Common law developed in England, probably starting around the eleventh century. Civil law predates the birth of Christ. The Roman Emperor Justinian, with the guidance of the Jurist, Tribonian, was responsible for the historically most significant expression of early civil law in the sixth century, referred to as the *Justinian Codes.* Civil law was greatly influenced by Canon Law of the Roman Catholic Church. Socialist law originated with the Bolshevik Revolution in Russia in the twentieth century. Under socialist law all law is an instrument of political, social, and economic policy.

The United States of America is basically a common-law jurisdiction. But law here has been extensively codified. Codes (statutes) are enacted by the legislative body of the state. Codes must conform to the constitution of the state and the nation. The existence of codes within a particular jurisdiction does not mean that jurisdiction is a civil-law jurisdiction, however. Under civil-law systems, as in force in Europe and Latin America, the codes supersede all prior law. Civil laws are supposed to be stated in simple nontechnical language that the ordinary citizen can understand, but this is seldom the case.

Only the legislature can make law in a civil-law jurisdiction.

In a civil-law system, the judges merely apply the law.

In a common-law jurisdiction, the judges apply, interpret, and occasionally make new law.

In a common-law jurisdiction, the adoption of codes does not abolish all prior law on the same subject. The codes merely restate, modify, or clarify it. At times a statute may be enacted to abolish the ruling of a specific court decision. Judges perform an important function in resolving conflicts with prior common law.

[1.2]   1.   Common-Law Tradition

The common law means that body of law as applied and modified by English courts and American courts. Most states have specifically adopted the common law, and when they have not, the courts have relied upon common-law decisions for precedents.

All states have adopted codes, many of them extensive, and most states have adopted some uniform national codes such as the Uniform Commercial Code.

Common-law rules may be expressly changed by the Constitution of the United States or the constitution of an individual state, or by state codes or federal laws.

The common-law system then, as it exists in this nation, consists of the prior decision (*case law*) of English and American courts, and the codifications of law that are based upon common-law decisions.

[1.3]   2.   American Tradition

Each state has its own system of law, largely derived from the common-law tradition, with frequent influence from the civil-law tradition (especially in those areas that were historically under French or Spanish influence).

Today the typical state has a comprehensive system of codes which restate the common law and cover most legal subjects. The typical state also has a system of courts which follow the common-law tradition in interpreting and applying statutes.

Federal law within the United States is based upon the Constitution of the United States, federal statutes, federal regulations, decisions of federal courts, and rulings of federal administrative agencies.

3.   Constitutional Law   [1.4]

Each state has its own constitution, modeled, more or less, after the Constitution of the United States. The typical state constitution describes the basic organization of the state government (including legislative, judicial, executive, and administrative departments of the government), sets up basic rights of citizens of the state, and makes provisions for amendment and for legislative enactments.

The Constitution of the United States, with the Bill of Rights and decisions of the Supreme Court, combine to encompass a unique system of constitutional law.

4.   Local Laws   [1.5]

Counties, cities, and other local governmental bodies make law by passing ordinances that regulate and control conduct and activities within their areas of concern.

B. HOW ARE LAWS ENFORCED?

[1.6]   1. Police

The police are the vanguard of the law-enforcement body. They are the tip of the iceberg projecting above the surface. On the average in this nation there is about one policeman for every five hundred persons.

[1.7]   2. District Attorney's Office

The district attorney's office is charged with the responsibility of enforcing the law by prosecuting those whose criminal activities are brought to its attention by the police or complaints of citizens.

[1.8]   3. Federal Law-Enforcement Officers

Federal agencies such as the Federal Bureau of Investigation, the Food and Drug Administration, and Customs and Immigration authorities enforce various federal laws.

[1.9]   4. Courts

At the federal level there are federal district courts—appellate courts to which appeals may be taken from decisions of district courts—and the Supreme Court. There are also tax courts, courts of claims, and other similar specialized courts. In addition there are military courts for trying cases involving military personnel.

At the state level there are trial courts having general jurisdiction to try most cases, and there are local courts, which go by various names, that have specialized jurisdiction to try certain types of cases. There are also state appellate courts and a state supreme court or highest court of appeals.

There are also juvenile courts which states have set up in order to treat youthful offenders differently from adults.

5. Prisons

We have various types of detention and correctional institutions in our nation, including county jails, state prisons, federal penitentiaries, and military stockades. About one person in one hundred in this nation will be sentenced, for some crime, to a correction or detention facility. The nature of these institutions varies from large maximum-security prisons to open camps, or farms.

6. Citizen Law Enforcement   [1.11]

Law observance by each and every citizen constitutes the broad base of the iceberg beneath the surface. Law enforcement in the final analysis depends upon law observance by the overwhelming majority of citizens. With only one policeman for every five hundred persons, the police cannot hope to cope with a major breakdown in law and order. The people themselves must uphold and respect the law at all levels, no matter what their personal stake may seem to be, and no matter what the issues happen to be. If each person observed only those laws that did not conflict with his personal moral code and felt free to violate all others, we would have no workable system of law and order in this nation without massive military intervention and supervision, or in short, a dictatorship. Thus those who advocate complete individual license are sowing the seeds of their own, and the society's, destruction.

C. HOW DO YOU KNOW WHAT THE LAW IS?

[1.12]   1. Research

The best place to read up on the law in general or to learn about a particular law is at a law library. You may find one at a local law school or go to the local county law library. The law librarian at the library will be available to help you find the law you are looking for, or to help find you a treatise on the general legal subject you are interested in. The librarian can also give you assistance in understanding case citations and abbreviations you will need to be able to read and understand in order to research a problem. If you want to engage in a substantial research project and do not have prior legal research training, the librarian can probably find a book on legal research for you.

[1.13]   2. Lawyers

If you have a complicated legal problem and cannot find the answer to it yourself, or are not inclined to a do-it-yourself approach to solving legal problems, then by all means consult a good lawyer and let him help you with the problem (see Part II).

II. Lawyers

A. TRAINING AND QUALIFICATION OF LAWYERS [2.1]

The vast majority of lawyers are graduates of law schools. Most states require a diploma from an *accredited* (approved) law school before allowing an attorney to practice. In addition, he has to pass a written examination. It is still possible in many states to get a law degree by studying on a part-time basis, either by going to night school or taking a correspondence course, followed by a successful State Bar Examination. This is the hard way to do it and not many people who try it this way ever make it. Some states still permit the age-old custom of "reading law." This means that a person wishing to become a lawyer gets a job as a clerk in a law office and studies the law while he is working for his employers. When he thinks he knows enough law, he takes the Bar Examination, and if he passes, he may be able to start practicing law. If you wish to become a lawyer, try to get into a good law school.

B. THE PRACTICE OF LAW

Most lawyers are *general practitioners.* This means that they tend to practice in many different fields of law. Lawyers generally are not as specialized as doctors. On the whole, lawyers handle more varied types of cases in their practice of law than doctors do in their practice of medicine. However there are very few lawyers who will handle all types of cases. Most of them will not attempt to handle patent law unless they are patent attorneys, and will not attempt to practice tax law, criminal law, workmen's compensation law, or administrative law unless they are experienced in those areas. Lawyers who practice alone (*sole practitioners*) by necessity have to practice in more areas than those who practice together in a partnership, an association, or a professional corporation. The larger the firm, the more highly specialized each of the members is likely to be. If you need a lawyer for a particular job, you're generally better off to have a specialist in that field. However, some people feel that they would rather have a general practitioner as a sort of family lawyer who can counsel them in many different types of matters. Hopefully he is fairly competent in several different areas of practice, and knows enough about them and their personal characteristics that he can give them valuable guidance and counseling of a highly personal nature over a period of time.

Although you are more likely to be able to find a specialist in a large firm, you may also find your legal business being shuffled off to some junior partner or associate, especially if you don't represent a potentially large fee to the firm. The junior partner or associate may be quite competent to handle your case, and may devote more time to it. If you don't feel comfortable with the lawyer assigned to handle your case, ask one of the partners in the firm to assign a different lawyer to handle it. Whether you choose a general practitioner or a specialist is a matter of personal choice.

Because lawyers cannot advertise or announce their specialty, how do you find out if a lawyer is specialized? You'll have to ask him when the time comes. You may also ask for a reference to a specialist when you're looking for a lawyer in the first place.

There are over a quarter of a million lawyers practicing in this nation. Most of them are sole practitioners. The average annual earnings for all lawyers is reportedly $10-20,000 per year. The nationwide average earnings for lawyers who practice in partnership is reportedly between $20-30,000 per year. The larger the firm, the more the senior partners tend to earn. On the average the legal profession is not as well paid as is the medical profession, but there are exceptional law firms and exceptional lawyers who make a great deal of money.

C. HOW TO CHOOSE A LAWYER [2.3]

If you need a lawyer and don't have one already, how do you pick one? First of all, the kind of lawyer you want depends upon the kind of case you have, or the kind of advice you are seeking. You want a lawyer who is experienced in handling the matter you are concerned about. If you don't have an immediate need, but want to establish a relationship with a family lawyer who can handle most legal problems that you expect to encounter, then you are probably more interested in the personality and reputation of the man than you are in his particular specialty. There are a number of ways to go about finding a lawyer. Lawyers who need to contact other lawyers outside their city or state usually consult a law directory. The most commonly used one is *Martindale-Hubbell.* This is available in most law libraries and law offices. It lists most but not all lawyers in private practice and gives biographies of varying length about each of them. It tells when they were born, where they went to law school, how long they have been in practice, and what professional associations they belong to. It may also say something about what kind of clients they represent, what books or articles they have written, and what scholastic honors they have received. The lawyers are also rated by the publisher on the basis of first-hand evaluations compiled from confidential questionnaires sent to lawyers in each community. The publisher uses two scales. The first consists of *A* (excellent), *B* (good), *C* (average), and *no rating* (usually in the case of lawyers recently admitted to practice). The second rates the lawyer's reputation for honesty, integrity, etc. He gets either a *V* (very high) or no rating. "A-V" is the highest rating. A lawyer has to have been in practice at least ten years to get an "A" rating. If a lawyer isn't rated or has a low rating, it does not necessarily mean you should not select him. It may mean he just is not that well known to a great many other lawyers. Also, not all lawyers who have A-V ratings are that good in comparison with other lawyers in their own community—some of them may have received their ratings many years ago and not have learned anything since. Once a man has an A-V rating, the publisher never seems to take it away from him, regardless of how incompetent he may have become. Generally if a lawyer has been in practice for about ten years and has a B-V or A-V rating, you can assume that he is pretty competent to handle your problems.

Another way you can find a lawyer is to ask a judge or several judges to recommend one. However judges (once they become judges) lose regular contact with most lawyers except those who specialize in trial work. Therefore if you want a good trial lawyer, a judge is a good person to ask, but if you want a lawyer to draft a will or a contract, or to advise you on a business deal, unless the judge practiced in the community himself for many years and is therefore acquainted with business lawyers and their abilities, he may not be the best person to ask.

Bankers, particularly bank trust officers, can generally make sound recommendations of lawyers who are experienced and capable of handling business law and trust law.

Experienced and reputable real estate brokers or title company officers can recommend lawyers who are competent to advise you in real estate matters. Accountants can advise you on tax lawyers and lawyers experienced in handling corporate and business affairs.

If you are interested in a good "all-round family lawyer," ask some of your friends who have been in the community for a long time whom they would recommend. Be careful about taking the opinion of just one or two people about a lawyer. Every lawyer has plenty of clients who will swear by him, as well as plenty of ex-clients who are more apt to swear at him.

Most local bar associations have a *Lawyers' Reference Service.* You may find this listed in the Yellow Pages under *Attorneys.* If you want an attorney who practices in a particular field of law, the service will give you the name or names of attorneys who specialize in that field. The best lawyers don't always have their names on the Lawyers' Reference list, however, because they may be so busy handling their own practices that they don't have time to take calls or referrals from Lawyers' Reference. The typical Lawyers' Reference Service plan allows you a brief (probably one half-hour) conference with an attorney for a nominal sum (maybe ten dollars). At the end of that time you and the lawyer make your own deal as to what he is going to do for you and how much it will cost. You can do this yourself by calling a lawyer you have selected after talking to some of the people listed above and telling him you would like a short appointment with him to discuss whether or not you can mutually agree upon his representing you and if so what the fee will be. Most lawyers will agree to such a conference and if you decide after a brief chat that you don't want that particular lawyer you can terminate the conference and leave without getting billed. If you decide you do want the lawyer to represent you, then you can discuss fees (see Section 2.4).

Most local areas have a *legal aid* program. This program is set up to furnish legal counsel for those too poor to afford it. Lawyers serve on the legal aid panel on a rotating basis. To qualify for legal aid you have to come within the income and asset requirements. If you have more than a certain amount of property or earn more than a certain amount per month, you won't qualify. If you do qualify, you can get a lawyer to handle your case for no fee. Certain kinds of cases (usually divorces and criminal cases) will not be handled by the legal aid program.

What lawyers should you avoid? Avoid lawyers with a shady reputation. The most flamboyant lawyers whom you read about most often in the newspapers are not always the best, although they may be the most notorious. If you work for a company, the firm that represents the company might be a good place to look for a lawyer. But don't ask the company counsel to handle your personal legal problem if he is the type of lawyer who spends most of his time on high-level corporate matters. If you belong to a union, the union may have an attorney, but he is probably a labor law specialist and not equipped to handle your particular problems.

Most lawyers who "double in brass" as politicians generally don't have time to handle your affairs efficiently and expeditiously.

It's a good idea to avoid using relatives for personal legal problems, particularly in-laws. You are generally better off to keep business and legal matters separate from family matters and avoid putting any unnecessary strain on your relationship with relatives.

Above all, pick an individual as a lawyer in whom you can place your trust and confidence—one you feel will always do his best to represent you, be fair to you, and act in a professional manner.

D. ATTORNEYS' FEES [2.4]

There are at least five different general categories of attorneys' fees: *Retainer* fees, *hourly* fees, *contingent* fees, *statutory* fees, and *court-awarded* fees. A *retainer* is a fee paid at the beginning of a case so that a lawyer will take the case. It may also be a regular monthly or annual fee paid by a business client to a lawyer so that the lawyer will be ready at all times to handle phone calls, routine correspondence, and routine legal questions. The amount of the retainer is set by agreement between the lawyer and the client.

Most legal work is done on an hourly basis. *Hourly* fees range from twenty dollars to one hundred dollars an hour or more, depending upon such factors as the geographical location, the size of the law firm, the age and experience of the lawyer, the ability of the client to pay, the nature of the matter being handled, the amount of time required, the difficulties involved, and the results obtained.

Contingent fees are generally used in accident and personal injury litigation. The lawyer agrees to handle a case on a percentage basis, and if there is no recovery, there is no fee. The typical contingent fee contract in a personal injury case will start at twenty-five to thirty percent for a case that is settled, and to up to forty or fifty percent for a case that is tried. Sometimes the percentage may include an appeal, and sometimes an appeal is handled separately. Other cases frequently handled on a contingent fee basis include: condemnation cases, will contests, collection matters, and workmen's compensation cases. The attorney may advance costs (court fees, investigator's fees, etc.), but the client is expected to pay them even if there is no recovery.

Statutory fees are those set by state statute. Most states set probate fees on a sliding scale according to the amount of dollars involved in the estate.

Court-awarded fees are those awarded to the prevailing party in a lawsuit. Occasionally the court may award a sizable fee in such a case, but usually court-awarded fees tend to be less than the average fees charged by attorneys who practice in that court, and if you are the prevailing party in a law suit and have attorney's fees awarded to you, it may be necessary for your lawyer to charge you a fee that is larger than the fee awarded by the court (although this is not always true).

The American Bar Association has established some guidelines for attorneys' fees. These guidelines include some of the following factors: the attorney's time involved, and the novelty or difficulty of the case; the fact that handling the matter might keep him from handling other business or cause him to lose other business; customary charges by other lawyers for similar services; the amount of money involved in the case and the benefit received by the client; the certainty or uncertainty of payment of the fee; the skill and experience of the lawyer.

The following are some examples of average fees that you might expect to pay for particular legal services:

Type of Service	*Average Total Fee*
Trial (daily charge)	$100-400
Power of Attorney	$ 25
Appeal	$750-2500
Bankruptcy	$300 and up
Adoption	$150-500
Felony	$500 plus trial
Misdemeanor	$150 plus trial
Uncontested divorce or dissolution of marriage	$150-1000
Contested divorce	$500 and up
Organization of corporation	$250-1000
Handling purchase or sale of home	$ 50-250
Simple will	$ 25-100

Type of Service	*Average Total Fee*
Complicated will or trust	$150-500
Partnership agreement	$250-1000
Purchase or sale of small retail business	$150-750 or 1% to 3% of sale price
Real estate title examination	$ 50 and up, depending on value
Employment contract	$ 50-200
Review of lease	$ 25-250
Drafting of lease	$ 50-500
Purchase or sale of real property	Hourly rate or 1% of sale price

For the most part you will find that lawyers are worth what you pay them and that you are better off to put a lawyer on an hourly basis after you have found a good one and have him bill you just for the amount of time that he spends on your case. Then the idea is to have him spend as little of his time as possible. That means that you plan your conferences with him in advance and don't waste time. Don't chat with him on the phone and don't spend a lot of time in the office making small talk. Stick to the point and let him do the talking unless he asks you for information. Don't try to tell him how to do his job, how to draft your letters or your documents, or how to negotiate settlements, etc. In most cases you are better off telling a lawyer what you want and letting him do the work than you are if you try to draft a document yourself and ask him to make changes and corrections. Most lawyers are experienced in doing things a certain way and it takes less time for thcm to dictate a document in the style to which they are accustomed, starting from scratch, than it does to work over a "home-made" document that the client has prepared.

Don't make the mistake of assuming that some former agreement that you used before in another case, or that a friend of yours used in another case, can be used again by you with just a few minor changes. Forms definitely do have their place, but it takes an experienced lawyer to know how and when to use forms.

Be sure you reach an early understanding with your lawyer as to what fees he will charge. Be sure that you stick to your part of the bargain and pay him his fee when you are billed. Most lawyers are very busy and will concentrate their time on matters they are handling for clients who pay them regularly. The "slow-pay" or "no-pay" clients get their papers shuffled to the bottom of the pile.

[2.5] **E.** WHAT TO DO WHEN YOU HAVE A PROBLEM WITH A LAWYER

Most (if not all) lawyers carry malpractice insurance. If the lawyer makes a mistake that damages you, you can make a claim against him and if the claim is good his insurance company will pay. If a lawyer's neglect hasn't cost you any money, but you still have a grievance against him, you can take it up with the grievance committee of the local bar association.

Lawyers are bound by very strict rules of practice called the *Canons of Ethics*. The Canons cover many different aspects of law practice.

Don't be critical of a lawyer for representing a notorious criminal defendant. Everyone is entitled to a defense and lawyers are charged with the duty of defending all persons accused of crime. It is not the lawyer's job to pass judgment on the client. That is reserved for the court or the jury.

It is generally unethical for a lawyer to give out press releases concerning a case he is working on currently. There are of course exceptions to this rule, but generally you will find that lawyers who seek publicity and attempt to try their cases in the newspapers are putting their own interests above those of their clients.

Lawyers are not allowed to solicit business and are prohibited from stirring up litigation. People who have been involved in accident cases who are approached by lawyers seeking the right to handle the case should report them to the local bar association (see Section 5.23).

Is it proper for lawyers to talk to the jurors about the case after the jury trial is over and the jurors have been discharged by the judge? Opinion differs on this question. Some lawyers believe that it is improper, and others believe that it is not improper for a lawyer to discuss the case with jurors and ask for their opinions, after they have been discharged.

Lawyers are charged with the duty of maintaining decorum in the courtroom, controlling their clients, and exhibiting an adequate amount of respect for the judge, for court personnel, for witnesses, and for other attorneys. Violation of these duties can subject the lawyer to a charge of contempt which may result in a fine, or even a jail sentence.

Lawyers are never supposed to represent conflicting interests. It's impossible for one lawyer to represent both husband and wife in a divorce or dissolution action. A lawyer by his very nature has to take sides, and should never try to be "neutral" toward two clients who do not have common interests. The conflict of interest rules also prevent a lawyer from taking a case against another client of his, or even against a former client without the consent of that client or former client. If a lawyer has represented one of two adversaries in the past, he can enter the case but only with the permission of both parties. He should reveal to the party he represents that he formerly represented the other party and he should get the other party's consent as well as the consent of his client to continue in the case.

It is improper for a lawyer who is employed by a company or a firm to offer legal advice to clients or customers of that firm. A lawyer on retainer to an accounting firm or a so-called "estate-planning" firm cannot ethically offer legal advice to accounting or "estate-planning" clients of such firms.

The lawyer has an obligation to keep confidential anything that passes between him and his client. The law protects this right by creating the *attorney-client privilege.* A client can prohibit his attorney from answering questions concerning communications between the client and the attorney in the event the attorney is subpoenaed into court and asked such questions. It is obvious that the confidential nature of communications between the attorney and the client must be protected if the attorney is going to be able to represent the client effectively. Only if the client knows that what he tells the attorney is confidential will he feel secure in revealing everything to the attorney.

III. Family Law

A. MARRIAGE

[3.1]

Marriage is a unique form of contract. It is more than a contract between two people. In a way, the state is a party to the contract. The law determines who can get married. The law defines how and when people can marry, and how and when they can separate or get divorced. The law has a great deal to say about marriage and related matters such as annulment, divorce, child custody, etc. If you are married or are planning to marry, this discussion of family law should be of interest.

1. Valid Marriage

[3.2]

For a marriage to be "legal," the law requires valid consent, the issuance of a *license*, and a marriage ceremony either before a minister or an officer licensed to perform marriages. A blood test may be required to get a *license.*

2. Consent

[3.3]

Like any other contract, *consent* is required as a basis for a valid marriage contract. A person who is mentally incompetent or a person under the influence of alcohol or drugs to such an extent that he is incapable of giving consent cannot be legally married until he becomes competent, sobers up, ends his "trip," or whatever.

[3.4]   3.   Age and Relationship Restrictions

There are age limits in all states, and they vary greatly. The laws of many states strangely discriminate in favor of girls by permitting them to marry at a younger age than boys. Presumably when these laws were passed it was felt that women were ready for marriage earlier than men. These laws are now being questioned on the ground that such discrimination against men is unconstitutional because it denies equal protection of the laws (see Section 11.10). In most states boys and girls can marry without consent of anyone else if they reach the minimum required age, and can marry even younger than that with parental consent. Some states have a third level which permits even younger children to marry with the consent both of their parents and of a court. A marriage can be annulled if either or both of the parties were too young and the proper consents were not obtained. There are laws prohibiting marriage of certain persons. Marriages between first cousins are permitted in some jurisdictions but a relationship closer than that makes marriage illegal in all jurisdictions. Certain in-laws cannot legally marry each other.

[3.5]   4.   Getting Married Out of State

Youngsters who journey to another state in order to get married because their own state will not allow the marriage until they are older may find that when they return, their state will not recognize the validity of their marriage (this is not the case in all states). However, if they go to the other state not just to get married and return but to live there for a time, then their marriage can become valid and entitled to recognition by any state, including the one from which they originally came. It probably doesn't make much sense for every state to have different laws about marriage, and hopefully someday they will all be the same. In the meantime there will be controversy and confusion surrounding the "quickie marriages" that occur when a couple goes to another state to avoid some legal technicality that prevents them from getting married in their own state.

5. Why Marriage? [3.6]

Why should people be that much concerned about whether a marriage is legal or not, or whether they are in fact married? Don't a lot of people live together as man and wife without any serious legal consequences? The answer is, as in most cases, "It depends." If a young couple does not plan to have children (or if they do have children and intend to put them up for adoption immediately), and if they make no demands upon each other for support, and make no claims upon each other's estate for property in the event of death, then much of the need for the legal bonds of matrimony is missing. More and more people today are living together as husband and wife without benefit of a legal marriage ceremony. Most states have abolished laws that prohibit a man and a woman from living together as husband and wife without being married. In most cases no real harm is done to society by such relationships and law-enforcement personnel have more important things to do than enforce such laws. The answer to the question "Why get married?", then, is that it depends upon what is important to you. Society has always recognized the inherent values in the stability, longevity, and harmony of the *family unit* which is based upon a husband and wife who are committed to each other and to their children. Marriage is a holy and revered institution to the overwhelming majority of the world's religions. Certain legal consequences flow from marriage that are advantageous, particularly to the wife and to the children. Income tax laws are designed to favor married persons over single persons. The same is true of estate and inheritance tax laws. The laws of succession make automatic provision for surviving spouses, but not for mistresses. Of greater importance is the fact that marriage is the accepted custom of our society in these times, and has been since the beginning of recorded history. Marriage is the beginning of a much deeper and more meaningful relationship than is possible for the couple that just decides to share bed and board for a time.

[3.7]   **6. Common-Law Marriage**

Many states still recognize the *common-law marriage*. In these states the couple that has been living together can "get married" by agreeing that they are man and wife and so representing themselves in their community. However, the failure to have their marriage validated by a clergyman or authorized official can result in loss of property rights for a survivor, as well as loss of social security and retirement benefits and certain federal or state aid that otherwise might be available to the surviving widow and children.

[3.8]   **7. Legal Obligation of Marriage**

Once married, the responsibilities of the marriage continue until it is legally dissolved. The husband has the legal obligation to support his wife and children. Because the trend in law is toward equality of the sexes, women may, in time, lose this privileged position. Both husband and wife have an obligation to support the children, although the wife's obligation is secondary to that of the husband. The husband in most states does not have the right to his wife's earnings. Must the wife ever support the husband? The answer is *yes*, under certain conditions. To give one example: in some states, when the husband has no property and is unable to support himself, the wife must support him. What about liability of the wife for debts of the husband and vice versa? The rules here are very complex and vary greatly from state to state. They also vary depending upon what kind of property is involved—separate property, community property, joint tenancy property, tenancy by the entirety, etc. (see Sections 6.45 - 6.52). If you are faced with a question about the responsibility of one spouse for the debts of the other spouse, you might be able to find the answer by reading the pertinent sections of your state's Civil Code, or the code which may go by a different name, but which covers family property law. If you don't find the answer there, you will have to ask a lawyer.

B. DIVORCE OR DISSOLUTION

1. What is Divorce? [3.9]

Divorce is legal termination of the marriage contract by the state.

2. Divorce under Fault Requirement [3.10]

Some states still cling to the rule that a divorce must be based upon *fault*. Therefore, a divorce cannot be obtained in such a state unless one party is proved to be *at fault*. If both parties (or neither party) are at fault, some states will not grant a divorce.

[3.11] ### 3. Dissolution

Recent laws in some states permit dissolution of marriages based on *irreconcilable differences* between the parties. In such states you need not prove that anyone is *at fault* in order to get a divorce. The marriage is *dissolved* and a *decree of dissolution* is received, rather than a *divorce*.

[3.12] ### 4. State Policy

Until recently the policy of most states was to make it difficult to get divorces because of the state's interest in preserving marriages. However, with the increasing divorce rate, there has been a relaxation in the rules and now divorces are easier than ever to get.

[3.13] ### 5. Waiting Period

Most states will require a waiting period, however, between filing for and obtaining a divorce.

[3.14] ### 6. Who Gets the Divorce?

Most divorces are *amicable*, in the sense that one party (usually the wife) gets the divorce and the other party does not even show up at the hearing, or is represented only by his attorney. It is customary for the wife to get the divorce, in most situations, because in the past it was thought that a woman who was divorced by her husband was somehow stigmatized, and that the same stigma did not apply to a man who had been divorced by his wife. This custom is of little validity today.

7. Grounds [3.15]

Each state has established certain *grounds* for divorce. The most common grounds are *cruelty, adultery, desertion,* or *abandonment.* Other fairly common grounds include *alcoholism, drug addiction, imprisonment for a felony, insanity, incapacity* or *impotency,* and *nonsupport* or *willful neglect.* Altogether there are nearly fifty different grounds for divorce. Recent legislation in some states has established *irreconcilable differences* or *incompatibility* as grounds for divorce or dissolution of the marriage (see Section 3.11).

Cruelty seems to be the most commonly used ground. Cruelty can be either mental or physical. It can range from painful physical beatings to such things as a wife criticizing her husband in front of his friends or vice versa. In between it can include such things as refusal to maintain personal cleanliness; refusal to perform household duties; continual unjustifiable nagging; statements of lack of love for spouse; statements of love for another person; indifference, coldness, or denial of sexual relations or insistence upon abnormal sexual practices. In short, cruelty is a very easy charge to prove. But proving it is not enough. The spouse charging cruelty must also testify, under oath, that the alleged cruel acts made him or her unhappy, and miserable, and as a result a divorce is desired. One of the reasons cruelty is the most often-used ground for divorce is that instances of cruelty, or conduct constituting cruelty, can be found in almost any marriage. This is particularly true in marriages in which other grounds for a divorce exist such as drug addiction, alcoholism, adultery, etc. The divorce is less "messy" and attracts less public attention if cruelty is charged than if adultery or bigamy or alcoholism, etc., were charged. Once in awhile, however, in a state where the degree of fault and freedom from fault determines how the marital property will be divided by the court, a greedy and vindictive spouse will "get the goods" on the other spouse by hiring a private detective, making movies, or gathering some other form of "hard evidence" that can be used in a divorce action based on adultery, or can be used to pressure the other spouse into a lopsided property settlement agreement.

[3.16]   **8.   Divorce Procedure**

Certain steps must be followed in order to begin a divorce action. The steps in the procedure vary from state to state, and the names of the various steps are sometimes different, but generally the overall framework is quite similar.

[3.17]   *a.   COMPLAINT OR PETITION*

Once the husband and wife, or either of them, have decided that they must have a divorce, the initial step in the legal proceedings is to file a *complaint*, or *petition.* Sometimes the parties reach agreement on procedural matters and the husband or the wife will get an attorney and ask him to file a complaint or petition. Does it matter who files the complaint, or who files first if both parties are seeking a divorce? Some attorneys and some clients feel there is a psychological advantage in being the first to file, particularly where the question of division of the property, payment of alimony, child support, and child custody will be debated. There is slight procedural advantage if a contested case comes to trial because the party filing first will be the plaintiff, and will get to present his or her case first.

The complaint or petition will recite the marriage facts, which include the names of the parties, the date and place of marriage, length of the marriage, and the alleged grounds for divorce or dissolution. The facts upon which the grounds are based need not be alleged in detail, and usually are stated as mere conclusions, such as: "defendant has treated plaintiff with extreme cruelty." The divorce complaint, like other complaints, must be filed with the court. A summons must be issued by the clerk. A copy of the summons and complaint must be served upon the other spouse. Sometimes the other spouse will have an attorney who will accept service. Once the summons and complaint have been served, the spouse receiving service has a certain number of days (usually thirty) within which to file an answer or other *responsive pleading* to the complaint.

In those states having the *no-fault* system and providing for dissolution of marriage, the petition for dissolution is a simple form that either spouse can fill in and file, without aid of an attorney. In such cases the other spouse may then file another simple form called a *response*. The clerk of the court provides these forms and can instruct on how to file them.

b.   RESTRAINING ORDER   [3.18]

Occasionally a wife may feel that her husband's conduct has become unbearable, and she may seek an order from the court restraining him from molesting her, or the children, or ordering him to keep away from the family home pending a hearing. Such a restraining order is temporary in nature, generally lasting only a few days. It can be obtained by the wife upon a showing (made usually by a sworn affidavit) of justifiable fear of physical harm based on the husband's actions or threats.

[3.19]

c. TEMPORARY SUPPORT

A wife may occasionally be able to obtain an order from the court requiring the husband to furnish her with temporary support, generally in the form of monthly payments, pending a hearing to determine her monetary needs and her husband's ability to pay. To obtain such an order for temporary support the wife would have to make a showing (by an affidavit) that she had an immediate need for funds, that funds were otherwise unavailable, and that her husband would not provide them to her unless ordered to do so by the court. Occasionally an order for temporary support will be accompanied by an order for the husband to pay something to the wife for attorneys' fees.

[3.20]

d. UNCONTESTED DIVORCE

Where the parties have agreed beforehand on who will take the divorce and what the terms of the property settlement and support agreements will be, then it is not necessary for the spouse that is served with a copy of the summons and complaint to file an answer. In such a situation they intend that the wife (if she is the one to file) will take the divorce in an uncontested hearing, and the property settlement agreement and support agreement worked out between the two parties or their attorneys will be incorporated into the divorce decree. Where the divorce is uncontested, the wife (or husband if he is getting the divorce) will appear in court with an attorney at the time of the hearing and present evidence upon which the divorce action is based. If the grounds alleged for the divorce are *cruelty*, then the wife will testify that the husband has done certain things or said certain things to her which constitute mental or physical cruelty, and will state that these have made her unhappy and that she wishes the marriage terminated. Her statement will then be *corroborated* by another witness who must testify under oath to some specific act of cruelty of the husband which has been witnessed and which made the wife unhappy. The wife will also have to establish the minimum required residency within the jurisdiction of the court. Residence requirements run anywhere from six weeks to three years.

After the wife and her corroborating witness have testified, if the evidence is sufficient and a proper showing has been made, the court will issue its judgment of divorce.

In states allowing dissolution under the no-fault system, the procedure is shorter. No testimony is given about fault. The party wanting the divorce states that irreconcilable differences have arisen in the marriage and asks the judge for an order of dissolution of the marriage, which is granted without question. It is even possible now in some jurisdictions to obtain a dissolution entirely by mail through the use of affidavits.

e.   CONTESTED DIVORCE   [3.21]

Where the husband and wife cannot agree on a divorce, or on the terms for divorce, then the matter will be contested. When the first one files and serves summons and complaint upon the other one, the spouse receiving summons and complaint can file either an answer or a cross-complaint. If one spouse wants the divorce and the other does not, an answer would be filed. The answer would deny the allegations of the complaint and would ask that the marriage not be terminated. If both spouses want a divorce but cannot agree on the terms, then the first spouse to be served would file an answer and a cross-complaint. The answer would deny the allegations of the complaint and allege that the complaining spouse was not entitled to a divorce. The cross-complaint would state the grounds which the second spouse claims existed in his or her favor and would seek a divorce. The cross-complaint for divorce would contain the same type of allegations as the complaint for divorce, only with the parties being reversed.

An answer would consist of a denial of the allegations of the complaint. In effect, the spouse being accused of cruelty, adultery, drunkenness, etc., would deny the alleged acts of cruelty, adultery, drunkenness, etc. The answer might also raise certain other defenses. One of these would be *forgiveness* or *condonation*. If a husband is accused of physically beating his wife, or of committing adultery, he may defend against her divorce action by claiming that she condoned the offense by forgiving him and continuing to live with him after the beating or the adultery. Once the wife has discovered the adultery, she would have to somehow separate herself from her husband and have no further intercourse with him pending the divorce action. If she forgives him, continues to live and have intercourse with him, then she cannot get a divorce for that specific act. If the husband repeated the adultery, she could then obtain a divorce based upon the new grounds.

f. COLLUSION

[3.22]

Occasionally, a husband and wife may try to get a divorce in a state where under the law they really don't have grounds for divorce. If the husband agreed to let the wife present false testimony concerning his cruelty toward her, this would be *collusion*, and if the court learned of it, it would not grant the divorce. The same would be true if the husband and wife agreed that one of them should commit adultery. In some states adultery was for many years the only grounds for a divorce, and when husband and wife decided they wanted a divorce, one of them would agree to commit adultery so the other would have grounds for the divorce. Such *connivance*, if discovered by the court, will prevent the parties from obtaining a divorce.

g. RECRIMINATION

[3.23]

In some areas courts allow the defense of *recrimination*. If the wife sues the husband and proves that he is a habitual drunkard, and he cross-complains and proves the same about her, then in jurisdictions permitting this defense, neither spouse can get a divorce. A modification of this rule permits the spouse who is the *least to blame* to get a divorce in situations in which recrimination exists.

h. WIFE PREGNANT
AT TIME OF MARRIAGE

[3.24]

Occasionally a husband may seek a divorce on the grounds that his wife was pregnant by another man when he married her. However, if she can prove that he knew this before they were married, he may not be able to get the divorce.

[3.25]
i. PROVOCATION AS A DEFENSE

A wife who provoked her husband into beating her would be barred from obtaining a divorce on grounds of physical cruelty.

[3.26]
j. DELAY IN SEEKING DIVORCE

An unreasonably lengthy delay in suing for a divorce may prevent the party seeking the divorce from getting it, if the acts constituting the grounds for divorce happened a long time ago.

[3.27]
k. FAILURE TO PROVE GROUNDS

If only one party wants the divorce, and he or she sues for it but the other party defends against it and proves that grounds do not really exist, then a divorce will not be granted.

[3.28]
l. SETTLEMENT

Sometimes a complaint and a cross-complaint for divorce will be filed, and the parties will settle the matter before it comes to trial, *stipulating* that either the complaint or the cross-complaint be dismissed and that the party who is to obtain the divorce will obtain an uncontested divorce that will incorporate the terms of a property settlement and support agreement to be worked out beforehand. Sometimes the first party to be served with a summons and complaint will file a cross-complaint just for negotiating purposes, intending all along to dismiss the cross-complaint after it has served its purpose in helping to force the other spouse to agree to reasonable settlement terms.

9. Interlocutory Decree of Divorce [3.29]

After the hearing (contested or uncontested), the usual procedure is for the court to grant an *interlocutory decree* of divorce. In effect this decree says that grounds for divorce have been established and that one or both of the parties are entitled to a divorce. The laws of most states provide for an interim waiting period before a divorce can become final. The purpose of this is to provide an opportunity for reconciliation because of the interest of the state in seeing marriages continue, if possible. The interlocutory decree varies in length from state to state but is usually a period of several months. A decree may order property divided between the parties, may award custody of the minor children to one or the other or both of the parties, and may order one party to pay alimony to the other.

10. Final Divorce [3.30]

After the period of the interlocutory decree has passed, either party may ask the court that the divorce be made final. In order to obtain a final divorce, the party applying for it must be able to state that there has been no reconciliation of the parties during the period of the interlocutory divorce. Once the final divorce decree is issued, the marriage is really terminated. The final decree will finalize any temporary property division, support, or alimony orders that were made at the time of the interlocutory decree. It will also enable either party to marry again.

11. "Quickie" Divorces [3.31]

For years some states have been notorious for the difficulties they present to people wanting to obtain divorces, while others have been Meccas for divorce trade. Some of the Mexican border towns used to do a flourishing divorce business. People who seek "quickie" divorces are generally those who have an immediate problem such as a pregnant mistress. There are certain legal risks involved in obtaining a quickie divorce. Some states just plain don't recognize them. The key to the validity of any divorce is satisfying some reasonable residency requirement, and doing so with some degree of *good faith*. Six week Nevada divorces are generally accepted if both parties consent, but the residency requirement is a hard and fast one. Few states will accept twenty-four-hour Mexican or Caribbean divorces as being valid. On the other hand, an invalid quickie divorce isn't really a problem unless you have either children or substantial and complex property interests. If both parties agree to a quickie divorce, neither one can later argue that the divorce was invalid in an attempt to get some advantage over the other. However, if either party dies after a quickie divorce, complicated problems of inheritance may arise, particularly if one of the parties had remarried but hadn't prepared a new will, and left children surviving from the first marriage. *Bigamy* normally isn't a problem because district attorneys have more important things to do than to prosecute people who get married after a quickie divorce. The usual procedure for a quickie divorce is to have one party appear in person in Mexico (or wherever the divorce is being obtained) while the other party is represented by local counsel. This type of divorce is not worth obtaining unless both spouses agree to it. The cost is probably no less than a regular divorce, and may be more because two sets of lawyers may be involved, one set to handle the local matters, such as property settlement, and the other set to handle the out-of-state divorce proceedings. The client should find out in advance what the cost will be.

12. Reconciliation Court

[3.32]

Some states have established a system of *reconciliation courts*. In these courts either party may bring an action which requires both parties to appear before the court to seek its help in reconciling their differences in order to save the marriage. Such a procedure is sometimes valuable where one party wants a divorce but the other does not and feels that the marriage can be saved.

[3.33]

13. Property Settlement

In any divorce, questions arise concerning the division of property. In some states the court has the discretion in a divorce case to divide the property in such a way so as to give more than half of the property to one spouse. In many cases this results in the wife getting more than half of the property, particularly where the husband is the "bad guy" in the divorce action. However, the more enlightened view of divorce proceedings is that neither party should be penalized, and that the property should be more or less divided equally. In states (such as California) having the no-fault divorce rule, the court has to divide the community property equally (unless one of the parties has fraudulently tried to hide some assets). There is some property the court may not have any power to divide. For example, in community property states, the court has no power to divide or award separate property belonging to one of the spouses. In such a case that spouse keeps his or her separate property and the court can only divide the community property. In such an event you will find the parties arguing over what is community property and what is separate property.

Such arguments raise very complex legal and factual questions which can only be resolved with the help of a competent attorney and some records. Once in a while you find a husband who wants to be tricky and hide some of his assets so that neither the court nor his wife will know of their existence. This may work for him in the divorce, but if his wife finds out afterward that he held out on her, she can easily come back into court and get her share of that property. The husband could find himself in very hot water if he has perjured himself in declaring his assets by failing to include some substantial items.

A key document in any divorce situation is the *property settlement agreement.* This is an agreement worked out between the two parties (or their lawyers) which lists all of the property and divides the assets between them. The property settlement agreement can be quite lengthy and involved. It is usually incorporated into the interlocutory decree of divorce, and later, into final decree. If the couple doesn't have much property aside from their home, the home may have to be sold in order to divide the proceeds. An alternative to this is for the wife to give a note to the husband which is secured by deed of trust on the home property. The note will be for the amount of the husband's half of the value of the home. The agreement would provide that the wife could continue to live in the home, but that if she tried to sell, exchange, or refinance the house, the note to her husband would then become due.

If the only asset were a family business, or stock in a closely held corporation, the same thing could be done, with the husband keeping the stock or the business, but giving his wife a note, payable upon sale of the stock or business, or payable over a period of time out of the income from the business.

14. Alimony [3.34]

Alimony is what the court orders one spouse (usually the husband) to pay to the other spouse after the divorce (interlocutory). Why should anyone be entitled to alimony? The theory is that one party (usually the wife) has been maintained in a certain style of living, is incapable of earning enough money to continue that style of living, and that rather than have that person become a welfare case, the spouse should continue to support him or her. The law imposes a duty upon the husband to continue to provide his ex-wife with a standard of living reasonably close to that to which she had become accustomed during the marriage. Occasionally this works the other way and a wife may be ordered to pay alimony to a husband, but it doesn't happen very often. The longer the marriage has lasted, the more alimony a wife is entitled to. If the marriage has lasted less than a year, then it is questionable whether a court would award any alimony to a wife, except perhaps some sort of temporary support until she could get a job. If husband and wife are equally capable of earning a living and each has about the same earning power, there is no need for alimony. However, if the wife is unable to work because she has to stay home and take care of young children, then the court might award alimony to her in addition to child support for the children, even though theoretically she might be able to go out and earn as much as the husband. When the children become older and her presence isn't required fulltime in the home, then the alimony could be reduced or eliminated, and the wife would have to go to work. The age of the wife, and the fact that she may be beyond a reasonable working or training age, should be considered. Alimony does not last forever. It always terminates when the wife dies or remarries. It sometimes terminates if the husband dies. (Otherwise it would be a continuing obligation of his estate, to the extent of the assets in his estate.) The amount of the alimony is measured not only by the length of the marriage but also by the needs of the wife and by the husband's ability to pay. As a rule of thumb, courts will split the net take-home pay of the husband down the middle, awarding half to the husband, and the other half to the wife. If the wife has custody of the children, the combined alimony and child-support payments will usually be about half of the total family income (or a little more, if there are many children). If both husband and wife work, the results are similar, only the combined family income is divided in half. If the husband earns a large amount of money, the wife may get enough to maintain her standard of living, but less than half. In some cases the parties may agree on a *lump-sum* settlement of alimony. The wife gets a single large payment and waives all future alimony. This gets into complicated legal and tax questions that should be resolved by competent counsel.

A husband becomes *in arrears* when he fails to make an alimony payment. In this event, the wife can go back into court and ask the court to order the husband to make the payments, or be found in *contempt of court,* subject to either fine or jail sentence. Most states have adopted the *Uniform Reciprocal Support Law* which provides that each state will recognize divorce decrees or alimony awards of all other states, and that the states will cooperate in requiring alimony payments to be made. This is to prevent a husband from escaping his alimony obligations by moving to another state. Alimony payments made by the husband to the wife are tax-deductible. This means the husband deducts them from his income before figuring his tax. The wife includes the payments as income in her tax return. In deciding how much alimony to pay, tax considerations often enter in.

Alimony payments may be increased or decreased by court order, based on a change in circumstances (husband starts earning more money, or husband loses job).

15. Child Support [3.35]

If the parties who are divorced do not agree upon the amount of child support, the court will decide the matter. The amount of child support can vary greatly. This seems illogical, because one child ought to cost as much to support as the next. However, the courts take into consideration the style of living to which the child "had become accustomed." This means that rich kids get more child support than poor kids. Child-support payments are not tax-deductible by the husband. They are not included as income to the wife. A lot of jockeying for position goes on between husband and wife where substantial income is involved in deciding how much of the "total support package" should be alimony, and how much should be child support. The ideal thing for both parties would be to figure it all different ways and settle on the way that saves the most total income taxes for both parties. There are some tricky rules that determine whether payments agreed upon are alimony or child support. This is where professional help from lawyers and accountants can be of considerable benefit.

Child support can include regular monthly payments of a certain amount per child, plus the requirement to pay extraordinary medical or educational expenses. Child support continues until the child reaches majority, gets married, or becomes emancipated (see Section 3.59). Also, in deciding how much alimony and how much child support to pay, the husband will take into consideration the ages of the children, the age of his wife, and the chances of her marrying again. Naturally, if she is likely to remarry, he would want the alimony to be high and the child support low. If she does remarry he then only has to continue making the lower child-support payments. If he guesses wrong and she does not remarry, then he could be stuck for large alimony payments for a long time, but of course they are tax-deductible so there would be an offsetting advantage.

[3.36]   16. Marital Finances

Sometimes questions arise about whether one spouse is liable for the debts or obligations of another spouse. Unfortunately there are no simple answers to such questions. The type of debt or obligation first has to be considered as well as the circumstances under which it arose. Then the marital status of the parties at the time it arose and at the time the payment is being sought must be considered. Finally, the source from which payment is being sought must be examined. The separate property of the wife may not be reachable by creditors having claims against the husband.

Is the husband always liable for debts incurred by his wife, such as charge account balances, etc.? Under ordinary circumstances, he would be liable for his wife's charges. However, if the husband notified a certain store that his wife was not to be allowed to charge anything there anymore, and that if she did he would not pay the bill, the store might find it difficult to collect from the husband if they ignored him and continued to let his wife charge. Charge accounts should be closed when a divorce is obtained. Each party can then open a new account in his or her own name.

In any divorce situation the total debts and obligations of the family have to be taken into consideration and unless the parties work out the details in a property settlement agreement, the court will generally order certain debts to be paid by each of the parties.

17. Change of Name   [3.37]

Sometimes a woman getting a divorce wants to revert to her maiden name. This is easily done by including in the petition filed with the court a request that the maiden name be restored. The divorce decree will include an order that the woman's maiden name be restored to her and from then on she can use her former name.

If the wife gets custody of the children, and subsequently remarries, can she change the names of the children to the name of her new husband? In most cases she would need to petition the court for permission to do this and would have to notify the father. The father would have the right to appear and object. If the child wanted to change his name, he could have a temporary guardian appointed to petition the court to allow a name change.

18. Cost of Divorce   [3.38]

There is no getting around it, divorce is expensive. The amount of money used up in attorneys' fees depends upon how cooperative the parties are during negotiations. The least expensive divorce, with only one attorney involved, is probably going to cost no less than $250. With two attorneys involved, and some negotiating back and forth, even if the case is settled without a court fight, the total attorneys' fees will run between $500 and $1000. If the matter is contested in court, or if substantial amounts of property are involved, the fees can go much, much higher. After the divorce both parties will find it necessary to cut back on their prior standard of living because the same amount of money just doesn't go as far between two households. The husband pays attorney fees for both sides, unless the wife has sufficient income of her own to pay her counsel fees.

[3.39] C. ANNULMENT

Where no valid marriage ever existed because of some defect that was present at the time of the marriage, the marriage may be *annulled*. Annulment means the dissolution of a marriage by court order. Only if there was something legally wrong with the marriage at its inception, can it be annulled.

[3.40]   1.   Grounds

The grounds for annulment are specified by state law. Grounds for annulment include *minority* (the party seeking annulment was under the age of consent); *unsound mind* or physical *incapacity* of either party; *force* or *fraud* in obtaining consent; *concealment of pregnancy*; *impotence or sterility* of one of the parties that existed before but was discovered by the other party after marriage; and a secret determination to refuse sexual intercourse. There are other grounds, but these are the ones most frequently used. Some marriages are void from the beginning. Examples would be *incestuous* and *bigamous* marriages.

2. Procedure

[3.41]

An annulment is obtained by the party wanting it filing a petition or complaint for annulment in the appropriate court. Grounds for annulment must be set forth in the complaint, and a copy must be served on the other party. At the hearing, evidence must be presented of the grounds upon which the complaint for annulment is based. The action may be contested by the other party, or the other party can file a cross-complaint. The action can be defended by one spouse on the grounds that *cohabitation* of the two took place after the spouse seeking annulment arrived at the age of consent, acquired knowledge of the alleged fraud, or became free from the force or duress used, etc. Statutes of limitation apply to an annulment action. The person seeking an annulment who has been married for any length of time would have to check the applicable statute of limitations to see whether the annulment could still be sought.

3. Distinguished from Divorce

[3.42]

The *corroboration of testimony* and *residency requirements* of divorce generally are not required for annulment. Persons other than the two spouses can bring action for annulment (for example, the parents of one). The court lacks power to grant permanent alimony when a marriage is annulled.

D. SEPARATION

Instead of bringing an action for divorce, a spouse may bring an action for *separate maintenance* in some states. The grounds upon which an action for separate maintenance may be based are the same as the grounds for divorce. A wife seeking separate maintenance may also obtain custody of the children, alimony from the husband, and the division of property. After a separate maintenance action, the parties remain married, and neither one can remarry (unless a divorce is obtained). The procedure for obtaining a decree of separate maintenance is similar to the procedure for obtaining a divorce decree. The defenses that can be raised in a divorce action can also be raised in a separate maintenance action.

[3.44] **E.** CUSTODY

Parents are natural guardians of their children and are entitled to *custody* and control. If the child is illegitimate, the mother is entitled to custody, but if she refuses it, the father may obtain custody if he petitions the court and can show that he is able to provide a home for the child. In case of dispute between the father and mother as to who is entitled to custody, the court has to decide based upon the *best interests of the child*. Many courts will give custody to the mother, in a custody fight, if the child is young. If the children are old enough to form intelligent preferences, the court may consider these, other things being equal. Once custody has been awarded, it may be changed at any time thereafter by order of the court, if conditions have been changed. After the death of one parent, the other parent is then entitled to custody, unless he or she is *unfit*. In order for a parent to be unfit for custody, it must be shown that the parent has mental, moral, or physical limitations sufficient to endanger the permanent health or welfare of the minor. No matter which parent has custody, the other parent is entitled to reasonable visitation rights. Normally children cannot be moved permanently out of the state without court permission unless both parents agree. Custody can be changed from one spouse to the other, based on a change in circumstances, or based on the expressed desire of the child.

F. BIRTH CONTROL; ARTIFICIAL INSEMINATION [3.45]

Laws against the use of such birth control devices as drugs (the "pill") or instruments (such as the diaphragm) to prevent conception are unconstitutional. A pregnant woman has a constitutional right to an abortion during early pregnancy (see Section 8.6). The consent of both prospective parents is necessary for a wife to undergo *artificial insemination* in some states. The child will be treated as a naturally conceived child, under the law.

G. ADOPTION

Adoption is the legal creation of a parent-child relationship. An adopted child has the same legal rights that a natural child has. In order to qualify for adoption, the adopting parent must be an adult and must show that he can provide an adequate home and a healthy environment for the child. There are other requirements that vary from one state to another and statutes must be consulted. Consent of the natural parents (or of the mother, in the case of an illegitimate child) is required. Once the child is adopted, the natural parents no longer bear any responsibility or have any claim on the adopted child. Adoption results in a complete substitution of parents.

[3.47]   ## 1.   Procedure

Adoption procedures are set forth in state statutes. Basically the statutes provide that the person wishing to adopt the child must petition the proper court. Usually some state agency will investigate the situation to determine whether or not the petitioner can qualify for adoption. The investigation may include an examination of the petitioner, the child, and its parents. After proper notice to all parties, the court will hear the matter, and if everything is in order, will grant a petition for adoption. Most states provide for a temporary period of six months after which the adoption can be made permanent, provided things have worked out.

There are generally two types of adoption, *direct* and *agency* adoption.

[3.48]   ## 2.   Direct Adoption

Direct adoption, or *private adoption*, occurs when the child is placed directly with the adopting parents by the natural parent, without any agency being involved. Where this procedure is permitted by state law, the way it usually happens is this: A couple who desires to adopt a child may ask their minister, lawyer, or doctor if he knows of an adoption situation. He may have heard of a mother who wants to put up her child for adoption. The lawyer will arrange an interview with the natural parent or parents of the child. He will also interview the couple wanting to adopt the child. If all parties agree, the natural parent or parents and the adopting parents can all meet together. Some argue that a face-to-face confrontation is good because it gives all parties a sense of participation in the making of a decision on behalf of the child, and lets both sets of parents acquire some feeling of empathy and understanding about each other. Others believe that direct confrontation between both sets of parents is a mistake because it destroys the anonymous nature of the adoption and can cause trouble in the future if the natural parents have second thoughts or if they wish to interfere later by attempting to establish a relationship with their natural child.

If the child has not yet been born, it is customary for the couple wishing to adopt the child to establish a trust fund for the payment of medical and hospital expenses incurred during pregnancy and birth. The lawyer will prepare the papers for the setting up of the trust fund, which also provides for the payment of court costs incurred in connection with the adoption.

Whether the natural mother knows the identity of the adopting parents or not is up to the parties involved in a direct adoption situation. In this adoption situation the lawyer does all the work that is done by the agency in an agency adoption. Some people prefer direct adoption because they dislike the impersonal treatment they sometimes receive from agency adoption personnel. Other people resent the questions they have to answer and the forms they have to fill out when applying for an agency adoption.

[3.49]   ### 3. Agency Adoption

The state licenses adoption agencies to find homes for children and to place children with parents who want to adopt them. The natural parent or parents relinquish the child to the agency, and the agency then takes over the role of parent, caring for the child and finding a home for it. Some people prefer agency adoption because they feel that the people involved are professionals who know their job and because they think they are more likely to get a child who will match their racial and cultural background. Naturally there is a wider choice in dealing with an adoption agency than there is in dealing direct. The adopting parents are also better protected in an agency adoption against the possibility that the natural mother may decide she wants her child back and will attempt to interfere at some later date with the relationship between the adopted child and its parents.

[3.50]   ### 4. New Birth Certificate

After the adoption is completed and the adoption certificate is filed with the court, some states have a procedure for preparing and filing a new birth certificate showing the new name of the child as it appears on the adoption decree. The new birth certificate will contain no reference to the fact of adoption and it will appear as though the child were born to the adopting parents, although in some cases the name of the hospital where the child was born will be omitted. Some state laws require that the original birth certificate be sealed so that it is not open to public inspection. In such cases only the reissued birth certificate is available for inspection. For children born in another state or country, the local procedure should be looked into before having a new birth certificate issued.

H. GUARDIANSHIP

A *guardianship* is created when a person is appointed to take care of the person or property of another, called the *ward*. A *guardian of the person* has responsibility for care, feeding, education, and protection of the ward. A *guardian of the estate* has responsibility for management of the ward's property.

1. When Is Guardianship Necessary?

If a minor has received substantial sums of money or property by gift or inheritance, a guardian may have to be appointed to take care of the funds or property (see Section 3.62). A guardian can also be appointed for an incompetent person. A relative may be incompetent to continue managing a business, in which case a petition to appoint a guardian or conservator of the business might be filed. If a person is totally incompetent and dangerous to himself or to others, his relatives may apply to the court for his commitment to an institution. A minor receiving Veterans Administration benefits may need a guardian under circumstances in which his parents are not able to handle the funds for him.

2. Creation of Guardianship

A guardian may be nominated in the will of a deceased parent. The court may on its own appoint a guardian where necessary. Such a situation would obtain if both parents died, leaving children, and did not have a will or name a guardian in their will. A child over a certain age may nominate his own guardian, subject to court approval, or upon reaching that age, may request a change of guardian.

There is usually a standard form of *petition for appointment of guardian* which is filed with the appropriate court in order to start the guardianship proceeding. After the form is properly completed and filed, a notice of the time and place of the hearing of the petition must be given to persons having custody of the minor or the incompetent, and to the parents of the minor (if they don't have custody), and in some cases to other interested parties. At the time of the hearing the interested parties will appear in court and the judge will decide whether or not a guardian should be appointed, and if so, who, based upon the best interests of the potential ward. Medical testimony is required to establish incompetency if that is the reason for the guardianship.

After the hearing, the judge may order the appointment of the guardian, and letters of guardianship will thereafter be issued. The guardian may have to post a bond if he is to be guardian of the estate of the minor, unless the bond is waived. The bond can be waived by proper language in the will of a parent who wishes to nominate a guardian for his children, to serve, without bond, after his death. Where a bond is required, the size depends upon the value of the minor's estate. The cost of the bond is an expense of the guardianship. The guardian must sign letters of guardianship and be sworn in as guardian.

[3.54]   3.   Termination of Guardianship

Guardianship of a minor terminates when the minor marries or becomes an adult. The guardianship must be terminated by a court order and the guardian has to file a final petition and account requesting authority to terminate the guardianship and turn the assets (if any) over to the ward.

4.   Natural Guardian   [3.55]

Some states permit the parents to serve as *natural guardians* of a child without a formal court appointment. In such states a parent may act in the legal capacity of guardian with respect to his child, signing legal documents and making legal transactions.

5.   Temporary Guardian   [3.56]

A *temporary guardian,* or *guardian ad litem,* is a person appointed by the court to look after the interests of a minor who is involved in litigation, when the minor has no other guardian. Because the minor can't appear in court representing himself, an adult is appointed as temporary guardian either to defend the minor or to prosecute the minor's civil action against another person. This temporary guardian serves only long enough to take care of the litigation.

6.   Powers and Duties of Guardians   [3.57]

The guardian of a minor is in charge of the education of the minor and is responsible for his well being. If he is a guardian of the estate as well as the person of the minor, he must manage the estate competently, without wasting it, and he must apply the income as necessary for the maintenance and education of the minor. He should invest the assets of the minor's estate to get the best possible return, on a cautious or prudent basis. Investment in a savings account or in government bonds is always approved. However, if the guardian wants to get a greater return by investing the money in stocks or mutual funds he can apply to the court for permission to make such an investment. If he invests badly, without permission of the court, he may have to dip into his own pocket to make up the loss. Most states require a guardian to file an annual accounting with the court. However, it is possible to petition the court to account every second or third year in order to keep expenses down. A final accounting is required on termination of the guardianship before the guardian can be discharged. If a guardian ever has questions about how he should handle the minor's estate, or how he should carry out his duties as guardian, he can (and should) petition the court for appropriate instructions. A guardian is not entitled to fees for services. The estate of the minor bears the cost of the guardianship including accountant's fees, attorney's fees, and the cost of preparation and filing tax returns, etc. Where proceeds of settlement of a personal injury action filed on behalf of a ward by a temporary guardian are received, these are normally paid over to the minor if the amount is not large, and the temporary guardian is discharged, or the funds are deposited in an approved savings account to be kept until the minor reaches majority. In such case, a temporary guardian would again be discharged. The minor could petition the court for withdrawal of some or all of the funds prior to reaching majority for a purpose the court would approve, such as paying for a college education, or paying for medical expenses which the minor's parents are unable to afford (see Section 3.61).

I. CHILDREN AND PARENTS

1. Discipline and Control [3.58]

The law recognizes the need for family discipline as an important element in the preservation of social order. Both parents are permitted by law to use *reasonable* physical punishment to keep their children in line. What is reasonable depends upon the circumstances. Punishments may be inflicted to the point of physical pain or discomfort, but not to the point of real or serious injury. The use of *unreasonable* physical force constitutes the crime of *child-beating.* Parents are expected to set and enforce reasonable rules regarding the behavior of their children. A child is required to obey his parents as long as he is being supported by them and remains within their custody and control. A court will back up the parents if they seek its help in enforcing their rules—for example, to prevent an older man or boy from dating their teenage daughter.

2. Emancipation [3.59]

Emancipation is not exactly the same as becoming an adult, but is almost the same. A child can become emancipated by marrying, by working and living away from home, by entering military service, by agreement between child and parents, or by court order where parents are abusing their authority. Emancipation releases the child from the control of his parents. It also releases the parents from having to support the child. An emancipated child can enter into contracts that are binding upon him. He may also keep his own earnings. His parents will no longer be responsible for his debts. In some states an eighteen-year-old can move out of the home and qualify for welfare.

[3.60]   **3. Wages**

If a minor lives with his parents and is under their custody and control they may, if they wish, keep whatever wages he earns. In the case of the child with a large earning capacity, such as a child movie star, a contract will usually be entered into between the movie studio and the child actor and the court will approve the contract. In such cases the court may provide that most of the earnings will be placed in a trust fund for the child or be given to a guardian who will administer the funds under supervision of the court.

[3.61]   **4. Damage Awards**

Where a minor is successful as a plaintiff in a law suit for personal injuries or other damages, if the amount of the award is over a certain size, the court will order the money deposited in a special account, usually at a bank or a savings and loan association. Funds may be withdrawn from this account only by order of the court. When the child becomes an adult, the account is released to him (see Section 3.57).

[3.62]   **5. Gifts to Children**

When a child receives property by gift or inheritance, the property is his, and his parents do not have a right to dispose of it. If the amount of the property (or money) is substantial, then a guardian should be appointed to receive and manage it. To avoid the trouble and expense of a guardianship, laws have been passed for parents, relatives, or other persons to give property to minors and designate a *custodian* of the property who will administer and control the property until the child reaches majority, much the same as a guardian, but without the necessity of accountings and close court supervision. The law permitting this has been adopted in most states and is known as the *Uniform Gifts to Minors Act.* A person wishing to make a gift under the act designates himself or some other adult as the *custodian under the Uniform Gifts to Minors Act.* For example, a stock certificate would be registered in the name of *John Smith, Custodian for Mary Smith under the Uniform Gifts to Minors Act.*

6.   Liability of Parents for Torts of Children   [3.63]

Under certain conditions parents are liable for damages resulting from torts committed by their children. Parents who know they have a problem child on their hands and fail to control his actions may be held liable if their child injures someone else under circumstances where the parents might have prevented it if they had exercised a greater degree of control. Parents who equip their child with a gun, or allow him to use a gun, are liable if the child injures anyone. Some laws make the parents liable for any injury resulting from their child's use of the gun if they merely left the gun in a place accessible to the child. Parents are normally liable under statute for injury or damages caused by their child when driving the family automobile (see Section 12.5).

Many states have laws making parents liable for damages caused by vandalism or malicious mischief of their children. Some of these laws relate only to school property or other public property, and other laws cover any kind of damage, even damage to private property. Parents should figure that they are *targets* where their children are concerned, and will be named in any law-suit filed for injury or damage caused by their childrens' wrongful acts.

[3.64]   ## 7.   Liability of Parents for Crimes of Children

Certain laws make parents responsible for the crimes committed by their children. At times parents may be required to post a bond in order to have their child released on probation. Numerous laws make parents liable for destruction of public property caused by their children (see Section 3.63).

[3.65]   ## 8.   Liability of Minors for their Torts and Crimes

Minors over a certain age (which varies from state to state) can be prosecuted for their crimes. They are also liable for their torts. In other words, minors can be sued, fined, or imprisoned for their illegal acts. Children under a certain age are not considered capable of criminal activity and are not held liable for their torts. This is based on the theory that one has to have a certain mental capacity and a certain maturity in order to be held accountable at law for one's actions.

9.   Paternity and Legitimation

a.   *PATERNITY*

[3.66]   #### *(1)   Action to Establish Paternity*

An action to establish *paternity* can be brought by the mother of an illegitimate child, or by a guardian ad litem (temporary guardian), on behalf of the child. The action can be brought after conception, but before the birth of the child, or it may be brought after the birth of the child. The plaintiff has the burden of proving that the defendant is the father. The defendant must be given the opportunity to be heard and to present his evidence in the case.

(2) Custody and Support [3.67]

Both parents are liable for the support and education of an illegitimate minor child. The mother is entitled to the custody, earnings, and services of an illegitimate child.

(3) Evidence in Paternity Actions

(a)   RESEMBLANCE [3.68]

Some courts permit the child to be viewed by the judge or jury to consider the resemblance, if any, between the child and the alleged father, as a factor in determining the issue of paternity.

(b)   OTHER ACTS OF INTERCOURSE [3.69]

By way of defense, the alleged father can show that the mother had committed acts of intercourse with other men at or about the time the child could have been conceived.

(c)   BLOOD TESTS [3.70]

Where the statutes so provide, a blood test may be used in a paternity proceeding to determine whether the alleged father could really be the father. If the blood tests show that the alleged father could not be the father, the test is conclusive. If it shows that he could have been the father, then there must still be other evidence to show that he is or that no one else could have been the father.

(d)   IMPOTENT OR ABSENT FATHER [3.71]

If the alleged father can prove that he was impotent or that he was absent at the time when conception could have occurred, he may successfully defend a paternity suit.

b. LEGITIMATION

[3.72]

(1) Children of Invalid Marriage

If a marriage ceremony occurred, and it later turns out the marriage was invalid, most state laws provide that the children are still legitimate.

[3.73]

(2) Presumption of Legitimacy

Most states provide that children born to a married couple, or within up to ten months after the marriage was dissolved, are presumed to be legitimate. This means they are legitimate until legitimacy is positively disproved by either the husband or the wife (or by one of the children if they should wish to do so).

[3.74]

(3) Rights of Illegitimate Children

The mother and father owe a duty of support to illegitimate children. This right may be enforced by legal action. The parents may be prosecuted criminally for failure to support. Illegitimate children may sue for the wrongful death of their mother and vice versa. An illegitimate child may inherit from his mother's estate, but not from his father's (unless legitimacy is legally established).

[3.75]

(4) Subsequent Marriage

An illegitimate child may become legitimate if the mother and father get married.

[3.76]

(5) Adoption

The father of an illegitimate child may in effect adopt his child by publicly acknowledging it as his own, receiving it into his family, and treating it as if it were a legitimate child. This kind of *adoption* only works where there is a blood relationship, and is different from formal adoption that is not based on blood relationship (see Section 3.46).

10. Support and Nonsupport [3.77]

Parents are required to support their minor children. This continues until the child reaches majority or is emancipated. Liability for support rests primarily with the father, but the mother is also liable if what the father furnishes is inadequate. The obligation is to provide food, clothing, shelter, medical attention, and education. If a father fails to support his children, either the mother or the children can bring a civil action against him. The state can also bring a criminal action against him for nonsupport. Just how much support is awarded depends on the parents' income and the children's needs. For some youngsters that would mean just food, clothes, and medical care; for others it would mean such things as a car necessary for transportation to school, and tuition.

Some state laws provide that adult children have to support their parents or grandparents if they are unable to support themselves. If some children (who can afford to do so) fail to contribute to the support of their parents, any other children who contribute may be able to get a court to order their siblings to contribute also.

J. FAMILY LAWSUITS

The recent trend of new legislation and court decisions has been to allow husbands and wives, and children and parents, to sue each other for damages or injuries caused by intentional torts, and in many cases for damages or injuries caused by negligence.

K. PETS

[3.79]   1. Dog-Bite Statutes

There are two types of *dog-bite statutes.* Under one, the owner of a dog who bites someone for the first time is not liable. He is liable for every subsequent time his dog bites someone. Under the other kind of statute an owner is liable even the first time his dog bites someone.

[3.80]   2. Wild Animals

Under common law, a person who kept a wild animal was responsible for any harm that occurred if the wild animal escaped. This is still probably the law in most states. In addition, local laws make the keeping of most wild animals illegal. No one should attempt to keep a wild animal for a pet without first familiarizing himself with the laws on this subject that are in force in his area.

3. Leash Laws [3.81]

Most cities have a *leash law* which requires dogs to be kept on a leash. Owners who fail to observe this law can be held responsible for any damage done by their animals. In some cases they may also have to pay a fine if their dog is picked up.

4. Immunization Laws [3.82]

Immunization laws apply to dogs and sometimes to other pets. These laws specifically require an annual rabies shot. A person failing to get such a shot for his dog could be held liable in a civil action for the illness or death of any person contracting rabies from his pet. He could also be held liable under criminal law.

5. Licenses [3.83]

Most cities have local dog license laws which require the owner to pay a fee for an annual dog license. Failure to do so is a misdemeanor.

6. Liability for Harm by Animals [3.84]

Because the keeping of animals is no longer as important as it was to society in the days when most people lived on farms or in rural areas, the law becomes more and more strict in holding people who own animals responsible for any and all damage or injuries caused by their animals. This applies to such things as damage to the interior of an apartment done by a pet and the trampling of someone's garden by a runaway horse.

L. WELFARE LAWS

All states have some kind of welfare laws. These laws vary greatly from one state to another, and are also rapidly changing. There is a lot of controversy about such things as residency requirements. Other controversies revolve around mothers with young children who are receiving welfare and who have a man other than their husband living in their home who may or may not be the father of one or more of the children. Because of the complex nature of welfare laws and the constant state of turmoil in welfare departments in administering and interpreting them, if you have a question involving welfare laws, it is best to go to your local welfare department and talk to a social worker about your problem. If you don't get satisfactory answers, try to contact an attorney through the local legal aid society.

M. FAMILY INSURANCE

Every family should have insurance on their home or apartment, and on their car. In addition they should carry some kind of liability insurance that protects them against suits by other persons whom they may accidentally injure (see Section 9.39). If your domestic help (gardener, caretaker, maid, etc.) works fulltime you should have workmen's compensation insurance (see Section 3.87 regarding withholding of social security payments from domestic employees). There should also be a sufficient amount of life insurance on the father to protect the family in the event of his death. It is pretty tough for a family to get along on social security and welfare payments if the breadwinner dies unexpectedly and doesn't leave much in his estate. Insurance on the mother isn't a bad idea either. It costs a lot of money to hire a full-time cook, housekeeper, and babysitter. In a divorce case the wife will want to make sure the husband is obligated to maintain the insurance policies following the divorce, and to name her or the children as beneficiaries. The husband may be willing to maintain the policies, but may prefer to set up a trust fund for the children in the event of his death rather than leave the money to his ex-wife, particularly if she has remarried.

Social security, or *Federal Old-Age or Survivors Insurance* is sort of a combination of life insurance and retirement plan. The premium is paid through a payroll deduction tax on wages, the cost of which is shared by the employee and employer. Self-employed persons bear the entire cost. Theoretically the government takes the money paid in the form of these deductions and when an employee becomes disabled, retires, dies, or otherwise becomes eligible for social security (or if members of his family become eligible), benefits will be paid. The basic theory of the act is that employees or self-employed persons, as well as dependents and survivors, who are covered by the act are entitled to benefits if they have been paid *wages* and have contributed to the social security program for a minimum period of time.

The amount of monthly retirement or disability benefit is based upon one's average earnings (and contributions) over a period of years.

Benefits include retirement benefits, benefits for wives, widows, children, and parents. In addition, there may be funeral or burial expenses or lump-sum death payments. Application for benefits must be made on forms that can be obtained from the social security administration. You should see your local social security administration personnel for assistance in obtaining and filing application forms.

Earnings from work after retirement that exceed a certain total amount in a calendar year may cause social security payments to be lowered. Death, remarriage, divorce, adoption, and extended absence from the United States all have an effect upon social security benefits. Social security laws are complex. Advice should be sought from your local social security office.

If you pay your domestic help more than a certain amount per quarter (currently $50 a quarter) *you should file an earnings report* and pay social security taxes (the rate was 11.5% of their wages in 1973). You may deduct and withhold one-half of the social security payments from their wages, if you wish, or simply pay them yourself.

Most people sixty-five and over are eligible for Medicare, which provides medical and hospital benefits. You should enroll during the three-month period before you reach that age. Hospital care is available more or less automatically for all those over sixty-five. Additional medical service benefits (outside the hospital) can be obtained by enrolling in the medical insurance plan under Medicare. You should apply for social security and Medicare benefits before reaching the age of retirement. Delaying until after you reach age sixty-five (or sixty-two, in some cases) can cost you several months of protection. To apply you will need proof of age, your social security number, and a copy of your last federal tax return or W-2 statement. Widows may need marriage certificates, death certificate for deceased husband, and birth certificates for children.

O. RECORDS

There may come a time when you want to obtain copies of records of birth, marriage, divorce, or death. If you can't find out where to obtain such records, you may write to the U.S. Department of Health, Education and Welfare, Public Health Service, Washington, D.C. They will send you pamphlets telling you where to write to obtain such records in your own state.

P. CHILDREN AND SCHOOL

[3.89] ## 1. Clothes and Hair

Schools and school officials have the right to make and enforce reasonable regulations concerning the appearance of students. This includes hair and clothing. However, the law provides that in order for a school to restrict hair to a certain length or to restrict the wearing of beards, sideburns, or mustaches, or to prohibit the wearing of certain styles of clothing, it must be done on the basis that the prohibited style has actually caused an interference with or a disruption of the school decorum. In other words, the school has to be able to show that long hair or short skirts interfere with the educational process before they can ban either. The modern legal view here is that the school should concentrate on educating the students, and leave matters of grooming to the parents. The only exception to this is where health or sanitation problems have occurred, or where in spite of reasonable efforts on the part of teachers to enforce discipline in the classroom, a particular style of dress or grooming is so distracting to other students in the class that they can't concentrate on their work. Students who are sent home or suspended from school because of dress or grooming problems may have a right to go to court to force the school to let them return. In such a case, if the student has the support of his parents, he should see a lawyer about it. In some cases in which the school rules are obviously arbitrary and not related to furthering the educational process, the American Civil Liberties Union will provide a lawyer to represent the student and his parents.

2. Damage to School Property [3.90]

Students can be held civilly liable for any damage they do to school property. They can also be prosecuted criminally for destruction of public property. Many statutes exist which make parents liable for the cost of repairing school property damage done by their children (see Section 3.63).

3. Conduct at School

a. RIGHTS OF TEACHERS [3.91]
TO DISCIPLINE STUDENTS

Teachers have the right under the law to administer reasonable physical punishment to students, in most states. However, the trend of the law is away from use of physical punishment, such as paddling. Every school district should consult its own legal counsel on the question of physical discipline and should have a policy in effect which tells teachers exactly how far they may go under their local laws in administering physical punishment to students. If they go beyond what is permitted under the law, the teachers can be held liable either civilly or criminally for assault and battery. If the teachers stay within the law, the student has no legal complaint if physical discipline is reasonably administered to him under proper circumstances.

[3.92]

b. RIGHTS OF STUDENTS TO DUE PROCESS OF LAW

The courts are freely extending the area of student rights these days. In many states, students are entitled to notice and a hearing before they can be permanently suspended or expelled from school. They may even be entitled to have an attorney represent them at such a hearing, at the expense of the state if they cannot afford to pay an attorney. In these cases, the student must be notified of the charges against him and be given an opportunity to present a defense.

Q. JUVENILE COURT

1.   Juvenile Court Jurisdiction   [3.93]

Juvenile courts have jurisdiction over juveniles who become delinquent. A juvenile, in this sense, means a young person who is below a certain age set by state law—usually it is eighteen. The juvenile becomes *delinquent* when he violates any law or if he commits some act that endangers himself or society. Examples of noncriminal acts that could result in a minor being subject to the jurisdiction of the juvenile court, as a delinquent, would be: unexcused absences from school or from home; association with criminals or drug addicts; engaging in activity endangering life or health; desertion or neglect by parents; conduct uncontrollable by parents or teachers, etc. Once a minor becomes subject to the jurisdiction of a juvenile court, it may continue its control over him even after he reaches eighteen, or it may transfer him to a state prison if he has not been released by that time. Some juveniles who are accused of very serious crimes or who have previously appeared in juvenile court and show little promise of being rehabilitated will be transferred to adult criminal court.

2.   Juvenile Court Philosophy and Terminology   [3.94]

Juvenile courts were first established in this nation in the nineteenth century. They were and are based on the theory that the youthful lawbreaker should not be dealt with as harshly as an adult. Neither should he be removed from society in order to protect society. Juvenile court is supposed to guide and protect youngsters who are in trouble with the law. Minors are to be protected from themselves because of their own immaturity, and they are to be protected by the juvenile court from undesirable influences of other people and from harmful publicity. In order to accomplish this purpose a variety of experts are attached to the juvenile court such as doctors, probation workers, and psychology workers. The idea is to keep a juvenile who needs supervision and help under the guidance and control of a juvenile court for as long as he needs it, rather than to lock him up for a certain period of time. Because the philosophy is different in adult than in juvenile court, so is the terminology. Some of the differences in terminology are as follows:

Criminal Court	Juvenile Court
arraignment	detention hearing
arrest	intake
complaint	petition
conviction	finding of delinquency or involvement
trial	adjudication hearing
guilty	delinquent
sentence	disposition or commitment

Statistics show that perhaps one out of every five or six boys will appear before juvenile court before he becomes eighteen. Unfortunately, juvenile courts have not entirely lived up to their expectations. Like adult courts, they tend to be overburdened with cases, understaffed, and underfinanced.

[3.95]   3.   Rights of Minors in Juvenile Court

In recent cases courts have held that minors are entitled to the same rights in juvenile court as adults are entitled to in criminal court. This means that the minor has the right to be advised of the charges against him, the right not to answer questions, and the right not to testify against himself. He also has the right to an attorney, and one must be appointed for him if he cannot afford to pay his own legal fees. Witnesses who testify against him must be brought to court and be made available for cross-examination. There is no right to a jury trial in juvenile court.

4. Juvenile Court Procedure [3.96]

After *arrest* or *intake,* the juvenile offender is processed through the police station or juvenile hall intake area. The parents are then notified and in some cases the juvenile probation officer will ask the parents for permission to talk to the youth. Depending upon the situation, the youth will either be released to the custody of his parents or booked pending a *detention hearing.* The purpose of a detention hearing is to examine the charges brought against the minor and to determine whether he should be released, tried in adult criminal court, or held pending an *adjudication hearing.* If an adjudication hearing results in a finding of delinquency, then a *disposition hearing* will follow. The purpose of the disposition hearing is to decide whether the youth should be released to the custody of his parents, placed on probation, placed under guardianship of the court, or turned over to a public agency such as a youth commission or reform school.

5. Juvenile Court Records [3.97]

Juvenile court records are not supposed to be open to the public, as are criminal court records. Nevertheless they are subject to examination in certain cases, such as in connection with civil-service employment applications or enlistment in the armed services. Existence of a juvenile court record could also hinder or prevent a youth from being licensed to practice a profession in later life. In line with the philosophy of giving youthful criminal offenders a break, many laws now permit sealing or *expunging* of juvenile court records after a certain number of years have passed following completion of probation. Under such statutes, where the record has been expunged, it is proper for the individual to state on an employment application form that he has not been arrested or convicted (if that was his only prior arrest or conviction).

IV. Contracts

A. MAKING THE CONTRACT [4.1]

A contract is an agreement between two or more persons, both of whom are legally competent to enter into a contract, by which each of them in return for a consideration does something, refrains from doing something, or agrees to do or to refrain from doing something. In order for a contract to result, there must be an *offer,* an *acceptance,* an *exchange of consideration,* and a *mutual understanding.*

1. Offer and Acceptance [4.2]

If you tell a friend you will sell him your used automobile for $500, that constitutes a legal offer. If he agrees to buy it for the price that you are asking, that constitutes an *acceptance.* An offer has to be either spoken or written or made by sign language. An acceptance can be implied. If you offer a reward for your lost dog, the person who returns your dog to you has accepted your offer by his actions and is entitled to claim the reward. If you order something from a mail-order catalog, you are offering to buy something and at the same time agreeing to pay for it. Your offer is accepted by delivery of the goods.

2. Consideration [4.3]

Consideration is the inducement to enter into the con-tract—it may be in the form of money, benefit received, detriment avoided, or simply a promise. If your rich uncle promises to give you $1,000 if you stop smoking for a year, the consideration he receives for his promise to pay you the $1,000 might be the pleasure that he gets from believing he has helped to improve your health or prolong your life. It could also be the fact that he has caused you to stop doing something that you had a right to do. Either way you look at it, he has received consideration for his promise, and if you make it through the year without smoking, you're entitled to the $1,000.

[4.4]   3.   Meeting of the Minds

There must be a mutual understanding in order to have a contract. Suppose you went to a horse farm to buy a horse and pointed to the strawberry roan in the corral and said, "I'll take that one. How much is it?" The owner, who thought you were pointing to the palomino, said, "$500." You said, "I'll take it." Is there a contract? The answer is no. Each of you is thinking about a different horse, so there was no *mutual meeting of the minds.*

[4.5]   4.   Written Contracts

Only certain types of contracts are required to be in writing. Most contracts are oral, and the fact that they are not in writing doesn't matter a bit.

[4.6]   *a.   STATUTE OF FRAUDS*

Each state has a *statute of frauds,* which specifies what contracts have to be in writing. The purpose is to prevent dishonest people from falsely claiming that contracts had been entered into orally. Most contracts involving the purchase or sale of real property are required to be in writing. Likewise contracts for rental or services over a long period of time (usually more than a year) are required to be in writing. The statute of frauds is tricky, and any question involving the enforceability of an oral or partly oral and partly written contract should be referred to a lawyer. The statute of frauds does not require that the entire contract be spelled out in detail. There may be some provisions that are not contained in the writing. However, usually the written agreement must be complete enough so that at least the major items of importance are in writing. There are many exceptions to the statute of frauds. A mere memorandum of a contract, signed by one of the parties, can sometimes satisfy the statute of frauds. Performance by one party of his obligations under an oral contract can sometimes satisfy the statute of frauds. Where a contract is required to be in writing and is not, and the law does not provide some exception to the rule, the contract is then *unenforceable.*

b. IMPORTANCE OF WRITTEN CONTRACTS [4.7]

Regardless of the statute of frauds, it is a good idea to have most contracts in writing, even if the writing consists merely of a letter, the original signed by one party, with a copy signed by the other party, summarizing their oral agreement. Insisting upon having something in writing should in no way cause the other person to become defensive or to be insulted. It is easy to explain that putting it in writing is for the protection of both of you, so that your pleasant relationship will be certain of continuing and so that there will not be any possible misunderstandings in the future. This is just as important in the case of contracts with friends or family members as it is in the case of contracts with total strangers. You don't want to have to get involved in differences with friends or family members about what was agreed upon, and you want even less to have to settle these differences in court. The purpose of a written contract is not to give anybody some legal advantage over someone else, but to avoid misunderstandings.

[4.8]

c. IMPORTANCE OF READING CONTRACTS

Most people sign written contracts all the time without reading them. This applies to automobile or equipment rental contracts, leases, and the like. If you are tempted to sign a contract without reading it because of time pressure, ask yourself whether it is worth the risk. If there is something in that contract you don't know about or don't understand, your pleas to the court that you signed it without reading it will fall on deaf ears. Of course there may be exceptions to this (as there are to every rule), such as the case of the immigrant who was told to sign a contract printed in English that he couldn't read, or the person with feeble eyesight who was assured by the salesman that there was nothing in the agreement to be afraid of, or the person who signed a contract based on a misrepresentation of the other party made for the purpose of inducing him to sign the contract. Any contract you don't understand should be explained to you by a lawyer. It is a mistake to sign contracts with blanks in them, trusting the other party to fill in the blanks, unless your confidence is justified. Even if you trust the other party not to fill in the blanks incorrectly, what if they are not filled in at all and you later get into a disagreement about the contract? If you don't then agree on what was supposed to go into the blanks, there may be no enforceable contract.

d.   PAROLE EVIDENCE RULE   [4.9]

Suppose you have a contract that is in writing, and a dispute arises. The parties go to court and the contract is introduced into evidence. One of the parties attempts to explain, during his testimony, something that is not in the contract, but which he claims was agreed to. The other party's attorney can then object on the basis of the *parole evidence rule.* Under that rule, courts will not allow oral testimony that changes the terms of a contract that is in writing, and that is, or appears to be, a complete agreement between the two parties, containing all essential details. The parole evidence rule also will allow certain oral testimony to clarify a written contract that is ambiguous or uncertain in some respects. Oral testimony is sometimes admitted if it pertains to some additional agreements between the parties that do not alter the written portion of the contract. The theory of the parole evidence rule is that if the parties signed a written agreement, they must have intended the agreement to take the place of all their prior discussions, therefore (unless the contract appears incomplete or ambiguous) testimony about their prior discussions should not be allowed. The rule does not normally exclude testimony about oral agreements or modifications that occurred after the written contract was signed.

e.   PROOF OF TERMS OF CONTRACT   [4.10]

The parole evidence rule is sometimes confused with the *best evidence rule* (see Section 5.34). The best evidence rule requires that, to prove the terms of a written agreement, the written agreement itself is put into evidence (except under certain conditions).

[4.11]   5.   Revocation, Rejection, and Counteroffer

An offer may be *revoked* by the offeror (person making the offer) before it is accepted by the offeree (person accepting the offer), and no contract can then result. An offer can be *rejected* by an offeree, and no contract can thereafter result. The offeree, having received the offer, can make a *counteroffer,* or can accept the offer conditionally, which may amount to a counteroffer. There would be no contract until the counteroffer or the conditional acceptance is agreed to by the original offeror. An acceptance or rejection can be implied or it can be explicitly spelled out. Many lawsuits arise out of situations in which revocation, rejection, and counteroffer are involved. This is a technical area and the assistance of an attorney should be sought for guidance.

6.   Enforceability

[4.12]   *a.   MUTUALITY OF REMEDY*

This is a technical doctrine meaning that both parties to a contract must have some remedy available to them to enforce the contract. Otherwise, if one party has a remedy, and the other has no remedy, the contract may not be enforceable. There are, of course, exceptions to this rule and this is an area where the layman will have to call upon the assistance of counsel.

b. ILLUSORY CONTRACTS [4.13]

A frequent problem with contracts is that they do not really obligate either or both of the parties to do anything. For example, if you agree to furnish another person at a certain price with all of the goods he may *want* or *desire*, there will not be an enforceable contract because he is not obligated to buy anything at all. He can defeat the contract by saying that he doesn't want anything.

c. ILLEGAL CONTRACTS [4.14]

Illegal contracts are invalid. This means they are not enforceable. This includes contracts that are usurious (see Section 7.77); contracts of unlicensed persons (see Section 4.29); contracts that are in restraint of trade; wagering or gambling contracts; contracts obstructing the administration of justice; or contracts that violate public policy or some policy of the law.

d. FRUSTRATION AND [4.15]
IMPOSSIBILITY

Certain contracts may become unenforceable because performance becomes impossible. For example, a contract to remodel a house would be terminated if the house were destroyed by a tornado before the remodeling could begin.

e. VAGUE AND UNCERTAIN [4.16]
CONTRACTS

In order to be enforceable, contracts must be specific as to the essential details of performance by both parties.

If a contract is vague to the degree that a court cannot fairly well determine what it is the parties are required to perform, then the contract may be found to be unenforceable. The most frequent weakness of contracts drafted by laymen is that they tend to be vague on some important details such as time of performance, price, quantity, quality, method and manner of payment, etc.

[4.17]

f. IMPORTANCE OF CAREFULLY DRAFTED DOCUMENTS AND USE OF FORMS

It is essential that any contract, either written or oral, contain all of the important details to which the parties agree. The absence of a single essential element of a contract can prevent it from being enforceable. Even if you enter into an oral contract it is still a good idea to have at least a written memorandum of the agreement so that there will not be any question about the terms of the agreement in the event something happens to one of the parties. Some laymen can draft adequate, simple, written contracts without help of counsel. Most people, however, are not able to do this without getting themselves into trouble. If you insist on drafting your own contracts, it doesn't cost much to have a lawyer briefly review your draft and give you some helpful comments.

There are many contract forms you can purchase at a stationery store or copy out of form books. In many cases these contracts can be used by simply filling in the blanks and perhaps by adding a few handwritten provisions. Commonly used forms are: leases, rental agreements, bills of sale, and deposit-receipt agreements for the sale of a residence. However, even form contracts can get you into trouble if you are inexperienced, or if you try to use a form for a purpose for which it was not intended. A brief review of your self-prepared agreement by a lawyer can save you a lot of legal expense later on, and the small amount you spend will be well worth it (see Part II).

7. Capacity—Minors and Incompetents   [4.18]

A person legally judged incompetent cannot make binding contracts. Temporary (mental) incapacity may also prevent formation of a contract. One under the influence of alcohol or drugs to such an extent that he was not able to comprehend the nature of his act might have a defense to an action brought against him for breach of a contract which he had agreed to in writing under those circumstances.

Minors lack capacity to enter into some contracts. Minors (under an age that varies from state to state) cannot contract for *luxuries*. They may be able to enter into binding contracts for *necessities* or *necessaries* (which include things like food, clothing, medical supplies, and shelter), but only if they are *emancipated* (living outside of the home and responsible for their own self support); otherwise not.

A contract entered into by a minor (unless a contract involves necessaries purchased by an emancipated minor) is said to be *voidable*. This means that the minor may refuse to perform his obligations and cannot be liable for breach. However, the adult must perform, the contract being voidable only by the minor, and at his option. There are different rules for minors above and below a certain age (usually eighteen) and there are different rules concerning the responsibility of a minor to pay for the use of or damage to an article which he wishes to return after having purchased it. The minor who wishes to avoid a contract must notify the other party of his election to do so within a reasonable period of time after he reaches majority (or any earlier time).

B. KINDS OF CONTRACTS

1.   Purchase Contracts

The purchase of a home requires the making of a contract and performance of that contract by both parties. It starts with the seller offering the house for sale. Seller may be the owner of the house or a builder-developer who has constructed the house and is offering it for sale, or who is offering lots for sale with homes that he will build on the lot according to certain plans and specifications. A seller may offer his property direct, through advertising it in the newspaper, or by signs posted on the property. Normally the price will be specified. The price is the "asking price," and experience tells us that in most cases the price is "negotiable." An exception to this, of course, is the standard subdivision house where the price is the same for every house of a given model. Of course, extras may add to the basic cost of the house. The next step in the formation of the contract occurs when a prospective buyer appears. He may accept the offer by agreeing to pay the purchase price, or he may make a counteroffer, if he thinks the offering price is too high. The seller of the house is the *offeror,* and his offer consists of his statement (which may be contained in an advertisement or a *listing*) that he wishes to sell his house under certain conditions and for certain terms. The *acceptance* would be the agreement of the purchaser to buy the house on those terms. The *consideration* would be the delivery of title by the seller and the payment of money by the buyer. A sale of a house usually involves several other parties such as a real estate salesman, a real estate broker's office, a title company, a termite inspection company, a bank or financial institution, and possibly lawyers for either or both parties. (For more details on purchase and sale of property see Part X.)

The purchase of an automobile is another common

contractual arrangement. In addition to the usual terms of the purchase including the offer to sell and the acceptance of that offer and the agreement to pay the purchase price, certain documents of title are also involved. Because automobiles are registered with the state, a certificate of title must change hands and the vehicle must be registered with the state in the name of the new owner. If the new owner is paying cash, he will become the legal owner of the vehicle. If he is borrowing the money from a bank or financial institution and it is using the vehicle as security for the loan, then the buyer will become the registered owner and the bank or financial institution will become the legal owner. When the loan has been paid off, the legal title will be transferred from the bank or financial institution to the registered owner, who then becomes both legal and registered owner (see Section 12.1).

a. THINGS TO WATCH OUT FOR WHEN BUYING A USED CAR [4.20]

In contracting to buy a used automobile, make sure that any representations as to the condition of the car (such as recent overhauls, new parts, mileage, etc.) are put in writing. Also make sure that the price of the car is within limits set by the automobile *blue book* (call any local automobile dealer and ask him for the blue-book price on the car you are buying), unless the car is either very good or bad. Be sure that the person you are dealing with has legal title and can pass it to you with proper documents. Don't pay the money until you get a properly endorsed certificate of title. Don't expect to get the same implied warranties from an individual that you would get from a car dealer (see Section 7.42).

[4.21]

b. THINGS TO WATCH OUT FOR WHEN SELLING A USED CAR

Make sure that you do not misrepresent the condition of the automobile to the buyer. Make sure the buyer is legally competent to enter into a contract. If he is a minor, get his parents to agree to purchase the car for him or to guarantee that the minor will not attempt to avoid the contract at a later date. Sell the car for cash and let the buyer obtain his own financing. Unlike a house, a car depreciates rapidly, and you don't want to get involved in complicated and messy procedures of repossessing the car for nonpayment and attempting to sell it over again after it has depreciated in value. Don't deliver the car and the keys until you have the cash, and make sure that the vehicle is or will be promptly registered in the name of the new owner so that you will not continue to be liable for damages or injuries as the registered owner of the automobile (see Section 12.6).

[4.22]

2. Mail-Order Contracts

An ordinary mail-order purchase from a catalog normally presents no more problems than the purchase of goods from the store itself. If the goods are defective, they can be returned for refund or credit. There are some kinds of mail-order contracts that are more complicated. You may receive in the mail an offer to join a book or record club. The typical solicitation will say that there is no need to send money, simply fill in and return the enclosed card and you will receive the first offering of merchandise which you have ten days to examine. At the end of ten days you may return it and not be charged, or you may keep it and be billed for it. You will then continue to receive regular shipments of merchandise which you may or may not be obligated to take. Usually you have to accept a certain minimum number over a certain period of time, and must pay for them. Because of the problems involved in long-distance communication and the frequency of computer breakdown or error, this type of contract tends to result in a great deal of trouble, most of it based on this communication. The only way to protect yourself is to be sure to keep a copy (preferably a photocopy) of every agreement that you sign and send to the company, and of every letter that you send to them. You can get a photocopy made of almost any document for as little as 10¢ at a local document-copying center. It is a worthwhile investment because you don't have to rely on memory later on when it comes to trying to figure out what was in the agreement that you signed, or in trying to prove what you sent to the mail-order company. It also enables you to keep track of deadlines. If you have kept a copy of the original order, then when you receive the goods you can review it, see exactly how many days you have to examine the goods, free, and you will know when you will have to return them in order to avoid being charged. When dropping out of one of these mail-order clubs, be sure to keep a copy of your letter resigning your membership. If you want to be absolutely sure, send your letter certified mail, return receipt requested, and keep a copy of it. When you receive the signed copy of the receipt, fasten it to your "file copy," and keep it on hand for as long as necessary (at least a year would be advisable). If you haven't heard from the company in a year, you can safely assume they are not going to bill you further or sic a collection agency on you. There are, of course, exceptions to this, and some companies may press claims for old bills dug out by their auditors that have been gathering dust for more than a year. If you want to be absolutely safe, keep your file copies of materials pertaining to the mail-order contract for the period of the statute of limitations on written contracts in your state (probably four years).

Sometimes you will receive unsolicited merchandise in the mail. If you have done nothing to cause the merchandise to be shipped to you, you have no obligation to pay for it. In spite of what is said in the documents accompanying the merchandise, you do not have an obligation to pay return postage. What you should do is merely set the package aside somewhere where it will be kept safely, and wait for the mail-order house to request either payment or return of the goods. Then send them a post card (keep a photocopy) telling them that you did not order the goods and that they may pick them up at your house or send you the amount of postage required for a return shipment. If you like you can give them a reasonable period of time (thirty to sixty days) to pick up the goods before you dispose of them. After that time has passed, you may then dispose of the goods if you don't wish to continue storing them. It would be best not to make any use of the goods unless you intend to pay for them. However, watch for recently proposed legislation that may give the person who receives unsolicited goods through the mail the complete ownership of them without obligation to pay for them.

[4.23]   3.   Door-to-Door Salesmen's Contracts

Door-to-door solicitation is another troublesome area of contract law. Experienced and capable salesmen can talk the ordinary housewife (and her husband) into buying almost anything, once the foot is in the door. Most reputable companies represented by door-to-door salesmen have a policy that the goods may be returned without charge (provided they are unused and undamaged) if the election to return is made within a short period of time. However, many companies do not have such a policy, and the purchaser of goods from a door-to-door salesman often finds, after the salesman has left and "buyer's remorse" has set in, that he has signed an iron-clad contract binding him to make regular monthly payments and that if he fails to do so the company can and will have a collection agency sue him for the balance due under the contract—plus interest, plus expense of litigation, plus attorneys' fees. Protection exists in the form of laws that permit the customer to cancel sales contracts made with door-to-door salesmen within three days.

There are several simple rules to follow in dealing with door-to-door salesmen. First, demand proper identification. Know the name of the person and the name of his company. Many local jurisdictions require a permit from city hall for door-to-door solicitation. Ask to see the permit. A reputable firm will require its salesmen to obtain permits. Never buy anything you don't need just because it appears to be a bargain. Some vacuum cleaner salesman may show you a cleaner for $10, to get your interest up, and then will criticize, very subtly, the $10 machine as being too light to do a really good job and end up selling you a $50 machine. Book salesmen are particularly adept at appealing to your desire for knowledge and/or culture, and can make you feel very guilty by refusing to buy a twenty-five-volume set containing "all the knowledge in the world." Most offers to "put something in your home for public display, trial," etc. are phoney. Most pitches that begin with "You have been selected as the lucky winner," etc., but that end with a requirement that you pay some money, are phoney. Most contests whereby the salesman is seeking "votes" or some other expression of confidence from you that will enable him to win a scholarship, a trip around the world, etc. are phoney. This stunt is frequently employed by door-to-door magazine salesmen who move through areas in fleets of cars and flood the local neighborhoods with young boys and girls who are supposedly working their way through college by selling magazine subscriptions. Most of the subscriptions they sell are for long terms (three to five years), and are two to three times as expensive as the price you can get by ordering direct from the publisher.

The best rule of thumb prior to buying anything from a door-to-door salesman is to ask yourself whether you really want and need the article he is offering, and if you would have gone out and bought it on your own, had he not come to the door. If the answer is yes, and he has a permit, and it is from a reputable company, then the next question is whether the price is competitive. There is no harm done in asking him to come back the following day so that you can, in the meantime, compare the price of the article he is offering you with what it would cost you to buy it in a local store. If he is unwilling to come back the next day, he is probably a "fly-by-night" operator, who won't even be within fifty miles of your home the following day.

Finally, before signing a contract handed you by a door-to-door salesman, be sure that you and other members of the family that are affected (e.g., husband and wife) have read it and understand it. Ask for explanations or clarifications of provisions you do not understand. If you object to something in the contract, ask if it can be crossed out and initialed. Insist upon keeping a copy of the agreement after it has been signed and initialed. Be sure to get the name and address and telephone number of the salesman in case you have any complaints later (see Section 7.74).

On contracts that involve either no down payment or a small down payment, and a balance payable over a period of time, there will be (normally) interest charges on the balance, and the lending laws may require certain *disclosure* of the interest rates and other costs of financing. If the disclosure documents are not in the form required by law, you may have an absolute right to rescind the agreement and get back all of your money, and may even have a right to collect damages (see Section 7.76).

4. Leases

a. REAL PROPERTY LEASES [4.24]

A lease is a form of contract. It is basically an agreement between an owner of property and a person who desires to use the property for a period of time in return for payment of rent and observance of certain conditions. A lease for less than a year can be oral, but most leases are written. Standard printed forms tend to be used, and in most cases are adequate. In spite of the fact that printed forms of lease tend to be used, the provisions are nevertheless negotiable, in most cases, and because printed forms tend to favor the landlord over the tenant, the tenant should carefully read the form and not be afraid to suggest modifications or changes or even additions to the printed lease form, which will tend to make the contract less one-sided. It doesn't cost much to have a lawyer look over a lease before you sign, and it's probably a good investment. For more details on provisions of leases see Part X.

b. LEASES OF PERSONAL PROPERTY [4.25]

Other familiar leases are the car, appliance, or equipment-rental agreement. Car leases are generally standard printed forms, and the lessors will not permit modifications in their form. About all you can do is be sure you read the lease carefully before you sign it, and if you don't understand it, ask for an explanation. If you don't understand the explanation, see a lawyer and have him explain it to you. Be sure you know what happens at the end of the term of the lease when you wish to dispose of the automobile you have been leasing and lease another one. Also be sure you know what happens under the lease in the event of mechanical breakdown. Who pays for replacement of parts? Who pays for a substitute rental automobile during the time your disabled rental automobile is tied up in the garage? Are you allowed some trade-in value on the car you have been leasing at the end of your lease term to be applied toward purchase or toward leasing of a new automobile? Are you permitted to sell the car for more than the value placed upon it by the lessor at the end of the term, and pocket the excess proceeds of the sale? What insurance are you required to maintain? What maintenance are you required to have performed on the car, and who pays for that? If you are close to the end of your lease term when the car needs new tires, should you buy brand-new expensive tires, or inexpensive re-treads? (The answer to this question and similar questions having to do with batteries, muffler, etc., depends on whether you get "credit" for the remaining value of these items under the term of the lease you have signed, or whether you are obligated to return the car in whatever condition it remains at the end of the term without any adjustment being made on the price owing to the condition of the automobile.) Generally speaking, if you drive less than 15,000 miles per year, you are probably better off buying a car than leasing it. If you drive more than 30,000 miles a year, you are probably better off leasing a car than owning it. There are certain tax advantages to leasing. You can get similar results if you buy a car, but much more complicated bookkeeping is required in order to establish your depreciation schedule for the automobile and to keep track of your maintenance and expenses.

On appliance- or equipment-rental agreements, or miscellaneous lease agreements for items such as airplanes, boats, tractors, trucks, trailers, etc., be sure you read and understand the rental agreement before signing, and be sure to note carefully the condition of the equipment at the time that you first take possession of it.

5. Contract for Construction or Remodeling of House

[4.26]

One type of contract frequently entered into is a contract for the construction of a home or the remodeling of an existing home. It may be a separate agreement with the architect, with the general contractor, and with one or more subcontractors. Most experienced architects and builders will have their own printed or typewritten form contracts. Because they like to use the same forms on all jobs, the forms are necessarily brief and may not specifically cover your situation. They should be read carefully to determine whether portions of them are not at all applicable and should be stricken out, with the deletions initialed in the margin, and whether they are complete enough to cover everything that you need to have detailed in the agreement. Additional paragraphs should be added on a separate page to be attached, to take care of any additions you desire. A good rule to follow in the case of all contracts, as has been mentioned, is never to sign a contract that has blanks in it. The blanks should either be filled in before you sign or crossed out.

There are very few exceptions to this rule. It is generally a mistake to permit the other party to the contract to fill in the blanks at some later date with items or amounts that you have not approved in advance. You should also obtain and keep a copy of any agreement you sign.

Never pay in advance for construction or remodeling. Even if the contract calls for making progress payments as things go along, make sure that the final payment is large enough to cover the last installment of the work, if it has to be done by someone else, and make sure that the final payment is not made until the work has been done. In some states you have to post a *notice of commencement* before you make the first payment. If you have a contract with a builder and he has not paid the subcontractors or has not paid for the materials that have been delivered to the site, and you make the final payment to him, it is possible that the subcontractor or material-man may file a lien against your property. You should find out what your local lien laws say about filing a notice of completion after completion of the job and what the waiting period is after filing such a notice before lien claims are cut off. Your agreement should provide that the final payment does not have to be made until that period of time (the cut-off period) has elapsed following the filing of a notice of completion (see Paragraph 1, below).

a. NECESSARY ELEMENTS OF A CONTRACT

- The date, the names of the parties, their signatures, and a description of the property

- The total amount of money that is to be paid for the job

- A detailed description of the work that is to be done

- The time within which the work is to be commenced and completed

- The time for and the method of payment

- For protection of both parties, any changes, modifications, or alterations should be in writing and should be inserted into the agreement. If the contract does not call for a cash payment, but permits installment payments, it should also fully disclose the interest rate and any finance charges you will be called upon to bear (see Section 10.22).

b. AMOUNT OF DETAIL

The important thing to remember about a construction or remodeling contract is that no amount of detail is too great. If the contract is a remodeling contract, it can go into great detail as to the type of construction, materials to be used, method of application, grade and quality of materials to be used, etc. If the contract is for construction of a new home, the plans and specifications will have to be incorporated by reference into the contract. Unfortunately, this means you will have to be able to read blueprints. If you are unable to read blueprints and you have some doubts about whether or not you are getting exactly what you are supposed to get, you should hire somebody who can read blueprints to supervise the job for you and to act as a liaison between you and the general contractor or the architect. The architect, of course, is supposed to supervise the general contractor and make sure that the home is built according to the plans and specifications. However, architects are busy people and cannot always be on the job every day to make sure that little mistakes are not made by workmen who may not know much more about reading blueprints than you do. If you have the time and the ability, you can stay on the job and see that everything is done right. If you have neither the time nor the inclination to do this sort of thing, you might consider hiring an experienced blueprint reader to check the progress of the work at least once a day and tell you and/or the architect if any mistakes are being made.

It never hurts to put in a clause reading: "All materials shall be new, and of good quality, and all workmanship shall be of good quality." Be sure the contractor is obligated to pay for the building permit, or that it is included in the contract price. The contractor should also carry adequate Workmen's Compensation insurance. Consult with your broker on whether or not the policy the contractor carries is broad enough to protect you.

c. BOND

You might also consider whether or not the contractor is bonded; most experienced and reputable contractors are. This means that if they default on their obligations, the bonding company will make it up to you. Some small operators are not bonded because they don't have enough experience to get a bond or they can't afford the premiums. You should be extremely careful in dealing with a contractor who cannot get a bond, unless it is a very small job. In very small remodeling jobs, with less than $1,000 involved, it is probably not worth the trouble and expense of obtaining a bond. You may also be dealing with small contractors in such cases who can't afford to obtain a bond, or who may ask you to pay the cost of it (1 percent of the contract price, or more), or who perhaps just can't qualify for a bond. You can protect yourself in such cases by not paying until the job is complete.

However, on larger jobs ($1,000 or more) definite consideration should be given to a bond, and certainly a bond should be required on any really big job. The bond will guarantee performance by the contractor and payment of his bills for labor and materials and obligations to subcontractors. If you have a contract secured by a bond, no changes or alterations should be made without the bonding company's consent. No payments should be made to the contractor except those that are actually due under the contract.

d. DEFECTS

Your contract should provide that the contractor shall remedy or correct any defect in workmanship or materials, or any construction that does not comply with the terms of the contract. This obligation should run for a minimum period of time, preferably one year or more.

e. COMPLETION

In case the contractor fails to complete the job, your agreement should provide that you can give him written notice to complete the work, and if he fails to do so within the period of the written notice (ten days will do), you may then go ahead and complete the job, either yourself or using another contractor, and may deduct the cost of completion from the balance due him under the agreement and hold him liable for the excess cost, if any.

f. PER DIEM DAMAGES

It is a good idea to hold a contractor liable for per diem damages (i.e., $50 a day) for each day that he fails to complete the work beyond the completion date specified in the agreement.

g. SECOND THOUGHTS

For those who rush into home improvement or construction contracts without sufficient forethought, and who have second thoughts immediately after signing, the law provides some remedies. There is some federal legislation that gives the right to rescind a home-improvement contract within three days. Under the Truth-In-Lending Act, certain home-improvement loans may be canceled within three days. These are technical areas of the law and if you have an idea that you want to get out of an agreement you have signed and only a day or so has passed, you should see a lawyer immediately.

h. ADDITIONAL INSURANCE

It seems obvious, but you'd be surprised how many people wait until after the remodeling is done, or the house is finished, before they purchase additional insurance coverage. You should see your insurance agent before beginning.

i. FRAUDULENT LOANS

Stay away from contractors who will offer to increase the *bid* or the *cost* of the new or remodeling construction in order to enable you to get a larger loan. You don't want to get involved in a claim by the bank or financial institution that you defrauded them into making an unreasonable loan.

j. COST-PLUS CONTRACTS

As a general rule, *fixed-cost* contracts are better than *cost-plus* contracts. Only very experienced businessmen who have had longstanding relationships with contractors can safely enter into cost-plus contracts. The average homeowner is better off to get several competitive bids and then take the lowest fixed-price bid that has been offered by a reputable and capable builder.

k. INCREASE IN COSTS

What about strikes, sudden increases in cost of lumber, etc.? Unless the contract provides that you get stuck for these, you cannot be forced to pay more on account of them. However, you may have to negotiate with the contractor if he threatens to quit the job unless you pay at least part of the increase in costs. At the first sign of trouble here, you should see your lawyer.

l. MECHANICS LIEN CLAIMS

A bond will protect you against mechanics lien claims. Making joint checks payable to the contractor and to all subcontractors and material-men will also protect you. You can obtain the names of all subcontractors and material-men and ask them for acknowledgement of the fact that they have been paid (or waiver of their lien rights) upon completion of the job prior to your making final payment to the general contractor. In some states you may be required to obtain a sworn statement from the general contractor, acknowledged before a notary public, that he has paid all of his bills, or listing those that have not been paid. Check with your lawyer on this, because if you don't obtain such a statement, you may have to pay the bills twice.

A *mechanics lien* is a claim by a person who furnished labor or materials in connection with the improvement of real property. A lien is created by filing a claim with the county recorder and properly notifying the property owner (some states require notice in advance of filing as well as notice at the time of filing). After recording the lien claim (which establishes the date of the lien for priority purposes), the claimant must file suit within a certain time (ninety days in some states) to foreclose the lien (see Section 10.72).

[4.27]   **6.   Employment Contracts**

The basic elements of an employment contract should include:

a. *TYPE OF WORK*

This would include the job title and specific duties to be performed by the employee which can be described in detail or can be described as any duties reasonably required to be performed by his employer.

b. *TERM OF EMPLOYMENT*

This would include the beginning of the employment and the date upon which it will terminate, unless extended. It can be at will, or it can be for a period of a year or longer.

c. COMPENSATION

The compensation should be spelled out, whether an hourly wage, or monthly or annual salary. The time for periodic payments such as weekly, semimonthly, or monthly should also be specified.

d. FRINGE BENEFITS

Whatever fringe benefits are available should be described and referred to, or the agreement can state generally that the employee will be entitled to whatever fringe benefits are customarily made available to employees in similar categories.

e. WORKING CONDITIONS

The agreement should specify the hours that the employee will work, and whether or not extra compensation will be paid for overtime. In businesses subject to the Federal Fair Labor Standards Act, employees working more than a certain number of hours per day and/or per week must be paid at a higher rate of pay (usually one-and-one-half times their hourly rate). Employees who voluntarily work overtime are not entitled to extra pay. The employer does not have to pay overtime unless he asks his employees to work overtime.

f. TERMINATION

Some employment contracts will spell out what constitutes termination for *cause* and may go into details on circumstances under which the employment shall terminate. Some period of notice should be included.

g. TRANSFER AND MOVING EXPENSES

Large employers having many different locations may provide for travel and relocation expenses in the event employees are transferred. Such agreements should not be left vague, but should be carefully spelled out, particularly the provisions relating to the rules for qualifying for moving and relocation expenses.

h. NONCOMPETITION CLAUSE AND ASSIGNMENT OF INVENTION CLAUSE

Two types of provisions which quite often appear in employment contracts are the *noncompetition clause* and the *assignment of invention clause.* The noncompetition clause generally provides that an employee will not, upon termination of his employment, compete with his former employer by engaging in the same type of business, or by attempting to take away the employer's customers, etc. Such *covenants not to compete* are closely regulated by federal and state laws designed to foster free competition. Whether a particular agreement is enforceable and how to draft such an agreement to make it enforceable are technical questions that should be referred to a competent lawyer. The assignment of invention agreement generally provides that the employee assign all of his rights to any inventions that he produces, conceives, or works on during his employment to his employer. This type of agreement is generally used in the case of an employee who is hired because of his talent for designing or inventing things. To the extent that controversy arises out of this type of agreement, it generally revolves around the employee who claims that he developed an invention on his own time, in his own home, without using any company funds, materials, or working time.

7. Bailment Contracts [4.28]

A *bailment contract* is an agreement whereby personal property is transferred from one person to another person with the understanding that the property is to be returned after a certain period of time, or after certain services have been performed. The person who owns the property is called the *bailor*, and the person to whom he transfers the property is called the *bailee*. If you take your car to a garage to have it repaired, you, the bailor, have entered into a bailment contract with a bailee, the garage. If you loan your sailboat to a friend, and he agrees to return it, there is a bailment. The bailee of goods has certain obligations. He is responsible for the goods he has in his possession, and may be obligated to restore them in the same condition in which he received them when requested by the bailor, unless he has been requested to perform certain services that require alteration or improvement of the goods. A bailee who fails or neglects to perform his duty to restore the goods to the bailor when asked can be held liable for breach of his bailment contract. If you take a gown to the cleaner, it becomes a bailee of your gown and has an obligation to properly clean it and return it to you in good condition. If the bailee does not return the gown in good condition, the cleaner is said to have *breached* its duty as *bailee* under a bailment contract. The cleaner may have to pay for the loss in value of the gown, or buy you a new one. The amount of care which the bailee must use in safekeeping the article entrusted to him depends on the circumstances. More care is required if the bailment is for the benefit of the bailee (you loan your car to a friend). Less care is required if the bailment is for the benefit of the bailor (you ask your friend to drive your car to the station for you). A bailment for mutual benefit requires ordinary care (you leave your car at a parking garage). If you ship goods by truck, rail, or air freight, the carrier becomes a bailee. It is liable for loss or damage, but may limit its liability by contract. It may not be liable for loss or damage due to causes beyond its control.

[4.29] ## C. LICENSES REQUIRED FOR TRADE, BUSINESS, OR PROFESSION

State laws require many businessmen and tradesmen, as well as all professional men, to be licensed in order to conduct their business or profession. The penalty for engaging in trade, business, or profession without a license is twofold. On the one hand the unlicensed person may be guilty of a misdemeanor for which he can be prosecuted in a criminal action. On the other hand the law penalizes him by providing (most states have statutes so providing) that he cannot collect the fees he claims are due him for the work he has performed, if he cannot prove that he was licensed at the time the work was performed and the fees were earned. Licensing statutes are for the protection of the public, and even though the work has been performed satisfactorily and in accordance with the desires of the person ordering the work done, the unlicensed businessman, trades-man, or professional man cannot collect his fee if payment is refused on the grounds that he was unlicensed. For this reason no one who is practicing a profession or working in a trade or business for which a license is required should ever be without one. Similarly, any person owing money to a businessman, tradesman, or professional man for services rendered, who has reason to be dissatisfied with the services and has not yet paid for them, should check to find out whether or not the person performing the services is licensed before paying. Examples of people needing licenses are: real estate brokers and salesmen; stock and bond and mutual fund salesmen; insurance salesmen and brokers; contractors; subcontractors; termite inspectors; pest control companies; door-to-door salesmen (where local government ordinance requires a permit); doctors; lawyers; dentists; accountants; engineers; architects; surveyors; etc. (see Section 7.75).

D. AGENTS

[4.30]   1.   Principal and Agent; Power of Attorney

Agent and *principal* are words that are sometimes used technically in the law. A principal is a person who authorizes an agent to act in his behalf. An agent acts under authority given him by his principal. The authority may be given orally or in writing. It may also be implied by the conduct of the principal and agent in certain cases. Certain agency contracts must be in writing, as for example where the statute of frauds requires a real estate broker's contract to be written. The creation of an *agency* occurs when a principal gives an agent authority to do something in the principal's behalf. It may be the authority to negotiate for the sale of a house; the agent would be called a *real estate agent* (see Section 10.2). A movie star or professional athlete may hire an agent to negotiate employment contracts. Door-to-door salesmen are agents representing the company whose wares they are selling. There are some important aspects of agency law with which you should be familiar. An agent is said to be responsible to his principal for carrying out his duties. If he does not properly carry out these duties, his principal can collect damages from him for breach of his agency contract. Some agents have a *fiduciary* responsibility to their principals. This means they are required to be honest and trustworthy and if they are devious or dishonest to the detriment of their principal or to their own benefit they will be held liable to their principal. An agent may have authority to obligate his principal to a contract, depending on his authority. If the agent has the authority, or if the principal allows it to appear that the agent has such authority, the principal can be legally bound by the acts of his agent.

A principal can also bind himself by ratifying the acts of an agent who acted without authority. An example would be the acceptance of a deposit by a seller who had not previously

---

authorized an agent to receive a deposit or accept an offer on his behalf.

A principal may also be held liable for fraudulent acts of his agent. If a car salesman made false statements about a used car to get you to buy it, you could make the dealer (principal) take the car back and return your money after you learned the truth about the car.

A principal is not liable, however, for crimes committed by his agent unless he himself, directed or aided the agent.

Another important aspect of agency law is that the principal is held responsible to third parties for any wrongful acts of the agent which are within the scope of the agency. For example, if a milk truck driver, while on his route, negligently runs over a child, the company that employs him will be liable for the injuries to the child. In such a case, the milk company as principal is said to be liable for the *tort* of its agent, the truck driver.

Under certain circumstances an agent may be acting so clearly outside the scope of his employment that his principal will not be liable for his acts. The milk truck driver who, during his lunch hour, took his girlfriend for a drive in the truck is said to be on a "frolic and detour" of his own, and is no longer representing his principal, the milk company. Under such circumstances, the agent would be liable, personally, to any persons injured by the truck, and for all damages caused by the truck. The principal would not be liable for these injuries or damages except by virtue of a special motor vehicle statute making the owner of a vehicle liable to an injured party for damages up to a certain amount (see Section 12.6).

By use of a *power of attorney* you can make another person your agent to do something for you. A *general power of attorney* would enable your agent to do anything you could legally do — write checks, sign deeds, sell stocks, etc. A *special power of attorney* would enable your agent to act in your behalf for a certain transaction, such as selling your house after you have moved to another state. Power-of-attorney forms can be purchased at most stationery supply stores. An attorney will prepare one for about $15. The signature must be notarized.

[4.31]   2. Independent Contractor

There is an important distinction between an agent and an *independent contractor*. An independent contractor is a person who agrees to perform a certain task or to complete a certain project. He controls the method and the manner by and in which he works and is not subject to the direct control of any other person in completing the project, except by virtue of his contract. For example, you might hire a painter to come and paint two or three rooms in your house. He might be an independent painting contractor and would enter directly into an agreement with you for the painting of your house. On the other hand, you might contract with a company specializing in home remodeling jobs, and it might agree to paint your bedrooms. The painter that it would send out to paint your bedrooms would *not*, in such a case, be an independent contractor in his relationship with you. He would be an agent (or servant or employee) of the remodeling contractor.

Just why these distinctions are important is sometimes hard to see. The main thing is that in the event difficulties arise, you should know whether the person you are dealing with is an independent contractor and is solely responsible for his actions or for his lack of performance, or, on the other hand, is an agent (or servant or employee), and you should look to his principal or superior for satisfaction, correction, or damages, as the case may be.

E. PERFORMANCE

1. Performance   [4.32]

Performance, as used in contract law, means the completion by one party of the obligations imposed upon him by the contract. Performance may consist of the actual doing of an act, the substantial completion of an obligation, or the offering (*tendering*) of the thing that is to be delivered or done. Whether or not a party has adequately performed his obligation is one of the major areas of potential conflict when agreements between parties break down.

2. Conditions   [4.33]

There may be certain *conditions* attached to a contract. A condition, as used in contract law, means the thing that can either create or extinguish a contractual duty. If you agree to buy a used automobile on condition that a mechanic friend of yours inspect it and approve it, you are not obligated to complete the purchase until the inspection and approval. You have agreed to a *conditional purchase*. If a contractor agrees to build a house for you and you agree to pay him in installments, the payment of each installment is a condition that must occur before he is obligated to continue and complete his performance (building the house). In every contract there is said to be an *implied condition* of good faith and fair dealing. In any employment contract there is an implied condition that the employee will pursue his duties with reasonable diligence.

3. Impossible Performance   [4.34]

Sometimes one or both parties cannot perform a contract because the performance has become impossible. In such a case the party whose performance has been made impossible (through no fault of his own) may be excused from his duty of performance. An actor who has agreed to perform a play in a certain theater at a certain time would be excused from his obligation to perform if the theater burned down and a suitable alternate location was not available. Prevention of performance by so-called acts of God may excuse performance of a contract. Examples would be lightning, flood, or earthquake. If such an event occurs, or if an *act of war* prevents performance, performance may be excused. If performance is made slightly more difficult by some unforeseen event, this will not usually excuse the parties from having to perform their agreement. However, if performance is made many, many times more difficult than it would otherwise have been (although still not impossible), such an occurrence may excuse the parties from their obligations to perform under the contract.

F. BREACH, ENFORCEMENT, AND DAMAGES

1. Breach
[4.35]

A *breach* of contract means an unjustifiable failure to perform contractual obligations. Failure of performance that is legally justified or excused is not equivalent to breach of contract (but may be termed *failure of consideration*).

A breach of contract can either be slight, material, or total. A total breach of contract excuses the other party from having to perform and gives him a right to damages. A very slight breach of contract that does not materially affect the other party does not result in termination of the agreement, and the other party must still perform his obligations. He may have a right, however, to damages as compensation for the slight breach if it has caused him measurable injury or damage. Prevention or hindrance of the other party from performing his obligations is a breach of contract. Sometimes a party may breach an agreement in advance by repudiating his obligation to perform before the time has arrived for his performance. Under such conditions the other party may possibly have a choice between suing at once for damages or waiting until the time for performance arrives and then bringing an action for damages.

2. Enforcement
[4.36]

Suppose you have entered into a contract and the other party either breaches or threatens to breach his part of the agreement. You could sue him for damages, if he does make good his threat, but that might not be what you want. If he has agreed to sell you his house, can you force him to go through with the deal even though he has changed his mind? The answer is yes. *Equity* is a special part of the legal process designed to achieve maximum flexibility within the framework of the law.

A court can grant equitable relief in certain situations where unique solutions to unusual problems are required. Specific *performance* is an equitable remedy available under contract law. The law theorizes that every piece of real estate is unique, and therefore the buyer of real estate is entitled to purchase the property for which he contracted, even if the seller becomes unwilling to sell. The buyer can sue in specific performance and the court will grant him equitable relief consisting of an order that the seller convey title in accordance with the terms of the contract. An equity court will also *enjoin* a party from breaking a contract in certain situations. A basketball player who did not want to play with his NBA team could be enjoined by that team from playing for a rival team in the ABA league if he were still under contract to the NBA team.

[4.37] **3. Damages**

The object of *damages* is to *compensate* the injured party for having lost the benefit of the contract. The law attempts to award to the injured party, as nearly as possible, the equivalent of what he would have received had the contract been fully performed. The injured party should receive an amount that will compensate him for all the damage that naturally arose out of the breach of contract and that would have been reasonably foreseen or contemplated by the parties to the contract. If no substantial damage is caused by the breach, or if the damages that result were not reasonably foreseeable, then only *nominal damages* will be awarded. The plaintiff may recover profits or benefits he would have obtained by performance of the contract only to the extent that he can establish them with reasonable certainty. Interest from the time of the breach may be recoverable where the amount of damages is clearly fixed at the time of the breach. Attorneys' fees are not recoverable as damages under contract law unless so provided by statute or by the contract itself (see Section 9.53). This is unfortunate in most cases, because the attorneys' fees that the plaintiff must pay will eat into his damage award, and even though he may win the lawsuit he may come out with far less than he was entitled to. In the future you may hope to see the law change to permit the prevailing party in a contract action to be awarded reasonable attorneys' fees by the court.

The plaintiff is said to have a duty to minimize his damages. That means that if he sees that the other party has breached the contract, he must take reasonable action to limit his damages and if he does not, he cannot recover the full amount of damages that result if they would have been less if he had so acted.

G. ARBITRATION

Because of the time and expense involved in going to court in breach-of-contract suits, an alternative system has been devised. It is called *arbitration*. The parties may agree, either in the beginning, as part of the contract itself, or after a dispute has arisen, to submit the matter to arbitration rather than to go into court. The parties may set up their own rules for arbitration and pick their own arbitrators. They may submit the matter to selected arbitrators in accordance with rules established by some society such as the American Arbitration Association. This body provides experienced arbitrators who handle matters in accordance with certain written rules, for fees that are generally less than the cost of litigation would have been. The advantages of arbitration are that it is usually faster, less expensive, and less formal than going to court, and therefore compromises can be achieved which might not be possible in a courtroom situation. The disadvantages of arbitration are that a party who is in a strong legal position in a breach-of-contract suit may not come out as well in an arbitration proceeding as he will in a courtroom. Some lawyers and some sophisticated businessmen shy away from arbitration when they feel they are in a strong contractual position, because they feel that the results of litigation in a court are more predictable than are the results from arbitration, and they don't want to take the risk of an unpredictably bad arbitration decision.

Decisions of the arbitrator can be made to have the force of law, the same as judgments of a court.

H. DISCHARGE [4.39]

Contractual obligations are said to be *discharged* when performance has been completed. A contract may also be discharged by *impossibility, rescission, release, accord and satisfaction, cancellation,* or *termination.* Death does not ordinarily discharge a contractual obligation (unless the contract was one that only the decedent could perform). The estate of the decedent will be required to perform.

I. RELEASE AND MODIFICATION

1. Release [4.40]

A party can *release* another party from his obligation to perform a contract, thereby discharging the contract.

2. Accord and Satisfaction [4.41]

An agreement to accept something different from that which was promised under the contract is said to be an *accord and satisfaction.* The agreement to accept this new performance is called an *accord,* and the acceptance of accord is called *satisfaction.* For example, if a legitimate dispute arises between you and your creditor, and you offer to pay him less than the amount he claims is due (but more than the amount you claim is due) and he accepts the sum you offer, then accord and satisfaction has taken place and your obligation to him has been extinguished.

[4.42]   ### 3.   New Agreement

A *novation* means a new agreement, one which replaces the prior existing agreement. A novation is simply a new contract which is intended to, and which does extinguish the old contract.

[4.43]   ### 4.   Modification

Any agreement may be modified or amended by mutual agreement of the parties. If there were errors in the original agreement, it may be modified without any new consideration being exchanged. Modifications that change the basic terms of the agreement require some new consideration to be exchanged.

J. ASSIGNMENT

An *assignment* means a transfer of rights and responsibilities under a contract. Assignments may be made orally unless they are required by statute to be in writing. Most contracts are assignable unless by their terms they call for some kind of special personal service that can only be rendered by a particular person, or unless the contract itself expressly prohibits assignment. In many leases and in many deed of trust forms you find a prohibition against assignment without the consent of the landlord or of the beneficiary of the deed of trust.

Most states have restrictions upon an assignment of wages by an employee.

The person who assigns his rights under a contract that involves reciprocal rights and duties cannot escape responsibility for his performance under the contract by an assignment. He still remains liable to the other party to the contract if the person to whom he has assigned his rights (and duties) does not perform.

K. RESCINDING A CONTRACT

If you find out you were defrauded by the other party to a contract, you may *rescind* the contract. *Rescission* means each party returns what he got from the other party. If you offer to give back the car you bought in return for the money you paid, when you learn the speedometer was turned back, the other party must give back the money and take the car or you may sue him for *rescission.*

V. Lawsuits

A. THE PLAINTIFF'S CASE

1. Cause of Action

[5.1]

Before you can think about becoming a plaintiff in a lawsuit, you must first have a case. Whether you have a case or not depends upon what your *cause of action* is. The cause of action is what a lawsuit is all about. If you get hit by a car while you are in a pedestrian crosswalk, crossing with the green light, you have a cause of action against the driver of that car. Your cause of action would be in *tort*, for *negligence*.

If you sign an agreement and pay a down payment for the purchase of a house and the seller refuses to go through with the deal, you would have a cause of action against him for breach of contract. Your lawyer will tell you what kind of a cause of action you have, and how good it is, or what your chances of winning are.

2. Complaint

[5.2]

A *complaint* is one of a number of legal documents that are collectively referred to as *pleadings*. A complaint names the *plaintiff* and the *defendant*, and has the title of the court in which it is to be filed on its first page. The body of the complaint sets forth the facts upon which your cause of action is based. Complaints are normally drafted by lawyers for their clients, and are filed with the clerk of the court having jurisdiction over the subject matter of the law suit. If planning to file your own case, see the chart on page ii to get an idea of the different courts that exist, and then seek help from the clerk of your local court in deciding which court is the proper one to hear your case. A filing fee must be paid to the clerk when the complaint is filed. The original copy goes into a new file which the clerk sets up under a new number. All later pleadings filed with the clerk that are connected with that action will be stamped with that same number and filed in that same file. This file becomes a public record and is open to inspection.

The complaint must set forth facts sufficient to state a cause of action. It must also be filed in the proper form, and on acceptable paper, etc. Each court has its own rules (which are fairly standard) regarding the form a complaint must be in to be accepted for filing. If you want to draft your own complaint, get a form book from the county library in order to find out what wording should be used in the complaint. Ask the clerk of the court in which you intend to file your complaint for some examples of complaints so that you can pattern yours after them. A complaint should be short and factual. It should not go into a lot of unnecessary detail, nor should it consist of a lot of arguments. It should be clear exactly what the complaint is and how the defendant was responsible. The complaint recites the damages sustained by the plaintiff and asks for relief in the form of money compensation or something else.

[5.3]   3.   Summons

When a complaint is filed, you or your lawyer can request the clerk to issue a *summons*. The summons is a form provided by the court which must be filled in by the plaintiff or his attorney. It directs the defendant to appear and answer the complaint within a certain period of time. The summons is issued by the clerk, and is served upon the defendant along with a copy of the complaint. It can be served by a sheriff or other qualified officer of the law, or by a private process server. (There are people or companies that serve papers for hire. They are usually listed in the yellow pages.) The serving of a summons is accomplished by handing a copy of the summons and the complaint to the defendant. It doesn't make any difference if he refuses to take it. An experienced process server will hand it to the person he has identified as the defendant, and if the defendant does not take it, the process server will drop it at his feet and tell him that he has been served. The same can be accomplished by slipping it through the window of the car in which the defendant is seated if he refuses to open the door. Summons can be served by an ordinary citizen, but he should not be a party to the lawsuit, and generally is required to be an adult.

What if the plaintiff can't find the defendant in order to have him served? Some defendants are not around because they have left the area or perhaps even the state. Other defendants are good at dodging summonses and can be served only by the most skillful professional process server. Most states permit service to be made by publication if the defendant is out of the state or is evading service, in which case the summons must be published in a local newspaper in accordance with statutory requirements. The cost of getting a summons and complaint served on the defendant can be anywhere from $2 to $3 paid to the sheriff, or from $5 to $50 paid to a private process server on a difficult case. If you have to publish summonses, the cost of publication can run the bill up even higher. These *costs* are recoverable from the defendant if you prevail in your action. Some laws allow you to mail a copy of the summons and complaint to the defendant. He can accept service by signing and returning a form. If he refuses to do so, he has to pay the cost of a process server, even if he wins the case. If a plaintiff sues you but you never get a copy of the summons because the process server lies about having delivered it to you, and as a result a default judgment is taken against you, what can you do? You can file a motion to have the judgment set aside as soon as you learn of it; you can also sue for damages the process server who lied, or have him prosecuted criminally for perjury.

[5.4]   4.   Attachment and Execution

Often the plaintiff has a good claim against a defendant, and yet has reason to fear that the defendant is in shaky financial condition or may suddenly dispose of his property if he is sued. The plaintiff naturally doesn't want to spend his money getting a judgment only to find that he can't collect it because the defendant doesn't have any property or money. In a few situations, law provides a remedy known as *attachment*. Attachment is available only in certain cases because appellate courts have held that laws permitting unlimited attachment before trial are unconstitutional. The decisions are based on the concept that one's property should not be taken from him without a trial, except in limited situations. In those cases in which attachment is permitted, the plaintiff, at the time he files his complaint and has his summons issued by the clerk, may also obtain a *writ of attachment*. In order to obtain this writ he must post a bond in the amount he is suing for. The bond is for the protection of the defendant. The plaintiff obtains the bond from a bonding company, paying a premium to the company for the bond. (A normal premium would be $10 for each $1,000 worth of bond.) He then posts the bond with the clerk of the court. He may also be required to file an *affidavit* with the clerk in order to get the writ of attachment. The affidavit must be a sworn statement relating the facts upon which the case is based and setting forth the facts necessary to entitle him to obtain a writ of attachment. The writ is then issued by the clerk (for an additional fee) and the plaintiff or his lawyer takes this to the sheriff's office. The sheriff then *attaches* the property identified by the plaintiff as belonging to the defendant. It can be a bank account, a house, a car, a boat, land, etc. The sheriff completes the attachment by posting notice on the property that it has been attached, taking physical possession of the automobile or boat, by notifying the bank that the bank account is attached, and so forth. The property is then *held* by or under the authority of the sheriff until the case is tried or settled.

If the plaintiff wins he gets a judgment and obtains a *writ of execution,* and takes that to the sheriff who then executes on the property that was previously attached by having it sold at public auction. The proceeds of sale are applied on the judgment.

If the plaintiff loses his case, the defendant may be entitled to recover his costs, and possibly may be entitled to other relief from the plaintiff. If he has been damaged because his property has been attached pending the outcome of the litigation, he may press a claim against the plaintiff for those damages. If the plaintiff is unable to pay the defendant for these damages, the defendant can collect the money from the bonding company (the bonding company will in turn ask the plaintiff to pay it back). It is not a good idea to use attachment as a remedy unless you have an airtight case and have reason to believe that the judgment may not be collectable unless you attach some assets initially. Some things are exempt from attachment (see Section 5.16).

5. Injunction [5.5]

Occasionally a plaintiff does not seek money damages, but wants to stop the defendant from doing something. A wife may want to get an order from the court restraining her estranged husband from molesting her. A property owner may want to stop a logger from cutting trees on his property in the area of a boundary dispute. In these cases the plaintiff would ask for *injunctive relief.* The plaintiff or his lawyer would prepare a complaint and also a petition for a *temporary restraining order* or a *preliminary injunction.* A temporary restraining order can sometimes be obtained from a judge upon presentation of a sworn affidavit containing the facts upon which the claim is based. The restraining order would order the defendant to stop doing something until a preliminary hearing could be held to determine whether or not the plaintiff has a good claim against the defendant. A temporary restraining order, when granted, is for a very short period of time. The plaintiff must usually post a bond in order to get a temporary restraining order so that if it turns out he does not have a good case, the defendant will have somewhere to look for any damages he has sustained by virtue or having obeyed the order. The next step in obtaining injunctive relief is to seek a preliminary injunction. A petition or request for this is filed with the clerk and then served upon the defendant. At the hearing the plaintiff then asks the court to issue the preliminary injunction, which means an order to the defendant to stop doing something until a full-scale hearing or *trial upon the merits* is heard at a later date. Sometimes a plaintiff will seek a temporary restraining order and be unsuccessful in obtaining it, will then seek a preliminary injunction and be unsuccessful in attaining it, and will go on to trial and succeed in obtaining a permanent injunction at trial. In other cases he may get a temporary restraining order and a preliminary injunction, but may be denied a permanent injunction at trial. In the latter case he is responsible to the defendant for any damages the defendant has sustained during the period he has been temporarily restrained or injoined.

6. Equitable Relief [5.6]

Your complaint may seek some type of *equitable relief,* such as rescission of a contract which you claim was entered into based on fraud or misrepresentation of the other party. You also may want the court to interpret an ambiguous agreement between you and another person. You would then file a complaint seeking *declaratory relief.* If you live in a subdivision and one of your neighbors is violating the recorded *covenants, conditions,* and *restrictions* that apply to all lots in that subdivision, you could bring an action to enforce the covenants. You might bring an action to prevent an upstream owner from polluting a stream or from cutting off your water supply. If you get caught in the middle between two other litigants, you might file an *interpleader* action, which means you would deposit the money or whatever you had that they both wanted into court and let them fight it out without involving you. (In other words, you do not claim what the other two parties are after.) Another equitable action would be *quiet title.* By such an action you would have a court determine the validity of your title to your real property and specifically determine whether or not someone else who claims an interest in your property has the right to do so.

7. Administrative Remedies [5.7]

If you sought a building permit from the building department of your city and it was denied for what you considered to be improper reasons, you might bring a *mandamus* action, which would in effect ask the court to order the building department to issue the permit. However, before bringing any such action, you would first have to follow the procedural or administrative remedies the city ordinances provide, which might include appealing to the planning commission and to the city council before going to court.

You might ask for a *writ of prohibition* if you wish to stop some governmental official from taking detrimental action involving your rights. The area of equitable relief is a complicated and technical one and requires the assistance of a lawyer.

[5.8]   **8. Statute of Limitations**

Every legal cause of action has a *statute of limitations* that applies to it, set forth in a written statute. It is necessary to file an action within the time limit. Normally there is a one-year statute of limitations on tort actions based on negligence. Some states have a two-year statute of limitations on oral contracts and a four-year statute of limitations on written contracts. One of the first things to find out about your case is what statute of limitations applies.

[5.9]   **9. Laches**

Equitable actions have something similar to a statute of limitations, referred to as the doctrine of *laches.* Laches in effect means an unreasonable delay in bringing your action. There is no set time within which an equitable action must be brought, but if the delay seems unreasonably long, the court may prevent you from bringing the action by the doctrine of laches.

[5.10]   **10. Exhaustion of Administrative Remedies**

In the area of administrative law, where governmental institutions are involved, there is a doctrine referred to as *exhaustion of administrative remedies.* What this means is that if you have been denied a building permit, for example, you must follow whatever administrative remedies have been set up by the applicable governmental ordinances before you can sue the city. This may mean that you have to file a written claim in a certain form, within a certain period of time. Then you have to take the matter up with certain administrative or governmental bodies. You can only file a legal action when you have given these bodies a chance to consider your claim and they have denied it.

11. The Prosecution of Your Case [5.11]

If you are representing yourself, note the time the defendant was served and check with the clerk of the court to see whether or not he has filed an answer within the time required. If he has not done so, then you ask the clerk to have the default of the defendant entered. Generally the court provides a form for you to fill out and sign requesting that a default be entered. If you have asked for a simple money judgment, some states then permit you to obtain a default judgment without having to appear and testify in court. You then prepare a form entitled *Judgment by Default* or something similar, and ask that it be submitted by the clerk to the judge for signature. When the judgment has been obtained, you then can obtain a *writ of execution* or similar document which entitles you to have the sheriff levy upon or attach property of the defendant in order to have it sold at auction to satisy your judgment. You can also ask the county recorder to record your judgment for you (for a small fee). The judgment then becomes a lien against property owned by the defendant within that county. If he tries to sell his property, he will have to get your release (and you can get his money) before he can close the sale to some third person.

If the defendant answers your complaint, then it is up to you to bring the case to trial. After certain preliminary events (see "Discovery," pp. 132-36), you can ask the clerk (generally by filing an approved form) that the matter be put on the calendar or scheduled for trial. One of the unfortunate things about our judicial system today is that some courts are months or perhaps even years behind on their calendars and it is not possible to get a case to trial within a reasonable period of time. If you want a jury trial (instead of letting the judge decide) it will take much longer to get a trial date. The law generally requires that you keep the defendant informed of everything you do by sending him a copy of every document you file with the court. If the defendant is represented by an attorney and you are not, you must correspond with and talk to his attorney. If you are represented by an attorney, your attorney will talk to the defendant's attorney, and will keep him informed—likewise as to the defendant if he does not have an attorney but is handling his own case.

If you have demanded a jury trial, you will be notified by the clerk when jury fees must be deposited with the court, and in what amount. Failure to deposit the fees on time means that you may waive your right to jury trial. The jury fees are *costs* that can be collected by the prevailing party from the losing party.

B. THE DEFENDANT'S CASE

1. Demurrer

[5.12]

If you are served with a summons and a complaint and you take it to your attorney, he may read it over and decide that it is defective because it contains some technical defects. He might then file a *demurrer*, usually accompanied by a memorandum (usually called a *memorandum of points and authorities*) which states why he feels the complaint is defective. The demurrer will normally be heard within a few days of the time it is served upon the plaintiff. The attorneys for both parties appear before the judge and argue as to whether the complaint is defective or not. If the demurrer is *sustained*, it means that the complaint is indeed defective and the plaintiff must try to redraft it in a proper manner in order to proceed with his suit. The judge may or may not give the plaintiff the privilege of amending or attempting to amend his pleading; in most cases he will be given this opportunity. He then drafts a new complaint and serves it again upon the defendant or the defendant's lawyer and the attorney can then either file another demurrer or an answer.

2. Answer

[5.13]

The defendant, having been served with a summons and a complaint, must either file a demurrer or an answer within the time stated in the summons. If he fails to do this, the plaintiff can have a default entered and get the relief he seeks without the court listening to the defendant's side of the case. An *answer* is a pleading that follows the same general form as a complaint, except that in the answer the allegations set forth in the complaint are admitted if true or denied if false.

[5.14]   3.   Cross-Complaint

If you are served with a summons and complaint and you feel that you have a claim against the plaintiff, you can file a *cross-complaint* or *counterclaim* against him. Sometimes you can file a cross-complaint against a third party and bring him into the suit. There are technical differences between cross-complaints and counterclaims which only lawyers and judges understand.

[5.15]   4.   Interpleader

As was mentioned in Section 5.6, a party caught in the middle of the lawsuit can sometimes file an *interpleader action,* which means that he does not make any claim to whatever it is that other parties are after, and that he deposits it in court and lets them fight it out. An example would be a title company that is holding a deposit received from the buyer of a house. The buyer might sue the title company for return of his deposit, and the seller might tell the title company not to return the money to the buyer. In that case the title company would file an interpleader action offering to deposit the money in court and let the buyer and the seller fight it out.

[5.16]   5.   Exemption from Attachment

If your property is attached, you may be able to obtain a bond from a bonding company by paying a premium (usually $10 per $1,000) to obtain an attachment release bond and then posting the bond with the court. Most states have exemption statutes which exempt all or a portion of your wages from attachment. Federal laws also exempt wages paid by employers involved in interstate commerce from attachment or garnishment. You may have to file a proper affidavit in the correct form with the court or with the sheriff, depending upon the circumstances, in order to get your wages released from an attachment. A federal statute prevents the firing of an employee of a business involved in interstate commerce the first time his wages are attached. If your wages are attached, you should either see your lawyer or check with the clerk of your court to find out what exemptions apply and what procedures should be followed in order to claim the exemptions. This should be done immediately. Most statutes also exempt certain property from attachment such as certain basic items of furniture, tools needed by a workman to make his living, some farm animals, an automobile having a relatively low blue-book value, etc. Other items of personal or real property are not exempt and can be attached. The attachment may be of no consequence to you (unless it is of wages), and you may be willing to wait until the case is tried before doing anything about it. If the plaintiff loses the case, the attachment is released and you may have a claim for damages against the plaintiff if it has in fact damaged you (for example, it may have prevented you from selling your property on very favorable terms). You may be able to exempt your home from attachment by filing a *homestead* (see Section 10.74). Household goods and personal effects are generally exempt from creditors' claims. Most states have a list of items that are exempt, and they vary from one shotgun and one pair of hogs to one grand piano, depending upon what state you're in. Some states exempt savings and loan association savings accounts up to a certain amount. Many types of pensions are exempt. Life insurance policies and their cash values may be exempt. If you get into a situation in which assets are being attached, check with a lawyer to find out what property is exempt, and then claim your exemption by filing the appropriate document with the sheriff or with the clerk of the court having jurisdiction over the matter. (See Section 5.4 regarding possible unconstitutionality of attachment statues.)

C. DISCOVERY

[5.17]   1.   Depositions

After the initial investigation of the facts has been completed, the first step in *discovery* usually involves *depositions*. Discovery is a term that refers to the finding out about the case of your adversary before the case goes to trial. You *discover* what evidence the other side has by asking questions and obtaining documents and other evidence. A deposition is the oral testimony of one of the parties or of a witness, taken under oath before a notary public, reduced to typewritten pages after the oral testimony has been transcribed, bound and filed with the court, with a copy given to each side. Depositions serve three main purposes:

> • To find out what the person whose deposition is being taken will say;

> • To learn as much as you can about the case prior to trial;

● To pin the witness down to a written sworn statement from which he cannot deviate at trial without having to explain his inconsistencies to the judge or jury.

A deposition can also preserve testimony of a witness who might not be around at the time of trial. Depositions are usually taken at a lawyer's office, with a court reporter, the lawyers for both sides, and the witness whose deposition is being taken all being present.

Careful lawyers will meet with their clients prior to the taking of the deposition to let them know what to expect and to give them a few "dos and don'ts." If your deposition is being taken, you should be very careful about the answers you give. Testifying at a deposition is not like being in a courtroom; a judge or a jury is not listening to your testimony and watching you, and it doesn't matter how long you take to frame your answer because the deposition will not indicate pauses. Therefore you have ample time to think. Never answer a question unless you clearly understand it. If you do not understand it, ask that it be repeated or state that you don't understand it. You have a right to make the attorney questioning you frame his questions properly. Another good rule to follow is never to guess or estimate if you do not know something.

Remember that the interrogator is after information. The more you talk, the more information he gets. The less information you give out at a deposition, the better off you will be. This means that you keep your answers as short as possible. If a question can be answered yes or no, limit yourself to that unless you feel you absolutely must explain an answer because a plain yes or no answer is misleading and might leave an impression that would be harmful to your case. Never volunteer information at a deposition.

Don't allow yourself to become emotional at a deposition.

Some lawyers will attempt to rile you to see what kind of a witness you will make on the stand. If you lose your temper at a deposition, they will figure you will do the same thing at trial, and mark you down as a witness having a major weakness. You should be as pleasant and as polite as possible—try to act natural and not display any nervousness. Don't try to be clever or to outsmart the lawyer asking you questions—he is far more experienced than you and you have everything to lose and nothing to gain by being a smart aleck.

If you don't know or can't remember something, be sure to say that, and don't guess or try to think out loud. Answer all questions that are put to you unless your lawyer (if you are represented by one) interrupts you with an objection or instructs you not to answer. Don't ask your lawyer whether you have to answer a question. Don't tell the attorney questioning you that he has no right to ask that particular question, unless you do not have your lawyer there.

If you are representing yourself or are not represented by a lawyer at a place where your deposition is being taken, just try to answer the questions put to you truthfully and as briefly as possible without elaboration or detail.

[5.18]   2.   Interrogatories

Interrogatories are written questions prepared by an attorney and served upon the attorney for the other party in the action. The questions must be answered in writing within time limits set by law. The answers must be under oath. The purpose of interrogatories is to discover something about the facts of the case which are unknown to the party asking the questions, or to pin down the party being questioned as to what his version of the facts will be at trial. In answering interrogatories, each question must be answered clearly and fully, and the written answers must be returned to the attorney from whom the questions were received within the stated time limit. Sometimes improper questions can be asked, either at a deposition or in interrogatories, and in such cases it is proper to object to them and, in some cases, to refuse to answer them. When this occurs, the party who asked the question may either agree that the question was improper and drop the matter or he may file a motion to have the matter brought before a judge for a ruling on whether or not the question must be answered.

3. Subpoena   [5.19]

A *subpoena* is a document issued by a court or some other legal authority that requires the person upon whom it is served to appear at a certain time and place in order to testify. It may be served by a sheriff or legal officer, or in some states it may be served by a private citizen—a professional process server, a lawyer, or any adult who is not a party to the action.

Anyone who receives a subpoena should appear at the time and place ordered or he may be found in contempt of court and be subject to fine or jail sentence. Sometimes the clerk of the court or the attorney for the party that subpoenaed can arrange a postponement, if an emergency has arisen. It is always better to phone before than it is to try to explain afterwards why you did not show up; this may avert a contempt citation or at least a tongue-lashing from the judge. If you are served with a subpoena, be sure to ask to see the original subpoena (you will be given a copy) and ask for your witness fees. In most states you are entitled to a small witness fee which includes a per diem allowance and mileage. It will not be much, but if you fail to ask for it then, you may never see it. Also, if the process server does not have a check or cash with him for the fees, the service is then invalid and he must return at another time. If he serves you anyway with the document and tells you that he does not have to pay you any fees, don't assume that you do not have to show up. In that case, call the clerk of the court and discuss it with him. He will tell you whether or not you have been legally served.

[5.20]   4.   Subpoena Duces Tecum

A *subpoena duces tecum* is like a subpoena except that it requires that certain documents be brought to court to be used as evidence. An accountant may have his books brought into court by subpoena duces tecum, or a doctor may have his medical records subpoenaed. In most states there are special procedures set up for doctors' records and clinic and hospital records. The *custodian of records* is the person upon whom the subpoena duces tecum is served and he or she brings the records to court at the proper time. If the records are needed by the person receiving the subpoena duces tecum and the originals are to be used at trial, a request should be made that the attorney stipulate to the return of the originals as soon as the trial is over, or stipulate to the substitution of photocopies for the originals if that is practicable. Most attorneys usually cooperate with such requests.

D. A TYPICAL TRIAL

1. Cause of Action: An Automobile Accident— [5.21]
Facts and Preliminaries

Assume that you are stopped in traffic on the freeway and have been sitting there for perhaps fifteen seconds when you are suddenly struck from the rear by another car. What is your next move? (See Section 12.7.) Stop your motor and get out of your car. If you have an emergency flare, light it and put it well to the rear of the vehicle behind you. If it is dark and no one has a flare, someone with a flashlight should walk back up the road and try to flag down or slow down oncoming traffic. If you are in the middle of a very busy freeway and you can't get a flare out immediately, the safest thing may be to get all the people out of the cars that are involved in the accident and get them off the road until the police arrive. If there is a phone nearby, the police should be notified. If anyone is injured, an ambulance should be called. Injured people should not be moved unless there is a fire or immediate danger of fire, or unless it is dangerous to leave them in the vehicle because of the traffic conditions.

It is important to immediately identify witnesses to the accident. Usually there will be at least two different versions of how the accident happened. Try to identify any witnesses that are in the area, and ask them if they will remain and give a statement to the police. If they refuse to do so ask them for a name, an address, a telephone number, a business card, etc. If they won't give you that, at least try to get the license number of their car so you can have them traced.

Try not to get involved with the driver of the other car as to who was at fault. What you want to do is to exchange drivers'-license information with him and make sure you record his name, address, telephone number, the make, model, year, and license number of his vehicle, and the date, time, and place

---

of the accident. If the police arrive in time to investigate the accident, they will usually take care of these things for you and write up a complete report. In such a case, all you should do is make sure that none of the witnesses get away in the confusion. Be sure they remain long enough for the police to get a statement from them or to get their name and address, etc.

Try not to make any comments about how the accident happened (except if asked by an officer) or to make any excuses or apologies for your own conduct. Avoid making any observations about your automobile and the damage to it, or about your health or your injuries or how you feel.

Make personal notes about what happened as soon as you return home, while the incident is still fresh in your mind. It is a good idea to draw a diagram of the accident showing the number of lanes, the position of the vehicles before and after the accident, the length of the skid marks (if there are any), and notations as to the damages to all vehicles involved and injuries of all persons involved. Make note of any traffic signals, speed limit signs, turn signs, etc. Photographs are great; if you have a camera, use it. If someone else in the area is taking pictures, get his name and address so you can get prints from him later.

If you are hurt or emotionally upset, try to avoid making any statements except your name, address, and information concerning your drivers' license and your automobile. Never admit responsibility for an accident without first getting legal advice. Don't argue with anyone at the scene of an accident about whose fault it was.

The police may ask you for a statement. What you say will be written down by the police officer and will become part of a permanent record, copies of which are available to other parties involved in the accident. For this reason you should be very careful about any statements you make to the police concerning time, speed, distance, injuries, etc. Under the facts given above, there would certainly be no harm in telling the police that you were sitting in your car, that you had stopped for traffic ahead, and that you had been sitting there for fifteen seconds with your foot on the brake when you were suddenly hit from behind. A statement like that is not likely to get you into any difficulty. However if you were involved in an intersection collision, it might be a different story altogether. If you give too many details in your statement to the police or make too many comments that are remembered later by the other party or by witnesses, you may find that you have said something you wish you had not.

Some state laws require an accident report to be filed with the Department of Motor Vehicles within a certain number of days after the accident has occurred. Some state laws also require you to post evidence of automobile liability insurance after an accident has occurred or you may lose your license. Of course, notify your insurance company as soon as possible after the accident.

If you are injured in any way, you should see a doctor as soon as possible. If you or any person was injured, or if you were charged with a traffic violation, you should see your lawyer as soon as possible.

In any automobile accident, the question of insurance is very important. The party who struck you may have insurance. If so, he may tell you to contact his agent or his insurance company, or he may not tell you, and after he reports the accident to his insurance company, the claims agent may contact you. The first contact by the other driver's insurance claims agent is very important. You must understand that the agent's job is not to take care of you; it is to save the company's money. He will therefore try to settle the case with you as quickly and as cheaply as possible if he thinks that the other person was clearly at fault. If there is some room for argument on the question of liability (as for example in an intersection collision), the agent's primary duty will be to prove that you (and not his insured driver) were in the wrong. If liability is going to be disputed, the company may send a professional claims investigator instead of a claims agent. His job is to get you to make a statement, which will either be recorded or written up for you to sign. This statement will be skillfully slanted in every way possible to favor the other party. Sometimes it is very difficult to do this, but in almost any case, there are little very subtle ways of stating facts and wording questions and answers that seem harmless at the time but that can have great impact at a later date. People who obtain such statements for a living are generally fairly experienced at it and can make you look bad if you are not careful. Unless you are going to handle your own case all the way through, you are better off not to give any statement at all to them, but instead refer them to your lawyer or tell them that your lawyer will be in touch with them if they will leave their card.

You have probably read about the person injured in the automobile accident who came out of anesthesia to find a claims agent there with flowers in one hand and a pocket tape recorder in the other. Statements made by parties under such circumstances can usually be discredited or thrown out later, but sometimes they stick, so don't get involved. Just say you're too tired to make a statement and ask the agent to go away. Of course if the man is from your own company, you should cooperate with him. Occasionally, however, both drivers will be insured by the same company. In such a case you should probably talk to your lawyer before making a statement if liability is going to be disputed or if there is some question about the extent of your injuries.

If the automobile that hit you sped off without stopping, then you may be covered under the *uninsured* motorist provisions of your insurance policy.

2. Investigation

Every accident involving personal injuries and most of those involving extensive property damage will be investigated by the company or companies insuring the parties involved. Some insurance companies have their own investigators; others hire independent investigators. The purpose of the investigation is twofold:

- To find out exactly what happened as quickly as possible, and establish it as a matter of record;
- To be prepared to defend any claim that may be brought, or to prosecute any claim that should be made.

A good investigation will include gathering of the following evidence:

- Photographs of the scene,
- Photographs of the vehicles,
- Copies of the police report,
- Copies of statements of witnesses to the accident,
- Estimates as to the amount of property damage,
- Description of the injuries,
- List of citations, if any, given as a result of the accident,
- Statement or evidence of the amount of medical bills incurred as a result of the accident,
- Statement or evidence of the amount of wage loss resulting from the accident,
- Statements of the parties themselves concerning the accident.

It is important to gather this evidence as quickly as possible. Skid marks should be measured and photographed before they fade or become obscured. Vehicles should be photo-graphed before they are repaired. In a case of injuries that are visible, such as black and blue marks, burns, scars, etc., these should be photographed (in color) as soon as possible, and if the injuries are prolonged, a series of photographs should be taken over a period of time. Insurance companies and investigators know that the first party to ask a witness to give a statement has the best chance of getting a good statement. That is why it is important to obtain statements as quickly as possible and hope you get there before the other side does. Insurance com-panies do not send inexperienced investigators to obtain written or recorded statements from witnesses in accident cases involv-ing serious injuries. Anyone involved in an accident should therefore make an immediate effort to get an experienced investigator working for him. You can do this either by contact-ing an investigator directly or by contacting an attorney. If you contact the investigator directly, you will have to pay him for his services. If you contact an attorney, the attorney may pay the investigator if you enter into a contingent fee contract with the attorney. In that event the attorney would reimburse him-self for having paid the investigator out of the amount he recovered for you. For more details concerning the contingent fee contract, see Part II.

Sometimes free-lance photographers get excellent pictures of an accident immediately after it has occurred. These pictures can be very valuable, and if you have reason to believe that a claim may be made against you, your insurance company would be grateful to have a set of such photographs and would gladly pay for them. If you intend to make a claim against some other party involved in the accident, you should obtain a copy of those photographs. The normal charge for a set of $8'' \times 10''$ glossy prints of the scene of an accident runs around $50. If an attorney is handling the case for you, he will advance that expense as part of the *costs advanced* in connection with your suit.

Sometimes the cause of an accident may be unclear. One party may claim that his brakes or his steering failed. In boating accidents in which the boat blows up or catches on fire, the exact cause is generally unknown at first. In such cases it becomes necessary to hire an expert to examine the wreckage and determine the cause of the malfunction or incident. These experts are expensive—they charge by the hour for their time and the time of their laboratory assistants. If a lawyer is handling your case for you, he will advance the costs of these investigations for you.

3.   Preparation: Lawyers and Doctors   [5.23]

If you do not intend to prepare your own case, you will consult your attorney, or if you do not have one, you will want to obtain one. Most attorneys handle automobile accident cases, although some who specialize in other areas do not accept them. But just because an attorney handles an accident case (usually called "P.I." for "personal injury") does not mean that he is especially competent at this type of case. Some lawyers can draft very fine contracts and wills but are not experienced or aggressive enough to adequately handle a personal injury case. Of the lawyers who specialize in personal injury cases, some are very good and some are very bad. For more discussion on this subject, see Part II.

The insurance company for the defendant (party against whom the claim is made) will generally retain the services of a personal injury defense specialist. He may either be full-time counsel for the company or an independent lawyer who special-izes in defending personal injury cases and handles them on a retainer basis plus per diem, or on an hourly basis, for the insurance company. Because he will almost always be a full-time trial attorney who handles this type of case almost exclusively, the lawyer representing the plaintiff should be very competent.

In the legal profession, the term *ambulance chaser* refers to a certain type of lawyer who specializes in handling personal injury cases and who solicits business, directly or indirectly, from people injured in spectacular accidents that receive newspaper publicity (see Section 9.51). Some of these lawyers brazenly approach the injured party directly at the hospital or at home, and offer their card and their services. Others pay ambulance drivers, hospital attendants, and private investigators to solicit these cases for them. Their ways of getting business are quite varied and in many cases very subtle. Any way that they do it, if it amounts to soliciting business, is strictly against their professional rules of ethics, and they can be barred from the practice of law. It is a good idea to stay away from any lawyers or any firms that use such tactics. If they can't be trusted to follow their own professional rules of conduct, you should not trust them to handle your case (see Section 2.5).

Unfortunately, it is necessary to emphasize strongly that you should never trust the investigator, claims agent, or lawyer for the insurance company on the other side of the case. Their job is to weaken your case or to destroy it altogether, if possible. They may appear friendly, solicitous, and interested in settlement, but the one thing they have in mind is preventing you from recovering anything, or at least keeping the amount as low as possible. Plaintiff's attorneys, insurance defense attorneys, and investigators on both sides can be very antagonistic and suspicious of each other. This is too bad, because this attitude sometimes stands in the way of fair settlement. Unfortunately this attitude is quite prevalent because of the many dirty tricks that have been pulled on both sides.

In any personal injury case, the doctor or doctors for the injured party play a large part. Just as there are good and bad lawyers, there are good and bad doctors. In every community there are certain doctors who sell their professional services to insurance companies. These doctors are *defense-oriented*. If you are injured in an automobile accident, you don't want to have a defense-oriented doctor treating you. There are also doctors in the community that specialize in plaintiff's cases, although they are less numerous. The presence of such a person in the case, although it may help you greatly at trial, may prevent you from being able to settle the case because the insurance company may assume that this doctor, whom they may have run into before, is exaggerating your injuries.

If your lawyer is experienced in handling personal injury cases, he will probably be able to tell you how to avoid getting involved with unscrupulous medical men. What you really want is a good competent doctor who treats the injury capably and hopefully, is capable of writing a good report and of making a good witness if necessary.

Few doctors who are not involved frequently in litigation realize how important their attitude may be in making or breaking a plaintiff's case. Some doctors tend by nature to be overly optimistic in their diagnoses and prognoses; in their reports they minimize injuries and predict early recoveries. When these predictions fail to come true, the insurance companies and their lawyers use the reports not to show that a doctor was mistaken but to show that he was right and the plaintiff is taking too long to recover and is faking in the hopes that he can get more money for his injuries. Sometimes doctors are very careless about what they put in their reports concerning how the accident happened, or what the injuries or complaints consisted of; once these reports are made, they become a permanent part of the medical records of the patient and can be *discovered* by the defendant's insurance company and used against the plaintiff. In Section 5.21 you are asked to assume that you are struck from behind by another car. Suppose that as your car is pushed forward by the sudden impact, your head snaps back, and as the front of your car strikes the rear of the car in front, your head snaps forward. This is the cycle that frequently results in the *whiplash syndrome.* There may be no immediate pain and no visible sign of injury, but in a few hours you may feel pain and stiffness in the neck or back. If you see a doctor before the pain starts, his records will note that you had no apparent ill effects from the accident. Most doctors understand and are sympathetic toward whiplash injuries and will delay any opinion about your condition until a reasonable time has passed after the accident. If you have a whiplash injury, a doctor who is totally unsympathetic to such injuries will not do you any good at all. In such a case, you should get another doctor. If your doctor is not a specialist in dealing with the type of injuries you have, you should get either another doctor or an additional specialist. You might also ask your attorney about a specialist because he may know something about which specialist you should see in your community. Remember that any doctor who earns a large percentage of his income from examining patients for plaintiff's lawyers or defense lawyers, and who spends a lot of time testifying in court, should be "suspect." Most competent orthopedists, orthopedic surgeons, neurologists, and neurological surgeons do occasionally, or even frequently have to appear in court and testify. But if a doctor spends as much time in court as most lawyers do, then he is more of a paid professional witness than he is a doctor, and you don't need him.

An important part of the preparation will be the depositions of the parties involved and of the witnesses. See Section 5.17 for details on depositions.

You or your lawyer should make at least one good attempt to settle your case before starting to prepare for trial. In order to make a settlement presentation, the investigation should be fairly complete, and you should have all of your evidence including photographs, statements, depositions, medical bills, evidence of wage-loss claim, doctor's statements as to extent of future disability, if any, and estimate as to future medical expenses, if any, all put together. You are then ready for settlement.

4. Settlement Negotiations [5.24]

The insurance company and the plaintiff approach settlement from opposite directions. Most insurance companies will put a low value on a case, and will authorize an even lower settlement offer. Some companies will set up a *reserve* on their books for settlement of the case. They may not offer that much money, but if you demand that amount and hold out for it, they will usually meet your demand. They seldom go above their reserve, however, without going to trial. The claims adjuster or the defense attorney wants to both save the company's money and look good, so he will always try to settle the case for less than the amount the company has authorized for a settlement offer. The plaintiff or his attorney will generally ask for more than he expects to get, and will be prepared to negotiate a compromise. Once in a while you will find an insurance company or a lawyer who will make one offer or demand and not negotiate further—sometimes this strategy works, and sometimes it backfires.

If you are represented by a lawyer, he is obligated to inform you of the exact terms of any offer made by the insurance company or its lawyer or claims man. If you wish to accept an offer, your attorney cannot prevent the settlement from going through (unless he can talk you out of accepting it). If your lawyer turns down an offer made by the company without telling you about it and then loses the case, and you would have accepted the offer, you can probably collect the amount that the company offered from him.

Most lawyers will try to pin you down on what you want or expect to get out of the suit fairly early in the game. A good lawyer will carefully evaluate your case and tell you what he thinks it is worth. You should give careful consideration to his evaluation. If your expectations are way out of line, you should lower them. It is a good idea to accept any "reasonable" offer, even if it is not quite as much as you hope or expect to get if you go to trial. Trials are expensive both in terms of time and money, and they take an emotional toll. There is always a risk in going to trial which can be avoided by settling out of court. Remember, a bird in the hand is worth two in the bush. Before turning down a reasonable settlement offer, you should know exactly what costs are involved in the case and how much you are going to have to pay if the verdict goes against you and you don't get anything. In such a case you may be considerably out of pocket when you have paid all your medical bills and the expenses of investigation, jury fees, etc. Remember that your lawyer advances these for you, but they are your responsibility to pay, whether the case is won or lost (see Part II). On the other hand, don't be pressured into accepting a ridiculously low sum just to settle a case if you really have a good case. Don't tie your lawyer's hands by telling him that under no circumstances will you go to trial and that you will accept any sum, no matter how small, rather than going to trial. If you take such a position, your lawyer has lost 50 percent of his effectiveness in bargaining for you.

There are several attitudes that get in the way of adequate settlements. One is the attitude of the malingerer. This person wants to milk every drop of sympathy for his injuries and every dime of compensation that he can out of the accident. He exaggerates his complaints and overemphasizes his injuries, and when he doesn't get the verdict he expected or loses the case altogether because he alienated the jury with his attitude, he always blames his lawyer. Another bad attitude, already mentioned, is the fear of going to trial. The person with this attitude is willing to accept a reasonable award for his claim, but refuses to go to trial if such an offer is not forthcoming from the insurance company. He forces his lawyer to run a bluff on the insurance company which can't be backed up if it is called. No lawyer wants to negotiate under such conditions.

Then there is the person who wants and demands an adequate award and who stands firmly on his request right up until the trial, and then suddenly turns chicken and tells his lawyer to settle for the amount of the last offer, perhaps made six months ago. This is most frustrating to the lawyer who has spent a considerable amount of time preparing for trial, only to be forced to settle a case for an amount he could have gotten six months ago had he known that the plaintiff would accept that amount.

A plaintiff who is trying to represent himself has a very difficult task. He must sell both himself and his case to the insurance company claims adjuster or investigator. If he does a good job on selling himself, he may not properly present the full extent and nature of his injuries and damages. If he does a good job in presenting his injuries and damages, he may create the impression that he is exaggerating his claims and the insurance company may figure the jury will penalize him for that and they will therefore favor going to trial.

If you have a case involving serious or permanent injuries, you should not try to settle it yourself. If you have a case involving a substantial wage loss, you should not try to settle it yourself. If you have no serious and no permanent injuries, and only a very minor, if any, wage loss and a modest amount of medical bills, you may be able to do better by settling your own case than by retaining an attorney and paying anywhere from 25 to 50 percent to him for his services (see Part II). It is true that insurance companies will raise their offer when a lawyer becomes involved in the case because they recognize that the plaintiff has to pay a percentage to his lawyer. However, for cases in which the company offers the same amount whether a lawyer is involved or not, in settlement, if you can get that same amount by yourself without a lawyer, you are obviously going to be better off. There are one or two settlement techniques you can use to advantage if you are going to settle your own case. In the past, insurance companies have used, from time to time, rules of thumb in arriving at settlement amounts. There are many such rules, but the two most widely used ones are the *three-times* and *five-times* rules. Most companies and claims agents will deny using these rules, but even so, they are good guidelines for you to follow in evaluating your own case for settlement purposes. The three times rule means simply that you take all of your special damages and multiply them by three. The product is the amount that you should demand for settlement purposes. Remember that your special damages include your medical bills, your property damage (out of pocket), and your wage loss.

The five-times rule is this: you take all of your medical bills, multiply that figure by five, then add your other special damages (wage loss, property damage, etc.) and that total amount is the amount that you demand. If you have an airtight case on liability and make a pretty good witness in your own behalf, then the insurance company will generally come close to meeting that demand. If your case is weak and you do not make a good witness, then you will not get that much and should be prepared to settle for less.

5. Trial

a. COURT TRIAL [5.25]

Once the case has been properly pleaded, discovery has been completed, and if settlement negotiations have failed, it is time to have the matter set for trial. One party or the other has to ask the court to have the matter scheduled for trial. Either party may demand a jury trial. If neither party demands a jury trial, the case will be tried by a judge. You may find that the particular court in which your case will be tried has more than one judge. In such a case, it is a good idea to find out something about the personality of each of the judges. Trial lawyers make it their business to know the personalities of local judges before whom they practice. If you are a defendant in a drunk driving case, you don't want a teetotaling judge to hear your case. If you are the husband in a domestic litigation case, you don't want to get a judge who has a reputation for being tough on husbands and sympathetic toward wives in such cases. Some attorneys are very skillful at maneuvering their trial calendars to avoid a particular judge, but generally, it is not possible for an inexperienced layman to accomplish such a result.

You also have a right to have another judge hear your case if you feel strongly that the judge assigned to hear your case is prejudiced against you. However, preparing and filing an affidavit of prejudice to have a judge replaced is again a technical proceeding that should be handled by an experienced attorney.

The parties or their attorneys will be notified of the trial date and are expected to show up ready for trial on that date. If one party does not appear, the other party is likely to win the case—if the defendant does not show up, the plaintiff will get what he is after by putting on a minimum amount of testimony; if the plaintiff does not show up, the defendant can have the case dismissed. Occasionally it may be possible to get a last-minute postponement or *continuance* for emergency reasons. If one party is just not ready to go to trial, and has a legitimate excuse, the matter may be continued to another date. It might also be dropped from the calendar, and be put back but this may take several months.

[5.26]

b. *JURY*

The constitutional right to a jury trial in criminal cases and in some civil cases is discussed in Parts VIII and XI. Jury trials are more time-consuming and expensive than court trials. They are more time-consuming because of the presence of twelve (or less) extra people that have to sit and listen to the evidence. Selecting the jury takes time. More recesses have to be taken in jury cases to rest the jurors and keep them alert. At different times during a jury trial the jurors may have to be excused while the attorneys or the litigants argue matters before the judge. When the evidence has been presented, the judge has to instruct the jury. The jury then has to retire and consider its decision. All of these things take time—you can figure that a jury will lengthen the time of any trial by at least one full day, even for a short trial, and by several days for a very lengthy trial. The jurors have to be paid, and the losing party must pay the jury fees. The art of presenting a case to a jury is very complex and sophisticated. An untrained layman would be very foolish to attempt to present his own case to a jury; therefore, the discussion here will not in any way attempt to tell you how to conduct a jury trial, because that is a job you should leave to a competent trial lawyer.

Prospective jurors are chosen from a panel of citizens within the area of the court's jurisdiction, and are summoned to appear on a certain day, assembled in the jury room and sent to the courtrooms where they wait to be called for cases that are getting underway (see Section 8.82). The procedure varies, but generally it goes something like this: The names of the jurors present in a court are mixed together and then selected at random from a box or basket. As each name is called the juror will take his or her place in the jury box until there are twelve (or whatever number) jurors. The judge and/or the attorneys may then question each of them and perhaps tell them something about the case (see Section 8.82). Some of the jurors will be excused by the lawyers, in which case other prospective jurors take the empty spaces in the jury box as their names are selected at random. Sometimes the process of selecting a jury can be very lengthy. No juror should be selected to serve on a jury who already knows the facts of the case, knows the parties involved, is friendly with either of the attorneys involved, or has a bias or prejudice against any of the parties involved in the lawsuit or against the positions that they intend to take at trial. Most of the questioning is designed to eliminate the jurors who would not be fair and impartial. Unfortunately, many attorneys also misuse the privilege of questioning jurors in an attempt to persuade them in advance that their client should win, or in an attempt to make friends or establish rapport with them. In some jurisdictions the judge questions the prospective jurors, and the attorneys are permitted very little opportunity to question them. Many trial attorneys use the process of examining jurors to eliminate certain ones because they think the jurors will not like them or their client. Attorneys have their own opinions about what type of juror is best for a particular case. Some attorneys, if trying a personal injury case involving a whiplash with general damages including pain, suffering, and anxiety, would be likely to eliminate accountants or engineers on the grounds that these people would tend to be less emotional and less sympathetic toward an injured person. Of course, no attorney representing a plaintiff wants to have any insurance company employees, executives, or stockholders on the jury, and conversely, defense attorneys love to have such people on the jury. The theory is that anybody who works for an insurance company or owns stock in it will do anything to keep the verdict down so that the insurance company won't lose money. This may or may not be true. It is true that the rules of evidence do not permit the mention in court of the fact that an insurance company may be defending or insuring one or both of the parties. It is also true that a plaintiff has a right to have insurance company personnel excluded from a jury. However, if he requests this, the other party has a right to have the jury instructed that an insurance company is not a party to the action and that the jurors should not decide the case based on the assumption that one of the parties may be insured (see Section 9.48).

The attorneys are permitted two types of challenges in selecting a jury, one *for cause*, and the other *peremptory*. Challenges for cause are unlimited in number; peremptory challenges are limited (see Section 8.82).

c. TRIAL PROCEDURES [5.27]

Once the jury has been impanelled, after all the questioning has been completed and both sides have agreed on the jury, then the jurors are sworn and the presentation of the case begins (see Section 8.80). Each attorney can make an opening statement of the facts that he intends to prove. The plaintiff then opens by calling his first witness and the trial is underway. As each witness is called, he is sworn, subjected to direct examination by the attorney calling him, and then cross-examined by the opposing counsel. Normal hours for court trials are from ten until twelve, and from one-thirty or two until four-thirty or five. There will generally be a morning and afternoon recess. The judge will tell the jury, the lawyers, and the litigants what time to return to court after the morning, noon, and afternoon recess and after conclusion of the trial each day. He will also admonish the jurors not to discuss the case with anyone.

d. WITNESSES [5.28]

In an automobile accident case, the witnesses consist of the occupants of the cars involved, any other persons who witnessed the accident, and probably the police investigator who prepared the accident report for the police department. In addition, there may be medical witnesses to testify as to the injuries and the treatment received. Each witness to be called is prepared for the testimony in a conference with the attorney. This is not true, of course, in the case of adverse witnesses, and might not be true in the case of a police officer, although in the latter case the attorney might have a short conference with him just prior to putting him on the stand. The attorney confers with the witness prior to calling him, going over the testimony that he expects to elicit from that witness. At the time he asks the witness the questions he expects to ask at trial, finding out what answers the witness will give. There is, of course, some coaching that is done by the attorney. He will caution the witness against making certain statements that might be misleading or damaging, and will also coach him regarding what answers he expects to the questions that will be put at trial. In doing this, the attorney does not attempt to put words into the mouth of the witness, but he may and should coach the witness on how to express what he will be trying to say on the stand. It is very awkward for an attorney to call a witness to the stand that he has not talked to before and attempt to get some essential factual testimony out of him if he does not understand what facts the attorney is after and cannot seem to remember everything or properly express himself. But an attorney who is examining his own witness cannot ask *leading* questions (see Section 8.93). These are questions which call for a yes or no answer, or which indicate to the witness the answer that is desired. Therefore it is very difficult for the attorney to lead the witness down any particular path on direct examination unless he has first talked to him, telling him what questions he is going to ask, in what order he will ask them, and what information he expects to get out of the witness.

Attorneys may coach their witnesses in the manner of answering questions and in the material to be covered, but they cannot instruct a witness to lie. The witness may be charged with the crime of perjury if he lies on the stand and is caught doing it. It is also very dangerous for the client to give false or misleading testimony, because if the other side can prove that it is false or misleading or expose the witness as being either a liar or unreliable, the entire case can be lost as a result. The good witness, therefore, is one who tells the truth, who has been properly prepared so that he will know what questions to expect, who knows fully the factual information that is supposed to be presented to the court through his testimony, and who listens carefully to each question as it is asked and gives the answer in his own words, without having previously memorized the answer. A witness who tries to memorize questions and answers is easily tripped up and confused on cross-examination. A witness should act natural, be polite, and not be overly nervous.

The same rules apply for a witness in courtroom that apply at deposition (see Section 5.17). He should answer questions directly and not volunteer additional information. He should not answer questions he does not understand and should be sure to wait until the attorney asking the question is finished, giving the other attorney a chance to make an objection if he is going to do so, before answering. Remember there can be only one person talking at a time in a courtroom, because the court reporter has to record everything that is being said.

Litigants and witnesses should be clean and neatly groomed. Hair should be combed, beards trimmed or faces shaved. In some courts men must wear coats and ties and women with slacks are not permitted. You may feel that this is archaic, but you are better off going along with it than trying to fight it. Both litigants and witnesses should conduct themselves well while in the courtroom—the judge and the jurors will be watching them the whole time they are in the courtroom, whether they are on the stand testifying or not. Chewing gum, talking, whispering, giggling, or grimacing should all be avoided. In recent times it has become popular for some witnesses or litigants, sometimes with the encouragement of their attorneys, to attempt to disrupt courtroom proceedings by creating noise, confusion, and disorder. Such tactics never contribute to the successful outcome of a case, but only prolong the trial, make it more expensive, and reduce the chances of success for the parties responsible for the outbursts. Criminals charged with a serious crime who attempt—either by themselves or through their attorneys—to turn their trial into a circus usually are unsuccessful in court. If a person has a good case and a competent attorney to present it, that is all that should be required in order to obtain justice.

Sometimes witnesses may be excluded from the trial except for the period during which they are on the witness stand. The purpose of this is to prevent one witness from influencing another. Unless the judge has ordered witnesses excluded from the trial, witnesses who are waiting to be called can sit in the courtroom and listen to the testimony of other witnesses.

A witness should speak loudly and clearly, and should not answer by nodding or shaking the head to indicate yes or no. If his deposition has been taken prior to trial, he should carefully review it once or twice the day before he is to be called as a witness so that he will remember what he said previously. He should also be pleasant and polite and at all times keep his temper. He should avoid sarcasm, and not try to be funny.

e. *EXPERT WITNESSES* [5.29]

Expert witnesses are those who are learned or skilled enough in some particular subject to be called to testify as experts. Doctors frequently testify as experts, as do engineers, architects, accountants, appraisers, and various members of the scientific community. To qualify to testify as experts, they will be questioned about their education background, training, and experience. Only if the judge decides that they are truly qualified to give expert testimony will they be permitted to do so. An expert may give an opinion on a subject, while an ordinary witness would be prevented from doing so. For example, only a doctor could give his opinion as to whether or not the pain in the plaintiff's neck was caused by the accident; the plaintiff himself or another person who is not a doctor could not give such testimony. Experts, naturally, are paid for their testimony. Doctors typically charge anywhere from $200 to $500 a day for their testimony in court, even though they may be on the witness stand for only one hour. Engineers or scientific accident reconstruction experts may charge $25 to $50 per hour for their time in investigating the cause of an accident and may charge $200 to $300 per day for court testimony. Whenever experts testify, there are usually conflicting expert opinions. It is up to the judge or the jury to decide what to believe.

f. *DIRECT EXAMINATION* [5.30]

Direct examination is the questioning of a witness by the lawyer who has called him to the stand initially. The typical direct examination starts with the attorney asking the witness to state his name, address, and occupation. In a series of preliminary or *foundation-laying* questions, the attorney establishes the importance of the testimony of the witness to the case and then leads him in a series of questions through the facts that the witness has knowledge of which are material to the issues in the case. When the attorney has completed his direct examination the other attorney then has an opportunity to cross-examine the witness.

[5.31]   *g.*   *CROSS-EXAMINATION*

Much greater latitude is allowed in cross-examination then is allowed in direct examination. In direct examination the questions that can be asked are more limited, and the way that they can be asked is much more restricted, than is the case under cross-examination. Expert cross-examination is never aimless—there is always a definite purpose. A good lawyer rarely asks a question in cross-examination that he doesn't know the answer to, for that leaves the opportunity for the witness to make an answer that may be surprising and damaging. Another thing to avoid in cross-examination is asking a witness "why"? This opens the door for him to say almost anything he wants to, and permits him to say many things he would not be able to say on direct examination. If a witness's testimony has not been particularly damaging to you, it is best not to cross-examine at all. If it has, however, been damaging, a good attorney will try to undermine it on cross-examination; if this fails, he may try to discredit the witness by showing that he is biased or prejudiced, or that he has not told the truth, or that he has a poor memory or was confused, or that in some other way he is mistaken in his testimony. A good cross-examiner will keep it short, make a few good points, and attempt to end on a strong point.

h. OBJECTIONS [5.32]

At times during the trial attorneys will object to some questions. An attorney must state the grounds for his *objection* and wait for the judge to indicate whether or not it is valid. If it is, the judge will say "sustained," and the question cannot then be answered. If it is not valid, the judge will say "overruled," and the question may be answered by the witness. Sometimes an attorney will make an objection after the question has been answered and will move to strike the answer. This means he is asking the judge to order the answer removed from the record and to instruct the jury to disregard that portion of the testimony containing the answer.

i. BASIC RULES OF EVIDENCE: [5.33]
HEARSAY, LEADING QUESTIONS

If a witness on the stand is asked what another person said concerning a fact that is important to the case and that other person is not a party to the suit and is not present in the courtroom so that he may be cross-examined about that statement, the question calls for *hearsay*, and can be objected to. *Leading questions* (those which tend to suggest the answer that should be given) are not allowed on direct examination. They may, however, be asked on *cross-examination* (see Sections 5.28, 5.30, and 5.31).

(1) Best Evidence Rule [5.34]

The best evidence of what a written document contains is the document itself; therefore if a witness tries to say what is in a document, the question can be objected to on the grounds of the *best evidence rule,* meaning that the document itself should be shown (see Section 4.10). Generally, original documents must be used rather than copies (unless both sides agree to or the court allows the use of copies).

[5.35]

(2) Foundation

Documents must be properly identified and authenticated before they can be introduced as evidence. The same is true of photographs or other physical evidence. The *foundation* would consist of establishing what the document or evidence is that is to be introduced, properly identifying it, and showing its relevance to the case. If it were, for example, a business record, it would have to be first established that it was in fact a record of a company that was kept in the ordinary course of business.

[5.36]

(3) Incompetent, Irrelevant, and Immaterial

A familiar objection is *"incompetent, irrelevant, and immaterial."* This is a shotgun objection frequently used by an attorney who can't think of a more specific objection to the question. The objection covers a multitude of sins, and is generally designed to eliminate a question that is outside of the issues involved and therefore is a waste of the time of the court and/or the jury because it doesn't lead to anything of any importance in the case. *Material* evidence is that which is important to the case; *relevant* means specifically related to the issues in the case.

[5.37]

(4) Argumentative or Repetitious

Argumentative or repetitious questions are not permitted under the rules of evidence.

j.   *FINDINGS OF FACT*   [5.38]

At the conclusion of a trial, where there has not been a jury, the judge may take the case under submission or he may rule from the bench. In either case, after he has granted his judgment, one of the parties may be required to prepare *findings of fact* and *conclusions of law*. This means that he must, in effect, write the judgment for the court which the judge will then sign. The other party can object to the findings of fact and conclusions of law that are prepared and can offer some of his own; the judge will then determine what the final findings are and they will become the basis for the judgment.

k.   *SPECIAL VERDICTS*   [5.39]

Sometimes a jury will be asked to render a *special verdict* rather than a general verdict. For example, in an intersection collision case it is possible that the defendant may be advised by the insurance company lawyers to admit liability so that trial will be only on the question of damages. This is a defense tactic that is used when the case is open and shut on liability and may be an aggravated case—such as when a defendant is intoxicated at the time, did something really stupid, or is the kind of person who would make a very bad witness. Any of these things might prejudice the jury to be overly sympathetic to the plaintiff. In such cases, where liability is admitted, the jury merely finds the amount of damages.

In some cases the jury may be asked a series of questions which it has to answer collectively. For example, it may be asked to determine whether or not there was negligence; whether there was contributory negligence on the part of any party; whether a vehicle was being driven with the knowledge and consent of its owner; whether the person driving the vehicle was acting within the course and scope of his employment at the time of the accident, etc.

[5.40]   6.   Jury Instructions

The jury first receives its instructions from the judge. The attorneys will have discussed the instructions with the judge in his chambers, usually, just before the trial begins, or at recess, or in the morning prior to the beginning of trial on the second day of the case. Most judges require the attorneys to submit complete written instructions prior to the beginning of the case. The judge and the attorneys then go over the instructions in his chambers, out of the presence of the jury, and the judge decides which instructions he will give. At the conclusion of the final argument the judge instructs the jury—this can take anywhere from fifteen minutes to an hour, depending upon how complicated the case is and how many instructions there are. Jury instructions are very important; unfortunately, they are also very lengthy and written in legal language that is difficult to understand, especially when it is being read and there is no chance to carefully examine it. Nevertheless, the members of the jury are expected to listen carefully to these instructions and to understand them the first time they hear them. They may ask that instructions be read over to them again, however, more than once if necessary (see Section 8.83).

[5.41]   7.   Jury Deliberations

After the jury has received its instructions, it is conducted to the jury room by the bailiff. No one is admitted, and the jurors then elect a foreman whose job it is to take charge of the proceedings and see that the jury goes about the business of reaching a verdict. Very little is known about how jurors really conduct themselves in jury rooms because of the secrecy involved. In theory, the jury is supposed to analyze the evidence and discuss the case in an orderly fashion, each juror being heard from, until finally a vote is taken. State laws generally require unanimous verdicts in criminal cases. The Supreme Court held in 1972 that in state court criminal trials a unanimous jury is not required by the Constitution. Most states require less than unanimity in civil cases. The judge may present the jury with two written forms of verdict before the members enter the jury room, one of which says "we, the jury, find for the defendant"; and the other "we, the jury, find for the plaintiff in the sum of $_____." The jury should first vote on the question of liability. If they find for the defendant, they have merely to fill in the verdict, have the foreman sign it, and notify the bailiff that they have reached a verdict. If they find for the plaintiff, they should vote again on the amount of damages, a matter that will have to be discussed until there is some consensus. There is very little written about how jurors should conduct themselves and what they should do in order to arrive at a verdict. Presumably most of them just exercise their common sense and use whatever parliamentary procedure methods they are familiar with. No juror should be brow-beaten into a verdict by other jurors. No jury should attempt to decide anything by compromising or by flipping a coin. When the verdict has been reached, the jurors tell the bailiff, who tells the judge, who asks the attorneys and their clients to return to the courtroom. When everyone is present, the jurors return to the courtroom and take their seats. The judge then asks the jury if it has reached a verdict. The foreman stands and says that it has. The verdict is read by the foreman, the clerk, or the judge. After this, the judge may ask the attorneys if they wish the jury *polled*. This means that each juror is asked whether or not this is his or her verdict. Their replies reveal whether the verdict was split or unanimous and how each juror voted.

Sometimes, during lengthy trials, it is necessary to use extreme methods to isolate the jurors from contact with other persons or things that might have an influence on their decision. In the *Manson* murder case in Los Angeles the jurors were driven from their hotel to the court and back in a bus that had the windows covered so they would not be able to see the headlines on the front pages of the newspapers on newsstands that they passed on their route. When Charles Manson, the chief defendant in the case, held up a newspaper headline in the court stating that the president of the United States had said that he was guilty, and the jury saw it, his attorneys moved for a mistrial. The trial judge questioned each juror carefully in order to find out whether he or she had been influenced by the glimpse of the headline, and after he decided that the headline had not had any prejudicial effect on any of the jurors, he permitted the trial to resume. If he had decided otherwise, he would have had to declare a mistrial and the case would have had to start all over with a new jury.

E. ENFORCEMENT OF JUDGMENTS

After the verdict has been rendered, judgment is then entered on the verdict. In an accident case in which an insurance company is defending the party against whom the judgment is obtained, in almost all cases the insurance company will pay promptly after receiving notice of the judgment. When any judgment is not promptly paid, the plaintiff obtains a *writ of execution* from the court clerk, takes the writ to the sheriff, and ask him to serve the writ by seizing property belonging to the defendant and having it sold at public auction, the proceeds to be paid to the plaintiff. If in doubt about the defendant's assets, the plaintiff can have the defendant served with an *order of examination*, which requires the defendant to come to court and answer questions under oath as to the nature of his assets.

F. APPEALS

Because writing an appellate brief is something the layman is not capable of doing without a tremendous amount of study and effort, the discussion of appellate procedure will be limited (see Section 8.115). The party wishing to appeal (*appellant*) must file a notice of appeal within the time limits prescribed by that court. The clerk must then be directed to prepare a *transcript* (written copy of all the testimony) and a summary of all the documentary exhibits that were introduced into evidence. This then becomes the record on appeal. The other side (*respondent*) then must file an answering brief. The appellate court reviews the briefs and the record, and may hear argument by the attorneys.

VI. Estates

A. FACING THE FACTS OF DEATH [6.1]

Sooner or later, we all come to it. Some are better prepared than others. To be prepared for death means to plan for it, something very few people ever really do. If you don't care what happens to your family, your property, or your heirs after you have died, then you can skip this part of the book. If you do have some concern, then perhaps you should consider your death. What shape would your estate be in in that event? Are there any people that are dependent upon you for their support? How will they get along after you die? What assets would your estate consist of? Who, besides yourself, knows about everything you own and knows where to find all the important documents such as pink slips or certificates of title for motor vehicles, deeds to property, stock certificates, savings account passbooks, bonds, safe deposit box keys, checking accounts, insurance policies, mutual funds, business interests, investments, etc.? Who do you want to get your estate when you die? How do you want your property to be handled? If you have children, how will they be cared for? If you leave a spouse, how will he or she fit into the picture? What funeral or burial arrangements do you desire? Do you want to donate your body or any portion of it to medical science? These are questions that the average person seldom asks himself; they are all questions that are asked by those that survive him, after his death. It is better for you if these questions are thought out and everything planned for while you are still among the living. If you do not do this planning and die without a will (*intestate*), the state will have to appoint someone to manage your property and to distribute it to your heirs in accordance with the statutes of succession. This means that your property will be divided among your closest relatives, starting with your spouse and your children and proceeding from there, depending upon the laws of the state in which you were domiciled at the time of your death. In some states this means that everything would go to your spouse; in others it means some would go to the spouse and some to the children.

B. PROBATE

When death occurs, whatever property the decedent owned or had an interest in comes under the jurisdiction of the probate court. Someone must be appointed to administer his property during the statutory period of *probate* (generally six months), see that creditor's bills are paid, income and expenses are accounted for, and that the estate is properly distributed to the proper persons after the statutory period of probate.

If you die having a will, the person appointed to manage your estate is called the *executor* (*executrix*, if female). If you do not have a will, the person appointed will be called the *administrator* (*administratrix*).

C. ADMINISTRATION

During administration of the estate, which is supervised by the probate court, the executor or administrator publishes in a newspaper a notice to creditors inviting them to submit their claims to him. The period in which these claims must be filed is set by statute in each state. Claims not properly filed within the time limit will not be honored. The administrator or executor takes the claims that are filed and pays them if they are valid. If he has a question about a claim, he asks the court for instructions as to whether or not to pay. He can deny a claim and if suit is brought, he can, through his attorney, defend against the suit. If the claims exceed the value of the estate, the court has to approve a method of paying each creditor a portion of his claim.

During the period of administration, the executor or administrator has the power to pay an allowance to the surviving spouse and/or children if they are in need of living expenses.

The executor or administrator must prepare the federal estate tax return, the income tax returns (federal and state), and the state inheritance tax return.

Through his attorney he petitions the court for final distribution when everything is ready. The court will order distribution in accordance with the petition, unless it is a contested matter, in which case the court will resolve any disputes and then order distribution of the estate.

D. WILLS

1. Why Have a Will? [6.4]

Everyone should have a will, even if it is very simple. There are those who say that they really don't care what happens to their money or property after they die, but if they really thought about it for a moment longer, they would be concerned. A husband may think that if he dies his wife will get everything and because that is just what he wants, there is no need for a will. However, if he lives in a state in which the children may inherit a share of the estate, even though their mother is still living, she will not get it all unless it is specifically willed to her. If the couple has no children and the husband assumes that his wife is going to get everything, what happens if they are injured in a common accident and she dies before he does? Who should get the property—his relatives or her relatives? Suppose there are no relatives at all? The balance in the estate after payment of debts and taxes would then go to the state. If he had thought about it, is that what he would want, or would he have preferred it to go to some specific charity, or perhaps to a college?

Who will be in charge of your personal possessions and your property when you die? You can name an executor in your will, someone you would like to see handle this responsibility. If you do not have a will, however, the state will appoint someone, and that person may not be the one you would have chosen for the job.

A will does not always have to be drafted by an attorney (although it is usually better if it is). You can find an adequate form for a will in almost any stationery store. There are many books on estate planning that have form wills in them that are not really too bad. This is provided, however, that you have a small estate and do not wish to do anything special or complicated with it. Keep in mind that there is a risk that the form will not produce the result you hoped for.

[6.5]   2.   Holographic Will

If you wish simply to leave everything you have to your spouse, or to the children, there is no reason you can't write your own will. A *holographic* will is valid in many states. That is a will which is entirely written in your own handwriting (not typewritten) on plain paper (not with a printed form, fill-in-the-blank type of document) and which is dated and signed by you. As for those states which permit holographic wills, some require witnesses, most require no witnesses.

[6.6]   3.   Witnessed Will

A witnessed will can also be handwritten, but is usually prepared by an attorney and is typewritten. Who may witness a will? There are different requirements in each state. A witness should be a disinterested adult (one who does not stand to gain or benefit from the will). A formal executed will must be signed under certain conditions, or else it is invalid. It must be signed in the presence of the witnesses, and all the witnesses must sign the will in the presence of each other and the *testator* (person making the will). Once a will has been executed, it cannot be changed by inserting different pages, crossing things out or changing them by writing between the lines or in the margins, etc.

The will should be witnessed by at least two adults (preferably three, because some states require that number). The will does not need to be notarized. Only the original copy should be signed and witnessed.

4. Codicil [6.7]

A will can be rewritten at any time and the new will automatically wipes out the old will. Just to be safe, however, the old will should be destroyed. A will can also be changed just slightly by another document called a *codicil*, which is an amendment to a will. It should be labeled as a codicil. Simple changes such as changing the name of the executor or adding or deleting some names of charities can best be done by writing a codicil. Extensive changes should not be made by codicil, but should be made by rewriting the whole will.

5. Of Sound Mind [6.8]

You must be old enough under the laws of your state to make a valid will. You must also be *of sound mind,* which means that you are mentally competent and understand or are capable of understanding what you are doing when you sign your will.

6. Proof of Will [6.9]

When you die, your will must be proved to the satisfaction of the probate court. That means its authenticity must be established. This can be done by the witnesses in the case of a witnessed will. In the case of a holographic will, if the document is known by someone to be your will, and it says so on its face, and it is obviously in your handwriting and is not a forgery, it will be admitted.

7. Moving [6.10]

Because of the differences in laws from state to state, you should see an attorney about changing your will every time you move from one state to another if you have a will that is anything other than a simple holographic will.

[6.11]   8.   Disinheriting

Many problems arise in connection with attempts to *disinherit* people. Disinherit means to cut somebody out of your will so they won't get a part of your estate. It is perfectly legal to do this, but some people nevertheless attempt to do it by indirect means—that is, they leave all their property to another person, and do not even mention the person they wish to disinherit. If the person that is not mentioned is a spouse or child, under some laws he will automatically get a share of the estate. Therefore, if a spouse or child is purposely to be disinherited, they should still be mentioned in the will; you can leave them a small token gift or you can specifically state that you are leaving them nothing. However you cannot prevent a spouse from taking his or her *community property interest* (in a community property state) (see Section 6.49) or his or her *dower interest* in states having that type of interest (see Section 6.53). If you are survived by a wife and children, some states will not permit you to disinherit them in favor of charities. Some states also limit the amount of your estate which you can leave to charity.

[6.12]   9.   Invalid Wills; Revocation of Wills

If your will is not properly executed or you don't qualify because of age, lack of capacity, or some other reason, or if the will is made under duress, it may be *invalid*, which means that the court will not accept it and your estate will be treated as if you had died without a will.

A will may be revoked at any time by the testator. A new (valid) will automatically revokes the old one. Tearing up, burning, or mutilating a will, if done by the testator or at his direction (voluntarily and while sane), revokes it. Some events will revoke a will, at least in part. A will written by a bachelor is automatically revoked when he marries and becomes a father. A gift in a will of specific property to a certain person is revoked if the testator later sells the property.

10. Executor's Bond [6.13]

In a will you can state that your executor will not have to post a bond. If you don't say this or if you die without a will and an administrator is appointed, then a bond will have to be posted, and the bond premium will be paid out of your estate. This is money that could otherwise be saved.

11. Contents of Simple Will [6.14]

What should the simple will contain? It should, of course, begin by stating the name and address of the testator. It should then name the executor and waive the bond. Next would be the provision leaving the property to the surviving spouse or to the children if there is no surviving spouse. It should go one step beyond that and state who is to get the property if there is no spouse or child surviving. In that case you can say the property will be left "to my heirs at law," or you can name certain relatives, or you can leave it all to certain named charities.

If there are minor children involved, the will should also nominate a guardian to look after them until the youngest reaches 21 (see Section 3.51).

[6.15]   12. Executor and Attorney for the Estate

Normally the surviving spouse is named as executor (or executrix). However, if this person is not experienced or capable enough to handle the job, you might want to appoint another qualified relative, or even your bank (this is more often done). Be sure the bank has the power to act as executor under the law (most banks do). Some people like to name their attorney as executor of their will. In many cases a lawyer can legitimately serve as executor for his client, and indeed may be the best-qualified and most available person. However, he is then exposed to a problem in some states of having to do the work of both executor and attorney for one fee, or to try to claim both fees. The circumstances under which an attorney may properly collect a fee for serving as both are really beyond the scope of this book. Naming an individual together with a bank as co-executors is very often done. Executor fees and attorney fees, next to taxes, constitute the largest expenditures of an estate going through probate. These fees are normally about equal, and are normally set by statute. They are usually based on a percentage of the total value of the property in the estate. The percentage usually starts higher, perhaps 5 percent or more for the first $10,000, then drops down to a lower figure of 1 to 3 percent for larger amounts. A $100,000 estate can have attorney and executor fees as high as $5,000 to $7,000.

[6.16]   13. Safekeeping

Once your will has been executed, it should be kept in a safe place, and your spouse or other survivor should know where to find it. You may keep it in a safe deposit box at the bank, if you have one, or your attorney may keep it for you, or you may keep it in some kind of a fireproof safe or box at home. If you keep the original will at the bank or your lawyer keeps it, you should have a copy at home to use for reference purposes. Occasionally when the original will is lost and the person dies, it may be possible to get a copy of it introduced in the court and accepted by the probate court as an authentic will.

14. List of Estate Assets [6.17]

It is a good idea to make a list of all of your property and keep it with your will. The list should be kept up to date. It ought to include such basic things as checking accounts, savings accounts, stocks, bonds, real estate holdings, interest in credit unions, profit sharing or pension plans, other business interests, life insurance policies, etc. If no one else knows about all of your property, they may not know where to look to find it and some of the assets may be permanently lost.

15. Undue Influence [6.18]

Occasionally a case makes the paper in which an elderly sick person dies after a long period of convalescence, leaving everything to nurse or housekeeper, to the shock and dismay of relatives. The relatives may file suit to have the will declared invalid on the grounds that this person exercised *undue influence* upon the testator and persuaded him to leave everything to him or her. If the case of undue influence can be proved, the court will invalidate the will and the estate will go to the heirs.

16. Husband and Wife [6.19]

Both husband and wife should have a will. If the wife dies first, the husband will find himself wishing his wife had a will. If the wife dies very shortly after the husband and his will leaves everything to her, and she does not have a will, the property may be distributed in a way the husband did not want. If husband and wife are going to have provisions in their will that are substantially different, some thought should be given to the problem that arises if they both die at the same time.

[6.20] **17. Substantial Estates**

If you have a substantial estate or a desire to do something other than simply leave everything to your spouse and children, then a simple will is not for you, and in spite of much advice that you will find to the contrary in books and magazines, you are better off to see a competent lawyer and get him to draft the will for you. There is a well-known toast that English barristers used to drink "to the man who drafts his own will, the lawyer's best friend." This refers, in jest, to the litigation that frequently arises as a result of "do-it-yourself" wills. The cost of any will contest will greatly exceed even the most expensive will.

[6.21] **18. Funeral Directions**

If your will contains funeral directions, the original copy should not be kept in your safe deposit box, because the box may be locked at your death and possibly can be opened only in the presence of a state inheritance tax appraiser. Funeral directions probably shouldn't be in a will anyway because people who are in charge of your funeral arrangements may not get around to reading it until after you are buried.

E. TRUSTS

1. Essential Elements of a Trust [6.22]

A *trust* is the name applied to a legal relationship in which one person holds title to property for the benefit of another person. There are four essential elements of a trust: the *trustor* (the person who creates the trust), the *trustee* (the person to whom title to property is transferred), the *trust property* itself, and the *beneficiary* (person for whose benefit the property is held in trust). It is possible for the same person to be trustor, trustee, and beneficiary. This occurs when you create a trust of your own property and name yourself as beneficiary. Why would anyone do such a thing? There are many reasons.

2. Types of Trust [6.23]

Before we get into that, we will discuss the two main types of trusts: *intervivos*, a "living" trust created by the trustor while he is still alive, and *testamentary*, a trust created by will which does not go into effect until the testator (person making the will) has died and his will has been admitted to probate.

3. Testamentary Trusts [6.24]

Testamentary trusts are used for a number of reasons. The most common is to maintain an orderly method of taking care of survivors, particularly a spouse, children, or grandchildren. Another major reason is to save on federal estate taxes upon the death of the surviving spouse (see Section 6.57). A typical husband's testamentary trust would name a bank as trustee, would designate the assets of his estate as the property to go into trust, and would name his wife as beneficiary during her lifetime, and his children as beneficiaries during their lives or until termination of the trust.

[6.25]   **4.   Intervivos Trusts**

Intervivos trusts have a number of purposes. One is to provide an orderly transition between life and death for the management of one's estate without the interruption of probate or the delays and expenses that are always involved.

Another purpose of an intervivos trust is to set up a method for managing the financial assets of a person who may be approaching a period in life during which he may not be completely capable at all times of managing his financial affairs.

[6.26]   **5.   Trust Powers**

The trustee can be given whatever powers the trustor wishes him to have. Certain powers are conferred by law, but the trustor can increase or decrease these powers by appropriate language in the trust document.

[6.27]   **6.   How Long Can a Trust Last?**

There are rules in every state which prohibit a trust from lasting longer than a certain period of time. Generally speaking (with many exceptions), this period of time is twenty-one years after the death of a person who is living at the time the trust goes into effect.

[6.28]   **7.   Termination of a Trust**

A typical trust terminates when the primary purpose for its creation has been fulfilled. Thus a trust for the benefit of wife and children would terminate when the wife has died and the children are old enough to take care of themselves and mature enough to manage their own money.

8. Trust in Place of Guardianship [6.29]

A trust is also a good alternative to a guardianship. If you die without a will, or have a will but leave your property to your children and your children are minors, a guardian will be appointed and the funds will be distributed to the guardian for management (see Section 3.51). The guardian will have to file periodic accountings with the court and will have to ask the court for instructions on how to deal with the property. Under the law the guardian has to distribute an equal share to each child who reaches the age of majority. You can improve this situation by creating a trust which provides that all the property shall be kept in the trust, administered by the trustee, until the youngest child reaches 21, or until all children have completed college. You can also provide for partial distributions to children upon reaching certain ages such as 25, 30, and 35. The trust offers many possibilities for financial planning that are more tailor-made to particular family situations than simply requiring guardianship until each child comes of age and then making a lump-sum distribution to that child of his share of the estate.

9. Saving Probate Costs [6.30]

An intervivos trust can also save probate costs. A testamentary trust takes effect only after the will has been probated. To get into the trust, the assets must first pass through the probate administration. This takes time and costs money. Time can be saved along with money with an *intervivos trust,* in which case the assets in the trust will escape probate and the trust can continue as if nothing had happened. The costs of probate include court costs, executor fees, attorney fees, costs of publication of notices, and other miscellaneous expenses of administration of the estate. These fees can be avoided or greatly reduced by an intervivos trust.

However, not all assets can be successfully put into an intervivos trust unless it is periodically revised. Assets acquired after the creation of the trust and before death may end up going through probate.

[6.31]   **10. Revocable or Irrevocable Trusts**

A trust can either be *revocable* or *irrevocable.* Most intervivos trusts are revocable, which means they can be terminated or changed at any time by the trustor. An irrevocable trust is a special device sometimes used for tax or other reasons. It should never be used without the advice of a legal specialist.

[6.32]   **11. Privacy**

One advantage of an intervivos trust over a testamentary trust is that the terms of the trust do not become public knowledge. The testamentary trust would be set forth in the will which, when it is probated, becomes a matter of public record. That is, a citizen or a reporter can go to the court where the estate has been probated and read the will, which would be kept in the clerk's file. This would not be of any concern to most people, but in the case of a very wealthy person whose name was widely known, the terms of that will might be of some interest to the public and a nosy reporter might read the file and write a story or a column about it in the newspaper. For those who are concerned about this possibility, an intervivos trust would be one way to avoid the publicity.

12. Pour-Over Will [6.33]

Of course, even with an intervivos trust, you should still have a will because there will always be some property that you did not put into the trust that must be disposed of at your death. In such a case you have a *pour-over will*, which takes care of that part of your estate, by having it distributed by the executor to the trustee of the intervivos trust after the probate has been completed.

13. How to Avoid Probate [6.34]

A device of increasing popularity is the intervivos trust with the same person as trustor, trustee, and also one of the beneficiaries. In his book entitled *How To Avoid Probate,* author Norman Dacey makes a strong pitch for this type of estate-planning. Some of the advantages of this device have been briefly discussed (see Sections 6.25, 6.29, 6.30, and 6.32). For many people it may be ideal; the problem is that no two people have the same estate-planning needs, and there just isn't one particular form that can be used, or one particular way of doing things that is good for everyone. It is a serious mistake for everyone to attempt to copy a form out of a form book, fill in a few blanks, and expect to have a workable and practical estate plan without any other unforeseen problems being created (see Section 6.64).

[6.35]   14. Cost of Intervivos Trust

In situations in which the intervivos trust is a good idea for you, and your primary purpose is to save the expenses of probate, you should be aware of the costs involved. Unless you plan to do it yourself (which in most cases would be a mistake), you will find that the attorney fees involved in setting up this kind of trust will be a little more than those involved in signing a will with a testamentary trust. Your attorney will advise you to execute a pour-over will anyway, in addition to the intervivos trust, and you should expect that it will cost slightly more to begin with. However, the increase in cost will be far less than the amount of executor and attorney fees that will be saved by not having the bulk of your estate pass through probate.

If a bank is to be named as trustee of your intervivos trust, it will probably charge a fee. If the bank is going to be an active trustee, managing the assets, keeping records, etc., during your lifetime, it will certainly charge an annual fee which will be based on a percentage of the total value of your trust property. The long-term cost of bank management should be compared with the estimated costs of going through probate in order to determine whether there is any real savings. If the trust is a *dry trust*, which means a trust consisting only of life insurance policies on the life of the trustor, then the bank may not charge any fee, or just a small one-time set-up charge.

There will also be one extra income tax return that will have to be filed each year if you set up an active intervivos trust, and you will have to figure the extra cost of that.

[6.36]   15. Adding Assets to a Trust

Once a trust is created, whether it is an intervivos trust or a testamentary trust, certain other assets can be put into that trust. The best example would be life insurance proceeds. The beneficiary designation clause of a life insurance policy could be changed to state that the proceeds would be paid to the trustee of the intervivos trust or to the trustee of the testamentary trust. The same is true of company pension or profit sharing plan benefits that survive the death of the employee. Your attorney should be consulted concerning the mechanics of doing these things.

16. Continuation of Family Business [6.37]

An intervivos trust may provide a means of continuing a small family business without interruption by death. The trust can provide for the trustee or successor trustee to continue the management of the business.

17. Trust for Charity [6.38]

You can also provide that gifts to certain charities will be accomplished by creating a trust while you are alive and naming the charities as beneficiaries of the trust after you are dead. If the trust is validly created, the gifts, if properly set up in the trust, would take effect at your death and would not be subject to the problems involved in leaving things to charity in your will, which may be subject to will contest or may be in violation of laws restricting the amount of gifts that can be left to charity by will.

18. Estate-Support Trust; Insurance Proceeds [6.39]

The trustee of an intervivos trust may also be authorized to use funds (such as insurance proceeds collected on your life insurance) (see Section 6.71) to buy assets from the executor of your estate or to loan money to the executor of your estate in order to pay funeral debts, taxes, etc. In some cases this would allow your executor to avoid selling assets at a bad time or under unfavorable conditions in order to obtain money to pay debts or taxes.

By placing insurance policies into trust, rather than have them go to the estate, the insurance dollars are immediately available upon death of the insured. The survivors don't have to wait for the money to go through probate. Probate fees are also saved.

F. TAXES

[6.40]   ## 1. Scope of Coverage

There are several subjects in this book which cannot be adequately covered in detail for a number of reasons. One of these subjects is taxes. There are several reasons for this. Tax laws are extremely complex and incredibly detailed; they involve a continual state of flux and change. This is an area best left to CPAs and tax attorneys. We will only briefly touch on the subject (see Section 6.55 for taxes in estate planning).

2. Basic Tax Structure [6.41]

The only favorable thing that can be said about our extremely complex tax structure is that it has become so bad that it now bears the seeds of its own destruction. Like anything that was based upon a faulty premise to begin with, it only gets worse if it is permitted to continue. Our tax structure is based on a premise that is contrary to the basic political-economic theories upon which our business and government operate. The basic fault is that it attempts to use a tool which is intended to fairly and efficiently raise money for the operation of government as a political weapon to achieve social and economic aims (such as redistribution of the wealth). Because the basic thrust of the tax laws is counterproductive in the economic sense, it has become necessary or expedient to create exemptions and exceptions and to devise loopholes. Unbelievably massive amounts of time, effort, and money have been spent by the government sector and the private sector in the last two or three decades to create the crazy-quilt, known as the *Internal Revenue Code.* The code includes countless revenue rulings, bulletins, tax court and other court decisions, and regulations. No one knows how many millions of people in this country earn their living by feeding off the tax system we have created. This includes tax attorneys, CPAs, Internal Revenue agents, accountants, tax advisors, estate planners, writers, book publishing companies, printing companies, teachers, lecturers, authors, and all the vast bureaucracy of governmental personnel concerned with the imposition, administration, and collection of taxes. The best thing that could ever happen in this country, next to permanent peace and prosperity, would be the total abolition of all existing tax laws and their replacement with a completely new simplified system which could be easily understood and efficiently administered, and would fairly apportion the burden of the costs of government.

[6.42]   3.   Proliferation of Taxes

As a citizen you are faced with taxes at all levels of government: federal, state, and local. There is a proliferation of taxes including, but not limited to, income taxes, sales taxes, estate taxes, inheritance taxes, license taxes, real property taxes, personal property taxes, and on and on.

[6.43]   4.   Income Tax

The income tax is the worst offender of them all. There is a continual flow of books, magazine articles, and newspaper articles on the subject of how to avoid, evade, or reduce income taxes. There is also a wealth of material available on how to fill out an income tax return. Most people, even those with some formal education and a lot of patience and concentration, find it a real struggle to successfully file their own income tax returns. For people with complicated income situations, some professional help is a must. The help of a professional is also indispensable in finding ways to reduce taxes. Because of the unfortunate way income tax laws are structured, the very poor and the very rich generally escape the payment of income taxes, leaving the heaviest burden to fall upon the shoulders of those in the middle. The Internal Revenue Service estimates that as many as 50 percent of the people do some kind of cheating on their tax returns, which says something about the regard of the average citizen for our tax laws.

[6.44]   5.   Income Tax Return Forms

Every person has some contact with federal and state income tax laws by virtue of the annual requirement for filing tax returns. Any income tax question you have that can't be answered by reference to the instructions accompanying your return, or that can't be solved by referring to any one of the number of handy guides to income tax law available at most pocket-book stores, should be referred to an accountant or a tax attorney (see Section 10.17).

G. TITLE TO PROPERTY

There are several different ways of holding title to property, that we will discuss briefly.

1. Joint Tenancy   [6.45]

Property may be held in *joint tenancy* by having in its deed that it is held by the parties as joint tenants, in the case of real property; securities may be registered in the names of joint tenants also, and a bank account may be registered in the name of two parties. (See Section 6.49 for a comparison with community property.) Almost any asset may be held in joint tenancy. Some states also permit you to convert everything to joint tenancy merely by having both parties sign a written agreement stating just that. However, such an agreement ought not to be signed without consulting a lawyer as to the legal and tax consequences. The most significant feature of joint tenancy is that title to the property passes automatically to the survivor upon the death of one joint tenant. No probate is necessary. At most, the surviving joint tenant merely has to get the court to order the joint tenancy terminated, which is done by filing a petition to terminate joint tenancy.

[6.46]   ## 2.   Disadvantages of Joint Tenancy

The major disadvantages of joint tenancy follow:

- The property passes outside a will and cannot be directed or given or disposed of by a will in any manner or form.

- In some cases property in joint tenancy may not receive a *stepped-up basis* upon the death of the first spouse to die. Property that is held as community property (see Section 6.49) receives a new *basis* when the husband or wife dies. That *basis* is the fair market value of the property at the date of death. If the property is thereafter sold at that value, there is no *gain*, and so there is no tax. If it is sold at a price higher than that value, the gain is only the difference between the value at the date of death and the price received at the sale. If the same property is held in joint tenancy, however, with certain exceptions it does not receive a stepped-up basis on death, and when it is sold the gain (if any) is the difference between the original cost of the property and the price for which it is sold. This could be a substantial gain in the case of property that appreciated greatly as a result of having been held for a long period of time, and a large tax might result.

● It is inflexible. If husband and wife own property in joint tenancy and the husband dies first, and the wife dies afterward without a will, the property would pass to the wife's relatives. This may or may not be what the husband wants. If husband and wife die in a common disaster, a court may be left with a difficult problem in distributing joint tenancy property. The final distribution may not be what the parties would have wanted.

3. Joint Tenancy May Mean a Gift   [6.47]

If the property belonged solely to one person before it was put into joint tenancy, the creation of the joint tenancy results in a gift, and a gift tax return may have to be filed. If the gift is large enough, a gift tax may have to be paid (see Section 6.60). Some property such as a home, a bank account, or a U.S. Savings Bond might not be treated as a gift for gift tax reasons at the time it was put into joint tenancy, but would become a gift when converted to cash or sold.

4. Estate Taxes on Joint Tenancy   [6.48]

Property held in joint tenancy may be fully taxed in the estate of the first joint tenant to die, unless it can be proved that it originally belonged to the surviving joint tenant or that part or all of it was paid for by the surviving joint tenant. Such proof is sometimes difficult to establish. Of course this doesn't become a problem unless the estate is over $120,000 in size, because the *marital deduction* would reduce the estate by half, and the $60,000 exemption from federal estate tax would reduce the remainder to zero (see Section 6.56).

[6.49]   5.   Community Property

If your state is among the eight or so having *community property* laws, you are probably somewhat familiar with the concept. In general terms, community property means property that is acquired by earnings of the husband or wife after they are married. This excludes property that they already had when they got married or property received by gift or inheritance during their marriage. As in the case of joint tenancy, community property can be converted to separate property, but unless the property is equally divided, a gift would result. Community property is owned by both spouses, each owning half and having the power to dispose of that half by gift or by will. The husband normally has control of the community property, although the expanding women's rights movement may change this. In a community property state, if one spouse dies without a will, the community property interests of the deceased go to the survivor and in some cases part of it will go to the children. Income from community property is taxed one-half to each spouse. On death, the entire community property may get a stepped-up basis (see Section 6.46). There may be a gift when separate property is transformed into community property or when community property is transformed into separate property. If husband and wife make a gift to their child of some community property, both are then subject to gift tax on their half-interest in the gifted property (if the amount is large; see Section 6.60).

6. Quasi-Community Property [6.50]

The laws of California provide that when a couple comes to California, the property that they acquired in another state that would have been community property had it been so acquired in California becomes *quasi-community property.* There are certain rules applying to such property that are similar to the community property rules.

7. Tenancy in Common [6.51]

Tenants in common each own an undivided interest in the property, which each can sell or leave to another in his will. If two people own some property in tenancy in common, each has a one-half undivided interest in the property. If ten people own property as tenants in common, each has a one-tenth interest in the property. When a tenant in common dies, his share does not go to the other tenants in common, but to his heirs if he dies without a will, otherwise to those designated in his will. Title is taken in the following form: "A, B, and C, as tenants in common."

8. Tenancy by the Entireties [6.52]

Tenancy by the entireties is recognized in twenty or more states. In those states, when husband and wife take title to property in both of their names, a tenancy by entirety, or estate by entirety, is created. When one of them dies, the survivor takes title automatically, just as if the property were in joint tenancy. In some states recognizing tenancy by the entirety, there is a unique document which provides that they both together own the entire property, and a creditor, therefore, has to have a judgment against both husband and wife in order to seize such property. Although a creditor can seize the half of property held in joint tenancy owned by the debtor, he cannot do the same in the case of property held in tenancy by the entireties.

[6.53]   9.   Dower and Curtesy

In some states the wife of a man who has died gets a share of the estate, ranging from one-third to two-thirds, which is called *dower* interest. *Curtesy* (or *courtesy*) was the interest which a husband had under English law in the property of his wife to which he was entitled after her death. *Curtesy* has been abolished in most states.

H. ESTATE PLANNING

Estate planning is a broad term, frequently misused, which can include a great many things. It includes the creation, conservation, and distribution of one's estate. Life insurance is a frequently used tool in estate planning—it is used to create or increase an estate, and to provide for survivors and for payment of taxes and expenses. Those who sell mutual funds occasionally refer to themselves as estate planners. The term *estate planning* can really be applied to almost anything having to do with the acquisition, ownership, and disposition of all kinds of property.

1. Taxes in Estate Planning

A large part of estate planning revolves around the federal income tax, the federal estate tax, the federal gift tax, and the equivalent state taxes. Income tax is of less importance after death than it is during one's lifetime, but it can still be important. The income tax bracket of a trust, an estate, the surviving members of a family, or beneficiaries of a trust must be taken into consideration by the estate planner. Any one having or anticipating enough income to make income taxes a problem should obtain some expert advice on how income tax planning fits into estate planning. As has been mentioned, it is risky for a book of this type to talk too much about taxes because of the rapid changes in this field. However, some general comments can be made about federal estate taxes.

2. Federal Estate Taxes

An estate is entitled to a $60,000 exemption. This means, in general, that the first $60,000-worth of property in an estate is not subject to federal estate tax. The tax is a graduated tax, the percentage going up with the size of the estate, in much the same way that income tax increases with the size of taxable income. When a spouse dies and leaves everything to the surviving spouse, there is a *marital deduction* of one-half of the amount so left. If a husband and wife, together, had $120,000 and the husband died, leaving everything to the wife, the marital deduction of one-half would reduce the husband's estate to $60,000, and because his estate is entitled to an exemption in that amount, there would be no federal estate tax. However, when the wife later dies, if she still has most of that $120,000 in her estate, the remainder after deducting the $60,000 exemption (less probate expenses) would be subject to federal estate tax. There are many ways to avoid the much larger tax on the death of the second spouse. A lawyer familiar with the field of taxes and estate planning should be consulted about such matters.

[6.57]   ### 3.   Balancing Estates

Because estate taxes become progressively higher as the amount of the estate increases, most estate planning revolves around the concept of attempting to equally balance the size of the estates of a husband and wife so that one-half will be taxed on the death of each. More exotic estate planning consists of attempting to reduce or eliminate taxes on the death of either spouse. For example, property can be put in trust for a spouse for life, and be passed to yet another upon that spouse's death and under proper conditions escape estate tax on the death of that spouse.

[6.58]   ### 4.   Gifts in Contemplation of Death

You can also escape estate tax by eliminating property from your estate by giving it away before you die. However there are special rules governing *gifts in contemplation of death* which have the effect of pulling gifted property back into your estate for estate tax purposes. Generally this applies to gifts given within three years before death, unless it can be proved that the decedent gave the property for some reason other than because he thought he was about to die.

5.   Annuities [6.59]

You can purchase an annuity from an insurance company and eliminate any estate tax by having nothing left when you die (the insurance company pays you a steady income for life). Some estate planners advocate *private annuities* whereby parents sell their property to their children in return for a life income, thus hoping to escape estate tax. There are many pitfalls in the private annuity arrangement and an expert should be consulted.

6.   Gift Tax [6.60]

The federal law taxes gifts (so do most states). Returns need not be filed unless the gift is over a certain amount ($3,000 per year, per person, for federal). Gift tax rates are also progressive, but are lower than estate tax rates (this may change). Taxes are due only if the gift is over a certain minimum. Every person has a $30,000 lifetime *exemption* from federal gift tax and a $3,000 annual *exclusion.* This means you can give up to $3,000 a year to any one person (or $3,000 each to as many people as you like) each year without having to pay federal gift tax. You can also give up to $30,000 (in addition to your annual exclusion) during your lifetime. If husband and wife give property they own together, each gets the benefit of the $3,000 exclusion and the $30,000 exemption. If a husband gives to a wife, or vice versa, the marital deduction applies (see Section 6.56). For example, a husband could give $6,000 to his wife; the marital deduction would eliminate paying tax on $3,000, and the annual exclusion would eliminate tax on the remaining $3,000, so there would be no gift tax. A husband and wife together could give $6,000 to one child and there would be no gift tax because each would get a $3,000 exclusion. A husband could give $60,000 to his wife in one year and there would be no gift tax because of the marital deduction and the $30,000 lifetime exemption. He could give an additional $6,000 to his wife in that year and there would still be no tax because of the marital deduction of $3,000 and the annual exclusion of $3,000.

[6.61]   7.   Family Gift Program

Parents who anticipate having very large estates which they plan to leave to their children would be well-advised to adopt a regular program of giving. The gifts would be small enough to stay within the annual exclusions or/and lifetime exemptions, but over a period of years would be large enough to greatly reduce estate taxes that would otherwise go to the government. This is also a good way for a family corporation or business to be passed from one generation to the next. The parents can hang on to 51 percent of the stock after giving 49 percent away to their children in amounts that are calculated to take maximum advantage of the annual exclusion and lifetime exemption rules. They could even go beyond the 51 percent if they have confidence in the interest and ability of their children to manage the business or to properly exercise their voting power as shareholders to elect directors who will properly manage the business. The stock that they (the parents) retain should generate enough income in the form of dividends to support them, taking into consideration other sources of income such as salary from the business, or income from other investments, and so forth.

8. Trusts in Estate Planning [6.62]

A trust is a very good estate planning tool (see Sections 6.22 to 6.39). It can be used to reduce estate tax on the death of the surviving spouse, and to provide income and financial supervision for children beyond the age of majority (see Section 6.29). An intervivos trust can be used to bypass probate and to serve as a means of administering the assets of an estate of an elderly person who may have need of some financial assistance in his declining years. A trust can also be used to reduce income taxes by creating a separate taxpayer—a valid trust pays its own tax. An income-producing asset can be removed from your tax return and be taken over by a trust under proper conditions; the combined income tax of the trust and the individual creating the trust would be less than the income tax of the individual if the income-producing asset remained in his possession and control.

9. The Will as an Estate-Planning Tool [6.63]

The will is the most basic estate-planning tool of all. There will almost always be some property in an estate that must be passed on by will, even where intervivos trusts (Section 6.25) and annuities (Section 6.59) have been created. For those whose estates are modest enough to preclude use of any other estate-planning devices, a simple will is still a must (see Sections 6.4 and 6.14). Remember, however, that not all property will pass under a will (see Section 6.46).

[6.64]   10. Do-It-Yourself Estate Planning

The do-it-yourself approach to estate planning is very risky and can have serious financial consequences (see Section 6.34). For anyone having an estate larger than $60,000 (leaving no surviving spouse) or $120,000 (leaving a spouse surviving), the wrong move can have serious tax consequences. For example, if a man dies owning stock in a company and he has reduced his interest in the corporation below a certain percentage of his total estate, he may lose (or his estate may lose) the opportunity to have corporate earnings used to redeem his stock with tax savings, or to have the estate spread the payment of estate taxes over a longer than normal period of time.

Putting property into or taking it out of joint tenancy can have adverse tax consequences (see Sections 6.47 and 6.48), and the consequences can be different depending upon which joint tenant dies first. In spite of the form books and the simplified approach to the problem adopted by some widely circulated publications, there is no fool-proof system of estate planning that the average person can adopt to his own use (see Section 6.34).

[6.65]   11. Estate Planners

There are many so-called professional estate planners who advertise and promote themselves by various means. Some of these people are extremely knowledgeable and competent. Many of them are former lawyers or accountants. Some of them know as much or more about the general field of estate planning than do many lawyers. However, there are certain dangers inherent in dealing with estate planners, or letting them advise you on how to set up your estate. Although states may at some time in the future license estate planners, they do not do so at the present time; consequently anyone can now call himself an estate planner, and you have no way of knowing whether he is competent or incompetent. The advice you seek in estate planning usually transcends the fields of law, taxes, insurance, and securities. A really thorough and complete estate-planning job for a wealthy man with large interests would require the services (and teamwork) of a lawyer, an accountant, a life insurance underwriter, an investment counsellor or securities broker, and a real estate broker or adviser. No one person is capable of furnishing all of these services, and doing it legally and without conflict of interest. The mutual fund salesman who is primarily motivated by selling you mutual funds (because he makes his living from his sales commission) is not the man to advise you on how much life insurance you need to pay your estate taxes and provide for your survivors. A life insurance salesman (who makes his living from his commissions) is not the man to advise you whether your wife should be the beneficiary of a marital deduction trust or whether your property should be left to your grandchildren by right of representation or per capita. Only an attorney is licensed to draft wills and trust instruments. If he makes a mistake, he is professionally responsible and can be made to pay for any damages (see Section 9.26). He also carries malpractice insurance to protect himself and his clients against his mistakes. Estate planners cannot obtain such insurance unless they are lawyers, in which case they would be practicing law and not doing estate planning solely. Estate planners solicit business; lawyers have to wait for the business to come to them. Because estate planners can't practice law and can't charge a fee for legal advice, how do they make their money? It could be that they are selling you something, and you should know what that is.

The proper approach to the professional estate planner is to find out (by making proper inquiries) whether he is competent and reputable or not. If he is, then listen carefully to all of his recommendations. Before committing yourself to whatever plan or proposal he recommends, whether it involves life insurance, mutual funds, real estate, securities, trusts, or whatever, take his recommendations to your attorney, accountant, life insurance underwriter, broker, etc., and get their opinions and their assistance. Beware of the estate planner who offers to line you up with an attorney who will take care of drafting all the necessary documents. Most reputable attorneys will not operate under such conditions, and if you run into one that does, he probably does a large volume of work for the estate planner and therefore his loyalty will be more to the estate planner's recommendations than to your best interests. Also beware of the professional (attorney, accountant, chartered life underwriter, etc.) who fearlessly ventures out of his field to give you advice or make recommendations in some other field. The real "professionals" in their own fields will not do this. For example, your attorney's recommendations on life insurance should properly be limited to the different ways that life insurance can be used and what effect each will have upon your estate, and what tax problems are involved. It would be improper for him to tell you how much insurance you should have, what kind of insurance you should have, or what company you should buy it from.

I. LIFE INSURANCE

1. How Life Insurance Fits into   [6.66]
Estate Planning

Life insurance and estate planning go together. A husband and father needs life insurance if the size of his estate is small in order to provide a reasonable standard of living for his wife and children in the event of his death. Larger estates may need life insurance for a number of reasons such as taking care of estate taxes or providing liquidity (cash) which might not otherwise be available on death where most of the assets consist of a family business or closely held company stock, or real property that cannot be easily converted to cash.

2. Types of Life Insurance Policies   [6.67]

There are many different types of insurance policies. The decision as to which type you should have should be based upon your total financial picture and your financial objectives.

Term insurance requires the least initial dollar outlay for the premium. As the age of the insured increases, the premium increases. Term is not the most economical type of policy where permanent insurance is needed. It is better for the short duration.

Ordinary life insurance costs more than term because your premiums buy more than just insurance. There is also a cash reserve built up over a period of time. The company permits you to borrow against this cash reserve.

Minimum deposit insurance is a variation on an ordinary life policy. The insured pays the premium for the first year and thereafter borrows back from the company each year the amount necessary to pay subsequent premiums. The advantage of this over paying the full annual premium on an ordinary life policy is that the cost in the early years of the policy is much less because you pay only the interest on the loan (plus some minor charges). As the borrowing continues, the amount of insurance proceeds left after payment of the loan decreases. To remedy this situation you can purchase a *term rider* on the policy which adds term insurance each year in an amount equal to the loan balance, so the total net payable insurance proceeds remain the same.

[6.68]   3.   Choosing an Insurance Man

How much insurance you should carry, what type of policy you should carry, and how your insurance should fit into your estate plan are all matters that you should discuss with an expert.

Before asking advice from any insurance salesman or broker, inquire around about the qualifications of the men that you are considering. You will find that some of them may put on a big show of being estate planners but have a reputation for being more interested in selling the greatest possible amount of insurance each year than in seeing that their client's interests are well served. It pays to shop around and pick your insurance adviser very carefully. If you are a person that has a need for some advanced estate planning, your insurance man will have to be able to work closely with your attorney and possibly with your accountant.

[6.69]   4.   Beneficiary Designations

Once you have purchased your insurance policy, there are a number of ways you can designate the beneficiary. It is very important to keep current on your beneficiary designations on insurance policies. These should be programmed to fit in with your estate plan. If your estate plan calls for a marital deduction trust with the income to be paid to your wife for life and then to the children for their lives or until the youngest reaches 25, you could defeat this whole plan if your insurance policy names your wife and children as beneficiaries (rather than the trust).

5. Ownership of Policy   [6.70]

There are a number of ways a policy can be owned. It may be possible to save estate taxes by having your wife purchase a policy on your life and have her actually pay the premiums. If properly done, this device may keep the insurance proceeds out of your estate and free from taxation on your death. However, the proceeds may be included in your wife's taxable estate at her subsequent death.

6. Life Insurance Trust   [6.71]

You can make your insurance policies payable to a trust that will manage the insurance proceeds at your death. The *life insurance trust* is a very flexible tool and is frequently used when most of the estate consists of insurance. Its use results in the insurance proceeds avoiding probate.

7. Settlement Options   [6.72]

The insurance company permits you several choices on how the proceeds will be paid. These choices are called *settlement options*. You may elect to leave the proceeds with the company and have the company pay them out to the beneficiary over a period of time. Some policies permit you to elect among lump-sum distribution, payment of proceeds over a period of time, including principal and interest, or the purchase of a lifetime annuity from the company. The settlement option can be made by the insured when the policy is purchased or can be left for the beneficiary to make when the policy matures.

[6.73]   8.   Group Life

Group life insurance is the coverage of a number of persons under a single contract at a lower cost than would be the case if each individual had his own insurance. Usually group policy premiums are paid by an employer, but a portion may also be paid by the employee. It may be possible to keep the proceeds of a group life policy out of your estate for estate inheritance tax and for federal estate tax purposes, but you should get the advice of experts before attempting to do this. If you are covered by a group life insurance policy and either quit or get laid off, check to see what effect this has on the policy and whether you can maintain the insurance.

[6.74]   9.   Special Features
             of Life Insurance Policies

There are some special features available on most insurance policies. One is an *automatic loan provision* which makes the policy continue in effect if you neglect to pay the premium. Another is *waiver of premium* by the company in the event of your sickness or disability.

10. Collecting Insurance Proceeds [6.75]

The insurance company may refuse to pay a claim under certain conditions. Failure to pay premiums, causing the policy to expire, is an obvious case. Most life policies have a thirty-day *grace period* beginning the date the premium was due. The insurance continues in effect during that period, but you must make the payment within that period to renew the policy.

Suicide may or may not bar recovery. It depends on the policy and upon how long the policy has been in effect before the suicide occurred.

Fraud may bar recovery of the proceeds. If the insured lied about his health to obtain a policy, the company may be able to avoid payment.

If the insured has borrowed up to the limit under his life insurance policy, there may be little or no net insurance proceeds when he dies. The payment will equal the face amount of the policy less the amount of the loan, including interest.

Where a policy provides for *double indemnity,* the death of the insured by accident will double the face value of the policy.

For those interested in increasing their estate through investments or in improving their income tax situation, there are many different potential investments. Insurance has already been discussed as a means of increasing an estate. In addition, it is possible to use insurance as a form of investment by buying ordinary life or whole life so that a portion of the premiums does not go for life insurance alone, but also goes to build up a cash value. This of course is a very conservative investment with a minimum return. Another form of investment would be a savings account or the purchase of U.S. Treasury Bonds. Although these are the safest kind of investment, they don't produce much of a return in an economy in which inflation is the long-term trend.

Stocks, common or preferred, offer a combination of opportunities for a modest return on investment in the form of dividends plus appreciation, which can range from moderate to substantial, depending upon the company. You can spread the risk of your investment somewhat by investing in mutual funds, which in theory offer a diversified portfolio of investments under expert management—this should provide a safer investment than investing in selective issues of common stocks, although not necessarily produce as great a return as some individual stocks would do. Recent trends have shown that mutual funds don't always perform as expected and sometimes go down just as fast as the market in general.

There are many different kinds of bonds that can be purchased in addition to U.S. Treasury Bonds. Many corporations issue bonds which provide a reasonable rate of return. Price fluctuations in bonds may provide opportunity for capital gains. Debentures are another form of investment. These are usually issued by a corporation in the form of interest-bearing notes which are convertible into stock. The advantage is that if the stock goes up you can convert to stock and get a capital gain and if it does not go up you can simply draw your interest. Warrants are another similar device. A warrant is a right to buy a share of stock sometime in the future. It is like an option.

Another form of investment is a pension or profit sharing plan. If you work for a corporation, it may have a pension plan or a profit sharing plan. If it does not, find out why not. Under some plans the employer takes care of everything and the employee simply gets what he is entitled to under the plan when he retires, dies, etc. Under other plans the employee may contribute part of his salary to the plan. The advantages of this are that he may escape paying income tax on salary contributed to a qualified plan, and the amounts contributed to the plan by him or in his behalf accumulate income, tax-free. You simply cannot match such a program by investing your own after-tax dollars (see Section 7.6). The *Keough Plan* legislation was an attempt to provide somewhat the same benefits for self-employed persons or members of partnerships. Efforts are now being made to extend the *Keough Plan* benefit so that self-employed persons and partnerships will be on an equal basis with corporations, because there is no reason to discriminate between them.

Once your money goes into a company pension or profit sharing trust, that trust can invest in stocks and bonds, including in some cases the company stock, and can sometimes make other investments such as real estate, etc.

Farm commodities are another form of investment. These can be purchased on a rapidly fluctuating market and speculators play this market, attempting to buy low and sell high and keep the difference. This is a highly specialized form of investment that involves predicting the future price of a certain crop or commodity based on complicated economic factors and forecasts.

There is a group of special investments having tax advantages which include cattle, oil, timber, Christmas trees, mining, and certain forms of real estate investment. This list is by no means exhaustive. There are certain advantages to be found by investing in such fields, particularly for people in higher-income brackets. Experts should be consulted before any such investment is made to determine the effectiveness and advisability.

Real estate is an excellent long-term investment, and can also offer many short-term tax advantages. A long-term investment in raw land may offer tremendous opportunities for appreciation or growth in capital. Investment in improved land in a rapidly developing area may result in a good combination of cash flow, equity build-up, tax shelter, and appreciation (see Sections 10.53 to 10.60). Investment in real estate can take many different forms. You can buy stock in a corporation that owns real estate. You can buy an apartment house yourself and either manage it or hire a manager. You can invest as a limited partner in a real estate venture or you can buy a limited partnership interest in a real estate syndication or put money into a real estate investment trust (see Sections 10.61 to 10.64).

VII. Business and Labor Laws

A. CORPORATIONS

1. Pros and Cons of Incorporating [7.1]

There are many different factors which should be considered by a businessman who is thinking of incorporating. The following are some of them:

a. CENTRALIZED MANAGEMENT [7.2]

If a business is large enough, there are certain administrative advantages which the corporate form has. Power can be delegated to a chief executive to make all important decisions. He in turn can delegate to subordinates. The chief executive is held accountable to the owners by means of the board of directors, who in turn are chosen by the shareholders. The corporate form permits lines of authority and responsibility to be clearly drawn.

b. CONTINUITY OF LIFE [7.3]

If a sole proprietor dies, or if a partner dies and the partnership is thereby dissolved, the business will certainly have problems in continuing its activities uninterrupted. Because the corporation has perpetual existence (until dissolved), death of an officer or of a shareholder does not directly interfere with the conduct of the business.

[7.4]

c.   TRANSFERABILITY

Ownership of the corporation is easily transferable by means of shares of stock. The same is not true of an interest in a sole proprietorship or of a partnership interest.

[7.5]

d.   TAXES

For some time the corporation tax rate has been 22 percent of the first $25,000 of net income. Also for some time the tax rate has been 48 percent of the excess above $25,000 net income—with an additional surtax sometimes being applied. (These rates may change). It is therefore possible that the same amount of money earned by a corporation would result in lower taxes than if earned by an individual. However, in order to get that income out of the corporation it may have to be paid in the form of dividends, which would be taxed, thus constituting a *double tax* which would generally exceed the tax an individual would pay on the same income even if he were paying at higher rates. The double tax can be postponed by accumulating earnings within the corporation. However there are limits upon the amount of earnings that a corporation may accumulate without getting hit with a penalty tax. The shareholders of a corporation may also make a *Subchapter S Election*. This means they choose to be taxed as if they were partners rather than shareholders. The result of this is that all the corporate income, whether it is paid out to them in the form of dividends or not, is taxed to the shareholders each year. This is advantageous if the corporation is expected to have losses during early periods of operation, and the shareholders want the losses passed through to them so that they can write them off against their other income.

Strict rules must be followed to qualify as a Subchapter S Corporation; these include having no more than ten shareholders, with all of the shareholders being either individuals or estates (no trusts or corporations).

e.   FRINGE BENEFITS   [7.6]

The corporation can set up profit sharing and/or pension plans which are not available to individuals. Although it is true that the *Keough Plan* legislation attempted to provide similar benefits for individuals and partnerships, it fell far short of providing benefits equal to those which are available to corporations. By adopting a profit sharing or pension plan a corporation can make payments into a fund for the employees without the payments being taxed to the employees as income. The employees can also contribute to the same fund and not be taxed on the amount of their income which they contribute to the fund. The interest or other income earned by the fund is not taxed; it therefore accumulates much faster than would otherwise be the case. There are certain tax advantages when the funds are withdrawn by the employee upon retirement, disability, or death (the funds going to his estate). In other words, the fund is not all taxed as if it were ordinary income when it is paid over to the employee or his estate. The basic difference between the profit sharing plan and the pension plan is that the corporation has to make regular payments into the pension plan fund, but it doesn't have to make payments into a profit sharing plan fund unless there are profits. Be sure to have your attorney pass on any pension or profit sharing plan before approving it. There are many pension and profit sharing "experts" who package and sell plans to corporations. If part of the package includes buying their insurance or buying their mutual funds, then you know they have a *conflict of interest* and cannot be counted upon to be totally objective in choosing the best possible plan for your corporation. Also beware of cut-rate packaged plans that have great appeal because they cost very little to put into effect. Every corporation has its own unique problems and it may be worth your while to pay a little more to get a plan that is tailor-made to your situation. A corporation can also save its officers and employees money on insurance through group insurance plans, including life insurance, income disability insurance, and medical insurance.

[7.7]

f. RAISING CAPITAL

A corporation provides a good vehicle for raising capital through the sale of shares of stock or the issuance of notes which are convertible into stock at the option of the lender (sometimes called *debentures*).

[7.8]

g. LIMITED LIABILITY

As a stockholder in a corporation, if things have been properly done, you can never lose more than you put into the corporation. The same is not true of a partner. A partner can lose everything he has. His creditors are not limited to just the assets of the partnership. However, it is possible to forfeit your limited liability in a number of different ways. One is if the corporation is *inadequately capitalized*. This means, simply, that not enough *equity* was put into the corporation. In other words, the stockholders didn't put enough money into the corporation to give it a reasonable chance of being able to survive and meet its obligations.

A sole stockholder can forfeit limited liability if he uses the corporation as his own personal vehicle. This is called the *alter-ego* (other self) doctrine. By running a corporation as if it were a sole proprietorship, a sole stockholder forfeits his limited liability.

Stockholders can also be treated as partners instead of stockholders if the corporation fails to operate as if it were a corporation. If adequate books and records are not kept and if meetings are not held and minutes of those meetings are not properly prepared, a court could find that the business was something other than a corporation.

n. EXPENSE OF INCORPORATION [7.9]

The initial expense of incorporating can run anywhere from $500 to $1,000 or more. The major expenses involved are the secretary of state's fees for filing the articles of incorporation, the minimum state income tax for corporations which in some states must be paid for one year in advance, attorneys' fees, and the state corporation commissioner's fees for stock issuance. There will be additional business expenses because of federal and state tax returns and many other corporate forms which must be processed and filed. To be able to make an intelligent decision about whether to incorporate a business or not, one would have to get together with his accountant and his attorney and consider all of the above factors, together with others.

2. Name of Corporation [7.10]

You can have almost any corporate name you want, as long as it is not the same as or similar to some other corporate name. To find out what names are available, you telephone or write the secretary of state (in your state) and ask if the name you want is available. If it is, you can usually reserve it for a month or more by paying a modest fee. This insures you that if you go ahead with the corporation the name will still be available.

If you are thinking in terms of expansion or doing business in other states, you would do well to search beyond the records of the secretary of state. Most libraries have reference books such as the *Thomas Register of Corporations*, which lists the names of corporations in all states. It never hurts to check as many different sources as you can before selecting a corporate name. Registration with the secretary of state in your state will not protect you against someone who has registered the name in another state.

[7.11]   3.   Articles and Bylaws

Most attorneys have standard form *articles of incorporation* and *by-laws* which only need to have a few blanks filled in. The articles are filed with the secretary of state and are usually required to be recorded in the county in which the corporation will have its principal offices. The bylaws are adopted by the board of directors at the first meeting. At the first meeting, which is usually held right after incorporation, the board will also appoint officers, approve the corporate seal, select a form of stock certificate, and establish a corporate bank account. At the first or at a subsequent meeting, the directors will approve the issuance of stock. If state law permits, be sure the bylaws authorize the directors to act, without a formal meeting, by unanimous written consent.

4. Meetings and Minutes [7.12]

The shareholders meet once a year. Adequate minutes of each meeting should be maintained. The directors also are required to meet once a year to elect officers. They should meet more often than that, preferably at least quarterly. Complete minutes should be kept of all directors' meetings. The bylaws should provide for special meetings of shareholders and/or directors, upon short notice.

5. Capitalization [7.13]

Before incorporating, you will have to decide how much stock you want the corporation to be able to issue. Because to some extent the fees you pay to the state are based upon the amount of authorized capital, you don't want to authorize more than you think the corporation will eventually need. However you should authorize as much as you reasonably believe will someday be necessary. This means more than the amount of stock you intend to issue initially. If you only authorize in the articles that amount of stock which you plan to issue initially, you will have to amend the articles later on if you wish to issue more stock. Enough stock should be issued so that the corporation will have an adequate amount of capital to start the business off with some reasonable chance of making a go of it. The capitalization may include loans as well as issuance of stock. However, the ratio of loaned funds to invested funds should not be overbalanced in favor of loans. If it is, the corporation is said to be *thinly capitalized*, and this can have two disastrous results: the repayment of loans may be held by Internal Revenue Service to be dividends and subject to taxes, or the general creditors may be able to have the loans treated as stock if the corporation becomes unable to pay its debts, so that the creditors would get paid first before the stockholders' loans were repaid.

[7.14]   6.   Stock Issuance

Stock can be issued for cash, for notes, for property, for patents or copyrights, or for services. Some corporations issue *promotional stock* to the persons responsible for forming the corporation and for getting it into business. Promotional stock issuances are tricky and raise difficult tax and corporate security law questions and therefore must be handled by a competent attorney. Permits must be obtained from the corporation commissioner (or an equivalent officer) of the state in which corporate stock is sold or issued. Some state laws permit issuance of stock upon notification to the commissioner under limited circumstances. Interstate stock sales require registration with the Securities Exchange Commission. SEC rules are very complicated and no one should venture into interstate sale of securities without the advice of competent counsel. Don't make the mistake of assuming that just because you are selling stock to a group of your closest friends you don't need permission from the state government to do it. Anyone who buys a share of stock under circumstances in which a permit is required but is not obtained has an absolute right to get his money back any time he wants it. Not only that, but the person who issued him the stock without a permit may have committed a criminal offense for which he could be fined or imprisoned. These laws regulating the issuance of stock are commonly known as *blue-sky laws* (so named because they prevent the sale of stock by a company whose only assets are the blue sky).

The *authorized stock* is the total amount of shares a corporation may issue under its charter. The *issued stock* is the total number of shares that have actually been issued by the corporation.

A *stock subscription* is an agreement to purchase stock in a new corporation when the corporation is able to issue it.

Treasury stock is stock that was once issued by the corporation, then repurchased by the corporation and held by it.

Most corporations have one class of stock, called *common.* Some corporations have more than one class of stock, the shares being *common* and *preferred.* Preferred shareholders get preference over common shareholders in such things as payment of dividends and distribution of assets.

7.   Corporate Supplies   [7.15]

The corporation needs a seal, and should have a minute book and stock certificates. If it is a shoestring operation, you can make up your own minute book by using a three-ring binder and some paper. You can also get your stock certificates from a stationery store. The other alternative is to buy a corporate package from companies specializing in such things. They will sell you a seal, minute book, and stock certificate book for a reasonable price. You will probably get an order blank in the mail from such a company within a week or two after you file your articles of incorporation.

8.   Converting Corporate Losses   [7.16]
to Personal Losses

A provision in the Internal Revenue Code (Section 1244) allows you to convert a capital loss to an ordinary loss in the event your corporation folds. Your attorney can advise you on the proper form for a Section 1244 plan and resolution.

[7.17]   9.   Buying and Selling Stock

It is a good idea for stockholders in a small closely held corporation to provide some mechanics for the transfer of shares among themselves. If anyone wants to get rid of his stock, he should be required by such an agreement to offer it first to the corporation, and if the corporation is unable to purchase the stock (because it doesn't have earned surplus or retained earnings, etc.), then it should be offered to the other shareholders, pro rata. If a shareholder dies, there should be some agreed method for purchase of his stock from his estate by the other shareholders. A typical corporate buy-sell agreement will provide for these things, and will include the purchase of insurance on the lives of stockholders so that there will be funds available to purchase their shares in the event of their death.

[7.18]   10. Shareholders' Rights

Shareholders, of course, are entitled to attend the annual meetings of the corporation and to receive adequate notice thereof. They are also entitled to an adequate and accurate statement showing the assets, liabilities, and profits and losses of the corporation. They are entitled to vote for directors at the annual meeting, either in person or by proxy. They have many other rights, including the right to sue in the event of dishonest or illegal conduct of the corporate affairs by officers or directors. One interesting and controversial right is that of a shareholder in a publicly held corporation to propose a resolution for inclusion in the annual proxy statement sent out by the corporation's officers to notify shareholders of the annual meeting and to solicit their votes or proxies in favor of management. A shareholder can have included in a proxy statement a proposal plus an explanation if management opposes the proposal. The proposal must involve a proper subject for action by stockholders, and not involve a personal matter or a matter relating to the ordinary business operations of the company.

Shareholders of record on the date a dividend is declared are entitled to the dividend. Dividends are not due unless declared by the directors. Laws regulate the declaration of dividends. A corporation may not declare a dividend if it doesn't have sufficient surplus or retained earnings. This protects creditors of the corporation.

Shareholders can bring suit to compel directors to declare dividends if the directors wrongfully refuse to declare them.

11. Directors' Liability [7.19]

Directors are responsible for the management of a corporation. They are responsible for hiring, supervising, and firing the corporate officers. It is inadvisable for an individual to serve as a figurehead director of a corporation. Directors must attend meetings and make a reasonable effort to find out about what is going on in the business. They are responsible for what is said in reports that go to the stockholders. Not only are directors liable, but accountants, attorneys, and underwriters may also be liable for misstatements or concealment of facts in reports that go to the public or to shareholders. It is getting tougher all the time to get and keep good directors because of the increased personal liability involved. It is possible to obtain insurance to protect the directors, but it is very difficult for a new corporation or a small corporation to obtain such insurance.

[7.20]   ## 12. Conflict of Interest

You hear a lot these days about *conflict of interest*. What this means is that someone has gotten himself into the position where he can't act objectively and independently because of competing or potentially competing interests. An example would be an officer or director of a corporation who has an interest in another company that is going to enter into a contract with his corporation. A person having a conflict or potential conflict of interest should not participate in the decision-making process. The minutes of the meeting should show that he abstained from voting because of the conflict. Full disclosure of the conflict of interest should be made at the earliest opportunity.

B. SOLE PROPRIETORSHIPS

A *sole proprietorship* is a one-man operation. It is probably the most common form of business enterprise. This is the typical small business run by a man with the assistance of his family. It doesn't require any incorporation or a legal partnership agreement. All decisions are made by the owner. There is no complicated income tax problem (other than the complexities of the individual income tax itself). The profits or losses of the business are reported directly by the owner. There are of course, some disadvantages. The owner is personally liable for all of the business debts. If he dies or becomes unable to work, the business may suffer or fail. He can't take advantage of some of the fringe benefits that corporations can offer.

C. PARTNERSHIPS

1. General Partnerships

[7.22]

a. NATURE OF PARTNERSHIP

A partnership is an association of two or more persons to carry on a business together. Each of the partners is the agent of the other partner. Each partner can legally bind and obligate the other partners.

[7.23]

b. ADVANTAGES AND DISADVANTAGES

There is less formality involved in running a partnership than there is in running a corporation. With a partnership you avoid the double tax problem that you may have with a corporation (see Section 7.5). Sometimes two or more heads are better than one in running a business. Partnerships are particularly valuable in professions such as medicine, law, accounting, engineering, etc. Each partner can specialize in a certain area. When one partner is away from the business (either sick or on vacation) the other partners can continue to operate the business without interruption. Partners can also enter into agreements with each other for the purchase of their partnership interest on retirement or death (see Section 7.32).

Each partner is personally liable for all the debts of the partnership. The partners will have to plan for the death or withdrawal of one of the partners to avoid the disruption that can otherwise occur.

[7.24]

c. FORMATION OF PARTNERSHIP

A partnership can exist without a formal partnership agreement. If two persons have the intention to carry on business as co-owners and they associate together for that purpose and conduct the business as if it were a partnership, they have in fact become partners, even though they may not have called themselves partners and may not have intended to create a legal partnership relationship. In such a case the courts would say that their intent to create a partnership is implied from their acts. Of course a partnership can be created by agreement, either oral or written. It is best to have a formal written agreement, even if the parties have known each other and have done business for a long period of time. This way any misunderstandings will be eliminated, and both partners will be protected in the event of a disagreement or the disability or death of one of the partners. If a formal written partnership agreement is to be prepared, the partners should go and see a lawyer together and ask his assistance in preparing it. This is one of those rare cases where a lawyer can represent both parties in preparing an agreement. That is, he may do so as long as the partners agree or reach agreement on what should go into the contract and resolve their differences before going to his office or in his presence without asking him to take sides. If a dispute occurs later on, the lawyer cannot continue to represent both parties, nor can he represent one against the other unless they both consent (see Section 2.5). The partnership agreement should include the names and the capital contributions of the partners; the name, place of business, and purpose of the partnership; the term of the partnership agreement; a provision for division of profits and losses; a provision on drawing accounts; a provision on management including the time each partner shall devote to the business; provisions on vote or voice in the making of management decisions; a provision on maintaining partnership books and records; a statement of what happens when a partner becomes temporarily disabled, retires, or dies; a provision for setting up a partnership bank account; a statement of what action may not be taken by a partner without the consent of all the other partners; a provision for the purchase and sale of partnership interests (see Section 7.32); and a provision governing dissolution of the partnership.

[7.25]   d   *DOING BUSINESS AS PARTNERS*

Partners are *fiduciaries*. That means that they owe special duties to each other. These are duties of *good faith* and *honesty*. Partners are required to act in the best interests of the partnership, and not to engage in actions which may be beneficial to themselves but detrimental to the partnership or to other partners. Each partner has the right to bind the partnership to certain obligations. These are obligations that arise in the ordinary course of the partnership business. Creditors of the partnership or plaintiffs who have been injured or damaged by someone acting on behalf of the partnership can sue the partnership and the individual partners. Sometimes one partner will put up some money and the other partner will contribute his services, and they will agree to split the profits, either fifty-fifty or in some other ratio.

[7.26]   e.   *FICTITIOUS NAMES*

Most states have statutes which provide that partnerships or individuals doing business under a *fictitious name*, or a designation not showing the true names of the individuals or partners, must prepare a certificate and file it with the clerk of the county in which they are doing business. The certificate is supposed to state the names and residences of the partners or individuals. Some laws require the certificate to be published in a newspaper a certain number of times. If there is a change in the membership of the partnership, a new certificate must be published and filed. The idea of this is that people who do business with the partnership or individual transacting business under a fictitious name will know or will be able to find out who they are really dealing with. Although state laws vary on this subject, the usual penalty for failure to file a fictitious name certificate is that the business or partnership cannot bring an action (sue) to enforce a contract or to collect a debt or an obligation until the certificate has been properly filed.

In suits by or against a partnership, the partners themselves, rather than the partnership, are parties to the action.

f.   DISSOLUTION AND WINDING UP   [7.27]

When a partnership is dissolved, it usually continues for a while until affairs can be wound up and assets distributed after payment of obligations. During this period the partners act as trustees for the purpose of completing the affairs of the partnership. Dissolution can occur as a result of agreement of the partners, expiration of the agreed-upon term of the partnership, or upon withdrawal, expulsion, or death of one of the partners. There are other events which can also cause dissolution of the partnership. Most states have adopted the *Uniform Partnership Act*, which spells out the law of partnership in great detail and includes provisions that take effect upon dissolution of a partnership.

2. Limited Partnerships

[7.28]

a. *NATURE OF*
LIMITED PARTNERSHIPS

A *limited partnership* is a partnership formed by two or more persons where one or more of them serves as a *general partner* and the others are *limited partners.* The limited partner contributes cash or property to the partnership. He has the right to inspect the books and to participate in the profits of the partnership in accordance with the partnership agreement. He also shares in the losses, but only up to the amount of his contribution to the partnership. In that sense he is like a stockholder in a corporation, and his liability is limited. However in order to remain a limited partner he cannot have any voice in or take an active part in the management of the partnership, or allow his name to be used as part of the firm name. That is the job of the general partner who is personally liable for all the debts and obligations of the partnership. The limited partnership is a vehicle similar to a corporation, and is used most frequently where there are some people willing to act as general partners but who need money to operate the business; it is also the type of business that lends itself to being operated as a partnership rather than as a corporation. An example would be partnership in owning an apartment house. The general partners could manage the apartment and the limited partners could put up the money or property to buy it. (A limited partner cannot contribute services for an interest in the partnership.)

b. FORMATION OF LIMITED PARTNERSHIP [7.29]

There must be a formal written agreement in order to form a limited partnership. Most states require a *certificate of limited partnership* to be signed by all of the partners and filed with the county clerk, recorded, and in some cases published in a local newspaper. The certificate names the partnership, lists the general and limited partners and the key provisions of the partnership agreement which are required by law to be in the certificate.

c. SALE OF LIMITED PARTNERSHIP INTERESTS [7.30]

Many states take the position that limited partnership interests are similar to the ownership of stock in a corporation, and therefore a permit from the state is required before limited partnership interests can be sold. In such cases the failure to obtain a permit may result in the limited partner having an absolute right to demand the return of his capital contribution at any time (see Section 10.63). Where such laws are in force, the sale of limited partnership interests without first obtaining a permit can result in criminal penalties for the promoters involved.

D. JOINT VENTURES

A *joint venture* is like a partnership. The joint venturers associate together in a business and agree to share profits and losses. The main difference between a joint venture and a partnership is that a partnership is usually a continuing business, whereas a joint venture normally involves just one single deal, like building a particular building and selling it and dividing the profits, or buying a particular piece of property and holding it for investment with the thought that the joint venture will be terminated when that particular property has been sold.

E. BUYING AND SELLING BUSINESSES

1. Buying and Selling Partnership Interests

With the consent of the other general partners, one general partner may sell his partnership interest to some other individual who will become a new general partner. The price will be negotiated between the selling partner and the purchaser. The purchaser will assume the position of the selling general partner, taking over his capital account and his share of profits and losses. A limited partner may also sell his limited partnership interest. Whether he needs the consent of the general partner or of the other limited partners depends upon the limited partnership agreement. Most partnership agreements contain provisions for the purchase and sale of partnership interests. The partnership agreement should include the method of figuring the price to be paid for a partnership interest, the terms for payment, the method of offering to sell, and the method of accepting an offer to sell. The purchase price can be paid in cash by means of a note with regular installment payments. Provisions should also cover purchase of a deceased partner's interest by the remaining partners. To provide for this event, it is a good idea for the partners to carry insurance on each other's lives, or for the partnership to carry a policy on the lives of each of the partners. In the latter case the partnership agreement should provide that the life insurance proceeds will not be part of the deceased partner's interest in the partnership.

2.   Corporate Buy-Sell Agreements   [7.33]

Many corporations place restrictions on the right of stockholders to sell their shares. These restrictions force the shareholder who wants to sell his shares to offer the shares first to the corporation, and if the corporation can't buy them, to the other stockholders. If neither the corporation nor the other stockholders want to buy the stock, the stock can be sold to an outsider. These agreements usually also provide for the purchase of shares of stock from the estate of a deceased stockholder. The corporation could carry life insurance on the lives of stockholders so that it would have the funds to buy shares from their estates in the event of death. Most states require corporations to have *surplus* in order to be able to buy (*redeem*) the corporation's own stock. Anybody involved in a situation of this nature should get advice from his attorney and his accountant.

Corporation buy-sell agreements have to establish a method for determining the price of the stock. Some people use *book value,* which is the *net worth* of the corporation. This is not always an accurate measure of the true value of a corporation or its stock.

Another method is to multiply the earnings of the corporation by a factor of 10, or perhaps a higher figure. The multiplication factor depends upon the size of the company and the type of business it is in.

Another method is to have the stockholders agree each year on what the value of the stock is and agree that that value will remain constant throughout that year. If everything else fails, you can always agree to appoint an appraiser (or appraisers) and let him set the price of the stock.

If you get involved in the purchase or sale of a corporation, you will certainly need legal and accounting assistance. There are many different ways by which a corporation can be purchased and sold. The stockholders can sell their stock, or the corporation can sell its assets. There are also *mergers* and *consolidations*; these involve the trading of stock for stock or assets for stock, or a combination of the two. Complicated tax and accounting problems will be present in any such transaction and the treatment of these subjects is beyond the scope of this book.

[7.34]   3.   Sale of Sole Proprietorship

The seller of a sole proprietorship should try to sell the business for cash so he won't have to worry about collecting the balance due from the new owner. However, because this is not always possible, he may have to take a down payment and a note for the balance. In that case his biggest concern is to make sure that he has security for the balance due. He will want a personal note from the buyer, and some kind of security agreement which gives him a lien against the assets of the business. This can be in the form of a mortgage on the property, or a chattel mortgage on the inventory and equipment. Some states have rules permitting the filing of a simple form (sometimes called a *financing statement*) with the secretary of state, which puts everyone on notice that you have a lien on the business inventory or personal property belonging to another individual. This prevents him from being able to sell it or mortgage it to someone else, and gives you the right to have it sold to pay the balance due you if he fails to make the payments on your note when they are due. The buyer of a small business of course wants to pay as little *down* as possible, and hopes to be able to pay off the balance out of the earnings of the business. The main thing the buyer should be concerned about is that the value of the business has not been inflated by the seller. The buyer should carefully inspect all the books and records of the business before purchasing it. The agreement should refer to a recent financial statement of the business and state that the buyer is relying on the figures contained in that statement in purchasing the business. That way if the figures turn out to be inaccurate (because the seller either deliberately or carelessly falsified them) the buyer can sue the seller and get his money back.

4. Bulk Sales Law [7.35]

Most states have a *Bulk Sales Law* which provides that whenever a business is sold and the business has an inventory which is included in the sale, the buyer and the seller have to get together and file a notice of their pending sale and publish such a notice in a local newspaper. Some states require registered mail notice to all known creditors of the business. The idea behind this is that creditors of the business who have advanced credit already and who are owed money should know that the owner of the business is selling out so that they can be sure to collect what he owes them at the time the sale goes through. It is also to protect future creditors who might be about to loan money to the business and who might not learn that the business has changed hands. In other words, it is to protect the creditors and to protect both buyer and seller from each other's creditors.

[7.36]   **5.   Transfer of Business License**

If you are buying a business such as a cleaning establishment or a drug store, you will need a license in order to operate it. If the buyer doesn't have a license of his own which he plans to use, arrangements will have to be made to transfer the license from the seller to the buyer. The agreement should cover this possibility.

[7.37]   **6.   Leases**

Because most businesses lease their property rather than own it, the buyer of a business will want to be sure that his seller's landlord will accept him as a new tenant. The seller should be obligated to get the consent of the landlord to the assignment of the lease to the buyer of the business. Advance rental deposits and security deposits should be covered in the agreement.

[7.38]   **7.   Financing**

Sometimes a seller already owes money to a lender which is secured by a lien on the assets of the business. In such a case arrangements will have to be made for the buyer to assume that loan (with the consent of the lender) if he isn't coming up with enough cash to pay off the loan. In other cases a buyer may want to borrow the money in order to buy the business or to make the down payment. In such a case he will have to arrange with the lender to put a chattel mortgage or some other form of security agreement on the assets of the business he is buying. A banker can help advise you on these matters.

8. Financial Statements [7.39]

A crucial document in any purchase and sale of a business is a financial statement. When large corporations are involved in purchases, sales, mergers, or consolidations, they almost always insist upon audited financial statements. This means that independent certified public accountants must go over all the books, records, and financial statements of the corporation to verify each item. These audits are time-consuming and expensive, but they are necessary when large sums of money are involved. In smaller transactions an audit may not be necessary or desirable, but if it is not required, there should be at least a preparation of a financial statement by a public accountant or a certified public accountant, and the seller should sign a declaration warranting the accuracy of the figures contained in such an unaudited financial statement.

9. Tax Factors [7.40]

There are many complex tax factors involved in the purchase and sale of a business, most of which are beyond the scope of this book. However in the sale of a small business, allocation of the purchase price is of great importance. There will always be several items that make up the total purchase price. They may include fixtures, furniture and furnishings, vehicles, leasehold interest, real property (if the business owns its own building or plant), inventory, work in process, cash, accounts receivable, etc. There are two special items that may or may not appear. These are *goodwill* and *covenant not to compete*. Buyers like to allocate a high value to depreciable assets like furniture and fixtures. This way they can take more depreciation on them, which is a write-off against income. Sellers like to allocate small amounts to these items because they may have already depreciated them and if they sell them for more than their depreciated value they may be charged with income. Inventory is usually valued at cost; if it is valued higher than that, the seller will have a gain and the buyer will have a higher *basis* for the inventory and will therefore have less of a taxable gain when he sells it. Sellers like to include goodwill and allocate a large part of the purchase price to it because that way they may get a capital gain. Buyers, on the other hand, don't like goodwill being included because it is not anything they can depreciate or write off. Buyers would prefer to have something allocated to *covenant not to compete* because they can write that off over the term of the covenant. A covenant not to compete means that the seller agrees not to go into the same business within a certain area during a certain period of time. This may or may not be important to the buyer.

[7.41]   **10. Sales Tax**

Be sure to find out whether a sales tax (or some other similar tax) will be imposed by the county (or other local governmental jurisdiction). Also find out who is supposed to pay it if the parties have not agreed. Then make sure the agreement covers this in a way that is most beneficial to you (this should be a negotiable item).

F. SALES

1. Warranties and Guaranties [7.42]

A *guaranty* is something that is provided by the seller, in writing, when an item is purchased. A guaranty states specifically how long the item is guaranteed, what kind of defects it is guaranteed against, and what the seller will do to make good on the guaranty. He may agree to repair it, with or without some charge, or replace it with another item, or refund the purchase price or a portion of the purchase price. In legal terminology, *guaranty* and *warranty* mean the same thing.

There are two types of warranties. One is an *express warranty*, the other is an *implied warranty*. An express warranty is a written (or sometimes oral) promise by the seller that the item will perform up to a certain standard, that it is without defects, and that it will be repaired or replaced, with the purchase price refunded in whole or in part if something goes wrong. In short, a written warranty is the same as a written guaranty. Express warranties can also be oral. You may rely on *a factual* statement made by a salesman, just as if it were contained in a written warranty. Be sure to separate opinion ("this is a fine car") from fact ("this car has been driven only 10,000 miles") when relying on what a salesman says. An *implied warranty* is different. The law supplies the terms of an implied warranty. The usual terms are that the owner has the right to sell the item and that the item is free from the claims of any third parties. However the most important elements of an implied warranty are that the item sold shall be *reasonably fit for the purpose for which it is sold*, and that it *shall be of merchantable quality*. What this means to a buyer is that even if he doesn't get a written guaranty or warranty with the product he purchases, if it turns out not to be fit for the purpose for which sold, or if it turns out not to be of merchantable quality, he should be able to return it and get his money back (as well as collect damages for any injury resulting from nonmerchantability). As you can imagine, many disputes revolve around the meaning and interpretation of the words "merchantable quality" and "fit for the purpose for which sold." Federal legislation requires manufacturers of consumer products to state terms of guarantees clearly and to conform to legal rules.

[7.43]   ## 2.   Defective Products

If something you bought turns out to be defective, first look to the guaranty. If there is no guaranty, you have to look further. If the guaranty has run out or does not cover this defect, you also have to look further. If it is covered by the guaranty, you simply notify the seller or the manufacturer and follow up on getting it repaired, replaced, or getting your money refunded. If you aren't covered by a guaranty or express warranty, then you will have to take the matter up with the seller or the manufacturer if you believe that the defect constitutes a breach of implied warranty. If the defective product is a food, beverage, medicine, or some product that might be dangerous to human life if it is defective, the law imposes very strict warranty requirements upon the seller and the manufacturer. If you are made sick or are injured as a result of a defect in such a product, the seller and the manufacturer will be liable to you for such sickness or injury (see Section 9.25). If the product does not fall within any of those categories, and you are injured as a result of the defect (for example a defective ladder that collapses) you again have a right to sue the manufacturer for your injuries. However in such a case you may have a slightly more difficult job of convincing the court that the manufacturer should be held liable. In a defective product case, the plaintiff has to prove that a defect existed and that it caused him harm. Sometimes he can prove this by expert testimony.

An expert can examine the product and say that it was defective because of some negligence on the part of the manufacturer. In other cases he can prove this by *circumstantial evidence*. An example would be a stepladder that appeared to be in excellent condition but nevertheless collapsed when used by the plaintiff in a reasonable manner. Don't give up if the defect is discovered after the time period of the warranty has expired. The author once collected a small claims court judgment against an automobile manufacturer for the cost of replacing brakes that burned out at 18 months and 17,000 miles, where the written warranty was only good for 12,000 miles and 12 months.

3.   Conditional Sales   [7.44]

If you buy a television set under a *conditional sales contract*, it means that you don't get title to the television set until you have made the last installment payment. Under such a contract the seller not only retains title to the television set, but he also may have the right to repossess it if you miss an installment payment (see Section 7.49). Because the buyer does not acquire title until he pays for the set, he cannot legally sell it to a third party. This is one difference between a *conditional sale* and an *installment sale* (see Section 7.48).

4.   Chattel Mortgages   [7.45]

A *chattel mortgage* is a mortgage on personal property such as the inventory of a store or a small business. It is a document which gives the seller or lender an interest in the property. When the business is sold, if the new owner makes a down payment and promises to pay the rest over a period of time, the seller may ask him to give back a chattel mortgage. This is like a mortgage on real property (see Section 10.69). If the buyer doesn't make the payments when they are due, the seller can foreclose and have the property sold at auction (through proper legal proceedings) to pay the balance due.

A chattel mortgage should be recorded or filed as required by state law in order to protect the rights of the lender (mortgagee).

[7.46]   **5.   C.O.D.**

C.O.D. means *collect on delivery*. When goods are shipped C.O.D., it means that the buyer pays the purchase price when he receives the goods.

[7.47]   **6.   F.O.B.**

F.O.B. means *free on board*. When goods are shipped F.O.B. there will usually be the name of the place immediately following, such as *F.O.B. San Francisco*. That means the goods will be shipped to that point or placed on a truck or train at that point without charge to the buyer for transportation or handling *to that point.*

[7.48]   **7.   Installment Sales**

When goods are purchased under an installment sale, the buyer makes a down payment and agrees to pay the balance off in installments. A great amount of merchandise is bought this way, with the seller having a *lien* on the property until final payment has been made. Most states have procedures for filing or recording these liens. Failure to file the mortgage doesn't affect the right of the seller to collect from the original buyer, but the seller cannot get the goods back from a third party who bought them from the original buyer if the mortgage was not filed and the second buyer did not know about the lien.

8.   Seller's Remedy for Default of Buyer   [7.49]

If the seller has a conditional sales contract or a lien and the buyer doesn't pay, it is necessary to look to the contract between the parties to see what the seller's rights are. The contract may say that he has the right to repossess the goods, to have them sold at public auction, and to collect any deficiency or balance due after the sale from the buyer. Most installment sales contracts give the seller the right to *accelerate* in the event of default. This means that if the buyer misses a payment a seller can demand the entire balance due all at once.

If the contract between the buyer and the seller doesn't state what the seller's rights are, it is necessary to look to the state statutes. If the statutes give seller a lien on the property, he has the right to have the goods sold at public sale. The seller has to send the buyer notice that repossessed items will be sold, and usually must also publish notice of the sale in a local newspaper. The goods are sold to the highest bidder. The proceeds of the sale are used to pay the unpaid balance, the costs of repossessing the merchandise, storing it, and reselling it. This means the buyer can end up losing his goods and still owe money to the seller. Legislation has been enacted to protect a buyer from having a large claim entered against him after the property he purchased has been repossessed and sold. If your property has been repossessed, be sure you know what your contract provides, and what your rights are. If you are in doubt, see a lawyer.

Where a seller has the right to repossess the goods, some

courts have said he may do it himself as long as he does not commit a breach of the peace or violate some law. These courts allow the seller of an automobile who has a right to repossess it to go to the buyer's house and pick up the car and either drive it away or have it towed away (without breaking into the owner's locked garage to get the car). However other courts have held that property can't be seized or repossessed until after a court hearing, and that a state law permitting repossession without notice and hearing is unconstitutional. In 1971 the California Supreme Court ruled that a law allowing the seizure of property on which loan payments are in default was unconstitutional. The creditor can't get the property before a court finds he is entitled to it.

Where no lien is provided either by contract or by statute, then the seller simply has a contract action against the buyer and will have to sue to collect.

[7.50]   9.   Buyer's Rights against the Seller

If the goods turn out to be defective, the buyer has his right to sue for breach of warranty (see Section 7.42). In some cases he may elect to return the goods and get his money back, or he may keep the goods and sue for damages. If the seller hasn't delivered and refuses to deliver the goods, the buyer who has a contract right to receive the goods can sue the seller for delivery of the goods. What if the seller has gone out of business, but has sold to a finance company the buyer's install-ment contract for the balance of the purchase price? The buyer may be in trouble. In that situation, some laws allow the finance company to collect the debt. Other laws deny the third-party finance company the right to collect if the merchandise was not delivered or was defective. Proposed uniform laws would add consumer protection in this area.

G. BANKING AND COMMERICAL LAW

1. Checking Accounts

[7.51]

When you open a checking account, you make a contract with the bank. The bank agrees to *honor* your checks. That means the bank agrees to pay money to a person who presents one of your checks for payment and who appears to have the right or the authority to do this. You agree to pay the bank a charge for this service, and the charge is usually waived if you keep a minimum balance of $300, the amount varying depending on the bank. Most banks offer *special* checking accounts which permit you to buy your checks for $0.15 to $0.20 each, or some similar charge, or you can pay the bank monthly at that rate for the checks you actually write. If you write few checks and keep a small amount in your account, you are better off with a *special* account. The bank will have you sign a signature card to indicate to it what signature on the checks will give them authority to pay money out of your account when they are presented. You also agree to examine the periodic statements that the bank will send to you with your cancelled checks, and to notify the bank within a period of time (usually thirty days) of any errors the bank has made in your statement. For this reason it is a good idea to check your monthly statements even if you only go over them briefly just to make sure that you have been credited with all the deposits, and to make sure that all checks that have been returned to you are really your checks and that the proper amounts have been deducted from your account. Careful people will go beyond this and actually balance their checkbook every month to make sure their balance agrees with the bank's balance. Believe it or not, banks do make mistakes. Some state laws let the bank off the hook for forgeries if the depositor failed to note them and so notify the bank within a definite period of time.

[7.52]   *a.   STOP PAYMENT ORDERS*

If you decide to stop payment on a check you have written, you will probably have to sign a written order and deliver it to your bank before the check is presented for payment. Then if your bank pays the check, it is liable to you. However, if the check is taken to another bank, or even another branch of the same bank, and is honored by that other bank, or if it is accepted after endorsement by some third party for value, it is doubtful your stop payment order will protect you. You should notify the payee that you have stopped payment before he tries to cash the check.

[7.53]   *b.   OVERDRAFTS (BAD CHECKS)*

It is a crime to write a check for funds you don't have (see Section 8.24). In most cases if you do this you will get a chance to make good on the check. The check will be returned to the person who tried to cash it or deposit it and he can then call you and ask you to give him another check or ask you to put some money in your account so he can put the check through again. Sometimes the same check can be put through again, but other times you will have to write a new check. If you don't make good on the bad check, you may wind up with a criminal charge against you. If you can prove that it was not intentional, but was a mistake because you made a mathematical error in your tabulations in keeping your checkbook balance, you might beat the rap, but you'll still have to make good on the check.

c. WRONGFUL DISHONOR OF CHECK OR NOTE

[7.54]

If the bank doesn't pay your check when it is presented, even though you have funds in your account, the bank may be liable to you for *actual damages*. You will have to prove you were damaged by the *dishonor* (non-acceptance). Sometimes *protest* is required before collection can be enforced against endorsers (see Section 7.60). Protest means getting a notary public to certify that a note has been presented (*presentment*) to the maker and he has refused to pay it. Sometimes *notice of dishonor* must be given immediately to all endorsers (orally or in writing) in order to make them liable (see Section 7.60).

The maker of a note or check may have certain defenses which he can raise to avoid payment, such as fraud (see Section 9.6) or failure of consideration (see Section 4.3). But such defenses will not be good against a *holder in due course* (some one who accepted an endorsed note or check in good faith, for value, and without knowledge of the possible defense). Forgery, however (see Section 8.23) is a good defense against anyone (see Section 7.64).

2. Checks

[7.55]

A check is an order to pay money which is given by the *drawer* (maker) of the check ordering the *drawee* (bank) to pay money to the *payee.*

a. FORM

[7.56]

To be acceptable as a negotiable instrument, a check must be in a certain form. It must be dated, signed by the drawer, and it must be drawn on a bank on a specific account at that bank. The check must be legible. The amount that is written next to the dollar sign should be the same as the amount which is written out in words on the next line. If there is any difference between these two amounts, some banks will not honor the check, others will pay the sum written out. Sometimes banks will not honor an undated check. If the signature is not the same as that on the signature card, it will not be honored (unless the bank makes a mistake).

[7.57]

b.   CHECKS PAYABLE TO ORDER

A check usually has printed on it, "Pay to the Order of____." When you fill in the name of a person or a business, that means that the check can only be cashed or passed on by the payee. To cash it or pass it on to someone else, he must then become an *endorser*. An endorser is someone who signs his name on the back of the check. The signature should be the same as the name on the front of the check. If the check is payable to Tom Jones, and Tom Jones endorses it by signing his name on the back, the check now becomes a *bearer check* (see Section 7.58). If Tom Jones wrote on the back of the check: "Pay to the Order of Macy's," it would still be an *order check*, and can only be cashed or passed on by Macy's.

[7.58]

c.   BEARER CHECK

A *bearer check* is almost like cash; it can be cashed by whoever holds it. A check payable to *cash* rather than to a named individual is a bearer check. A check payable to Tom Jones and endorsed "Tom Jones" on the back is a bearer check and can be cashed by anyone. However, if you found a check on the street that was payable to and endorsed by Tom Jones, and took it to the nearest bank to ask for cash, you might have problems. The bank might ask you to prove that you were Tom Jones, or it might ask you to endorse the check by signing your name on it before you get the money. By signing your name, you would then become an endorser (see Section 7.60). The person who lost the check might then be able to make you pay the money to him when he later found out that you found the check and cashed it. If a bank doesn't ask for an endorsement when you present a bearer check payable to and endorsed by Tom Jones, and gives you the money for the check, the bank is not liable to the drawer for that amount unless it knew or should have known that you did not have the right to present the check for payment. A check payable to *cash* is the kind of bearer instrument which can be passed around just like money until it winds up at the bank and is returned to the drawer.

d. POST-DATED CHECKS [7.59]

If you don't have money in your account and you still want to write a check, you can postdate it. However, you'd better be sure you get the funds into the account to cover the check. To be sure this is legal in your state, ask your banker. It is also a good idea to write on the check somewhere where it can be seen a note stating that it is a postdated check. It will still be good, but it will prevent anybody from being able to claim that you wrote a bad check if they overlook the date and the note and try to cash it before the due date (the date you put on it).

[7.60]

e. ENDORSEMENTS

An endorsement is a signature on the back of a check. It can be written, typed, or stamped. It should be the same as the name on the front. If your name is misspelled on a check, sign it as misspelled, and then sign your name again, spelling it correctly. There are different kinds of endorsements. A *general endorsement* means the payee signs his name on the back of the check. This means that the check can be cashed. It also means that the person endorsing it is guaranteeing that the check is good, that he has the right to cash it, and that he will pay the amount of the check if it is not paid by the drawer. A *qualified endorsement* is one where the endorser adds something besides his signature. He may say "without recourse," which means he is not going to guarantee the check and won't be responsible if it is dishonored by the bank. The *restrictive endorsement* occurs where the payee signs his name and writes "for deposit only." This means the check can only be deposited in his account. Another restrictive endorsement would be "pay to the order of John Smith only." Only John Smith could cash a check so endorsed.

Among several general endorsers, the liability is in order of their endorsements.

[7.61]

f. DELAY IN CASHING A CHECK

A check should be cashed or presented for payment within a reasonable period of time. The time is figured from the date on the check. Beware of accepting a *stale* (old) check. Don't carry a check for several weeks before cashing it. A check six months old will not be easily transferrable, although your own bank may cash it for you.

g.   DEATH OF DRAWER   [7.62]

Does the death of the drawer before a check is cashed invalidate the check? Sometimes but not always. It depends on such things as whether the person possessing the check knew of the death, or whether the bank knew of the death, or whether the check was a gift.

h.   ALTERED CHECKS   [7.63]

A check that has been altered by someone (other than the drawer) raising the amount payable is normally good only for the original amount of the check. But in some states, if you carelessly leave spaces in your writing and thereby enable a forger to fill in zeros and increase the amount of the check, you may be liable to your bank for the loss.

i.   FORGED CHECKS   [7.64]

The bank takes the loss if it pays out money on a forged check. But if you are negligent in reporting stolen checks or forgeries to your bank, the loss may fall upon you. If you sign your name to a blank check and then lose it, and the finder fills it in and cashes it, you (and not your bank) would take the loss, because you were the one who made the loss possible.

j.   CASHIER'S CHECKS   [7.65]
AND CERTIFIED CHECKS

A *cashier's check* and a *certified check* are special kinds of checks issued by banks. They are in effect guaranteed by the bank issuing them and so are more acceptable than ordinary checks in business transactions. The bank guarantees that the signature on a certified check is genuine, that there are sufficient funds to pay the amount on the check at the time of certification, and that those funds will not be withdrawn before the check has cleared. A cashier's check is one drawn on a bank by an officer of that bank.

[7.66]

k. MINORS' CHECKS

Minors can have checking accounts and can write checks. In states where the contracts of a minor for purchase of *necessaries* (see Section 4.18) are binding, a minor is liable for the check he writes to the same extent as an adult. In cases where a minor would not be liable for his contract, he may be able to refuse to accept (pay) a check after he has written it. He could do this if he had the right to *disaffirm* his contract because he was a minor (see Section 4.18). A minor's endorsement on a check will pass title to the check even though the minor may not be liable on the check.

3. Notes

[7.67]

a. FORM OF NOTE

A note is a written form of promise to pay money at a certain time in the future. If it is *payable on demand* it means that the holder of the note can decide when payment is due. If it is payable *on or before* a certain date, it is not due before that date (although it may be paid off early). A *straight* note means that the entire amount of the note counting *principal and interest* is payable at one time. An *installment* note is a note which calls for regular periodic payments to be made. If the periodic payments pay off the note in full, then the note is *fully amortized*. If there are periodic payments followed by a large payment at the end, that payment is called a *balloon* payment. Normally the interest is computed on the remaining principal of the note. A note providing for *add-on* interest is different. An *add-on note* is one written so that the interest is computed in advance over the entire term of the note and is added on to the principal. That total figure is then divided into an equal number of monthly payments. This has the effect of raising the *effective* interest rate. If you borrow money at 5 percent and sign an add-on interest note, the effective rate of interest will be close to 10 percent.

b. DEFAULT [7.68]

Most notes provide that if a payment is missed, the holder of the note can *accelerate* the balance. That means he can demand payment of the whole note. Notes usually also contain a provision permitting the holder to collect attorney's fees in the event he has to sue because of the maker's default. If you are the lender you should be sure that the note you get from the borrower contains provisions for acceleration and payment of attorney's fees.

c. NEGOTIABILITY [7.69]

If a note says, "pay to the order of," it is negotiable. That means the payee can endorse the note (see Section 7.60) and pass it on to another party. He may have to *discount* it, or transfer it for less than the face amount of the note, especially if he transfers it before the date the note is due.

[7.70]   *d.   GUARANTOR*

Sometimes a note will be guaranteed by a *co-signer*. A parent may co-sign a note for his minor child. The person who co-signs a note as a *guarantor* is liable if the maker fails to pay the note when it is due. If you lend money to a person who may have trouble in repaying it, try to get him to have someone else guarantee the note.

H. CREDIT CARDS

[7.71]   1.   Issuance

You no longer have to worry about a credit card issued to you without your request being used by someone else after you throw it away. If the card is mailed to you without your request and it falls into someone else's hands who forges your signature and then uses it to run up a bill, you can't be stuck with that bill.

[7.72]   2.   Lost or Stolen Credit Cards

Federal law limits your liability for the unauthorized use of your credit card to a maximum amount (currently $50.).

Note that this is *per card*. There is some doubt about whether this applies to business (as opposed to personal) credit cards. In addition, some states have laws that provide for no liability if the owner of the credit card notifies the issuer that he has lost the card or that it has been stolen (within a reasonable time after the loss or theft).

I. MAIL ORDERS   [7.73]

It has been estimated that 1 percent of mail orders are never properly mailed and delivered. That is a small percentage, but it amounts to millions of dollars every year. What can you do if you get cheated by a mail-order house (see Section 8.30)? If fraud is involved you can complain to the Fraud Section of the U.S. post office. If *fraudulent intent* can be proved, the post office can bring criminal charges against the mail-order house. It has been proposed that mail-order companies that require payment in advance be registered with the post office and have a federal registration number which they would have to use in all of their advertising materials. Any registered company that cheated a customer would have its registration number revoked. Until this comes to pass, there are certain things you can do to protect yourself. Check with the Direct Mail Advertising Association (230 Park Avenue, New York, N.Y. 10017) to see if the mail-order house is registered and in good standing. If the mail-order house permits it, use your credit card rather than sending a check or money order. If you don't get your merchandise you can then ask the customer service department of your credit card company to help you. They may charge the mail-order house and reimburse you when they collect. If the mail-order house refuses to reimburse you, the credit card company may then revoke the mail-order company's right to make credit card sales.

[7.74] **J. IN-HOME SALES**

The best way to protect yourself against door-to-door salesmen is to post a "No Solicitors" sign on your door. If you don't mind talking to door-to-door salesmen, then you should be aware of what protections are available to you under the law (see Section 4.23). If you have signed an agreement to buy something from a door-to-door salesman and change your mind after he leaves, be sure to call a lawyer immediately and find out how to cancel the contract.

K. BUSINESS LICENSES

[7.75]

It is illegal to conduct certain types of business or to practice certain professions without a license (see Sectiom 4.29).

L. LOANS AND INTEREST CHARGES

1. Truth-in-Lending Act

[7.76]

The *Truth-in-Lending Act* requires the lender to spell out for the borrower in great detail all the terms and conditions of the loan, in advance. This means the total amount of the loan, the interest rate, the amount of the monthly payments, any balloon payments (see Section 7.67), and any finance charges must be disclosed to the borrower in advance. The borrower must be given a *disclosure statement* and sign a receipt for a copy of it. He then has a certain amount of time (usually 48 hours) to reconsider before becoming bound under the deal. If the lender doesn't comply with these requirements, the law sets forth remedies for the borrower which may include getting out of paying anything back except the principal amount that he borrowed, and possibly giving him a right for damages.

2. Usury

[7.77]

All states set maximum interest rates by law. The rates vary. It is *usury* to charge more interest than the maximum rate permitted by law. Banks and other financial institutions or lending agencies are in some states permitted by statute to charge interest rates that would be *usurious* if the lender were an individual. Retailers in some states are also permitted to charge interest rates that would otherwise be usurious (1½ percent per month amounts to 18 percent per year). The logic of permitting retail merchants to charge 18 percent a year to the vast American purchasing public while prohibiting other individuals or businesses from charging more than 10 percent (which is, for example, the case in California) may escape you, but that is the law in many states and merchants take advantage of it. There are penalties for usury, which vary according to state law. Some laws permit the borrower to get away without paying any interest at all, and may even allow him to go so far as to collect additional damages from a lender if the loan is usurious. There are many tricky ways to get around the usury statutes, however. Some of these are perfectly legal. For example, a businessman may borrow money at 8 percent interest (where the legal maximum is 10 percent) and agree in addition to pay a percentage of "profits." If there are no profits he doesn't have to pay any more than 8 percent so no one can say that the loan is usurious on its face, even though he ends up paying more than 10 percent if in fact he does make a profit.

M. BANKRUPTCY

1. Who Can File for Bankruptcy? [7.78]

The purpose of bankruptcy law is to let a person in debt up to his ears have a chance to wipe out his debts and start over. To be eligible for bankruptcy an individual must have obligations or debts which exceed his total assets, or in other words, be *insolvent*.

2. How Do You File? [7.79]

Bankruptcy can be either *voluntary* or *involuntary*. It is voluntary if you file yourself, involuntary if one or more of your creditors files a bankruptcy petition against you. A bankruptcy proceeding is started by preparing a bankruptcy petition form and filing it in a federal district court. The forms can be obtained from the court or from a stationery store. They include a schedule on which you list all your assets, all of your creditors, and the amount owed to each one. You can also list any property that is exempt (see Section 7.84). Complete financial information must be given.

In an involuntary bankruptcy proceeding the creditors file a petition saying the bankrupt person has committed an *act of bankruptcy*. An act of bankruptcy includes any of the following: concealing property to defraud creditors; while insolvent, allowing a creditor to obtain a lien; giving a preference to a creditor (see Section 7.86) while insolvent; admission in writing of inability to pay debts and willingness to be declared bankrupt; making an assignment for benefit of creditors or allowing a receiver to be appointed for his property.

[7.80]   3.   Personal Bankruptcy

A single individual can file for bankruptcy. A husband and wife can file together for bankruptcy, or one of them can file alone. However, if you try to transfer all of your assets to your spouse and then file bankruptcy, the bankruptcy court would probably set the transfer aside.

[7.81]   4.   Corporate Bankruptcy

A corporation can file for bankruptcy and place all of its assets in the hands of the trustee in bankruptcy for the benefit of creditors. For a corporation in deep financial trouble, bankruptcy is sometimes the best way out for shareholders who have also made large loans to the corporation. If the corporation goes into bankruptcy they can then file claims based on their notes and share in the distribution of assets. If the corporation doesn't go into bankruptcy but other creditors sue and attach and have the corporate assets sold to pay their claims, the shareholders can wind up with a corporation that has no assets, so their notes will be worthless along with their stock.

[7.82]   5.   Debts Dischargeable in Bankruptcy

General obligations including notes, charge accounts, contract obligations, fees owed to professional people, and claims based upon ordinary negligence such as automobile accidents are dischargeable under bankruptcy. However there are many debts which are not dischargeable.

6.   Debts Not Dischargeable under Bankruptcy   [7.83]

The following claims are not dischargeable by bankruptcy: claims based upon willful or malicious injury such as assault and battery, taxes, alimony or child support payments, liability for misappropriation of funds, certain wage claims of employees, debts for money deposited as security or for trust funds, any debts which are not listed in the bankruptcy petition.

Claims of creditors will be discharged, but the secured creditors have the right to claim their security, whether it is your house, your car, or your TV set.

7.   Exempt Property   [7.84]

State laws establish certain exemptions such as the Homestead Exemption (see Section 10.74), and exemptions for certain furniture, clothing, household goods, older motor vehicles, life insurance policies, small balances in savings and loan accounts, pension benefits, and tools used in a trade, business, or occupation. You have to consult state statutes to know what is exempt in your state (see Section 5.16).

8.   Denial of Relief; Criminal Acts   [7.85]

You can only go through bankruptcy once every seven years. Certain acts can cause the court to deny bankruptcy relief to you. These include concealment of assets, making a false financial statement, failure to have adequate books or records, failure to make a complete disclosure of your finances, obtaining money or credit by means of a false financial statement, trying to conceal your assets by making fraudulent conveyances before filing bankruptcy, and refusal to cooperate with the court by answering questions and explaining any discrepancies in the papers which you file or in your testimony.

Certain acts are punishable by fine or imprisonment. Included are: making a false statement under oath, presenting a false claim, receiving money or property from a bankrupt after the filing of a petition with intent to defeat the purpose of the bankruptcy law, destroying records, and concealment of property.

[7.86]   9.   Preferences

A *preference* occurs when a person who is insolvent pays one of his creditors (but not the others) and then goes into bankruptcy within four months thereafter. The trustee in bankruptcy can make the creditor who is paid within that four-month period pay the money back to the court to be part of the debtor's assets that will be distributed to all creditors. A preference may result not only from payment to a creditor but also from transfer to a creditor for less than an adequate consideration, or from the debtor allowing a creditor to put a lien on his property.

[7.87]   10.   Expenses of Bankruptcy

The filing fee to file in bankruptcy runs from $50 to $1,000. Legal fees run from $300 on up, and these must be paid in advance. In addition, there are some administrative costs and trustees' fees which can further eat up assets.

[7.88]   11.   Bankruptcy Procedures

In a case of voluntary bankruptcy, the debtor files a petition asking that he be declared a bankrupt. He files schedules of assets and liabilities with the petition. He will be adjudicated a bankrupt, and then the referee will set a first meeting of creditors and notify all creditors listed in the petition of the time and place. Creditors may question the debtor and examine his records at the meeting. Creditors also receive notice that they may file proofs of claims with the referee within a certain period of time.

In a case of involuntary bankruptcy, the creditors file a petition stating that the debtor has committed an act of bankruptcy (see Section 7.79). The debtor is served with a subpoena, notifying him he has so many days to file an answer. If he fails to file an answer, he will be adjudicated a bankrupt. If he denies bankruptcy, there will be a trial on that issue. If he is declared bankrupt, the referee will appoint a trustee to represent the creditors. If necessary to protect perishable assets, a receiver may be appointed to take over assets or premises.

The trustee or referee totals all claims received from creditors, converts assets to cash, and distributes cash to creditors (after deducting fees and expenses). Each creditor receives his respective proportionate share of the distribution. *Secured creditors* are taken care of separately. They receive cash from the sale of assets which secure their claims, with excess proceeds above the amounts of their claims going to the *general creditors*.

12. Nonbankruptcy Arrangements [7.89]

There are other alternatives to bankruptcy. A debtor can get together with his creditors and persuade them to give him time to work out his debts. He can do this by means of a compromise with all of them whereby they all get paid some percentage of the total claims. He can also agree to make small monthly payments to each creditor until they have all been paid. Sometimes creditors will agree to give a debtor a little time to get back on his feet if they believe that he will make an honest effort to pay them off (see Section 7.94).

The federal laws provide for procedures similar to bankruptcy which can be undertaken by individuals, corporations, and partnerships that are in financial trouble. They can enter into certain arrangements which permit them to continue in business and at the same time prevent their creditors from suing them, attaching assets, and attempting to collect judgments, etc. Such arrangements are supervised by the court and are intended to permit persons and businesses to work their own way out of financial difficulty without being pushed into bankruptcy by their creditors. This is an area in which the advice of a lawyer specializing in this field is needed.

N. COLLECTION PRACTICES

1.   How to Collect a Debt   [7.90]

If money is owed to you or to your business, you may
try to collect it yourself or you may use an attorney or a
collection agency. The first step in collection is to write a letter
requesting immediate payment of a past-due debt. If this
produces no response, it should be followed by a tougher letter
which states that the matter will be referred for collection (or
will be turned over to your attorney) if payment is not made by
return mail. If this fails to produce results, consider a small
claims court action. You can file an action by paying a small fee
to the court clerk and preparing papers provided by the clerk.
There is a limit on the amount you may sue for in small claims
court (usually $200 or $300). If the amount owed you is slightly
over the small claims court maximum, you may be better
off to file in small claims court anyway and forget the difference. Attorneys are not allowed in small claims court. Each
party presents his own case. The clerk will tell you what the
procedures are.

Your other options are a collection agency or an attorney.
Most collection agencies work on a percentage. That means they
don't charge you if they don't collect, but if they do, the usual
practice is to take 50 percent. Some attorneys handle collec-
tions on an hourly basis (see Section 2.4) and some will handle
it on a contingent fee basis. If you can find an attorney who
will handle it on a contingent fee basis and charge a smaller
percentage than the collection agency charges, hire him. You
can also take it into civil court yourself, acting as your own
attorney, provided you get some help in drafting the pleadings
(see Section 5.2) and in getting the pleadings filed and served
(see Section 5.3). Once you get judgment, you can then proceed
to get a writ of execution and have the property of the debtor
seized and sold to satisfy the judgment, or have the debtor

served with a notice requiring him to come to court and testify under oath as to his assets (see Section 5.43).

If the debtor is an individual, you may go after any of his property if he does not pay the judgment. If the debtor is a partnership, you may collect either by levying on partnership property or by collection from any one of the partners (see Section 7.23). If the debtor is a corporation, you will have to go after the corporate assets and cannot go after shareholders or their assets unless you have some basis for legally disregarding the corporate entity (see Section 7.8).

What if a debtor sends you a check for an amount less than what he owes, but the check states either on the face or on the back above where you will have to endorse it, "paid in full"? If there is absolutely no dispute or question about the amount owed, you can cash the check and still collect the balance from him. However, if there is *any* dispute or question about how much is owed, your cashing of the check will prevent you from being able to recover the balance due.

[7.91]   2.   Costs of Collection

If you use a collection agency, it will generally cost you half the amount that is owed, payable upon collection. An attorney may cost you more or less than this, depending on the basis upon which he agrees to handle the claim. Sometimes you can get an attorney to write one letter for you and pay him for writing just that letter. If the letter produces payment, you are well ahead of the game. If it does not, you can then take it to small claims court, take it to a collection agency, or pay the attorney some more money to file suit (or have him handle it on a contingent fee contract). If suit has to be filed, the collection agency usually will not bill you for the costs of filing the complaint and service of process. These costs can run anywhere from $15 to $40. If an attorney handles it for you, even if he does it on a contingent fee basis, he may ask you to reimburse him for the filing fee and the costs of service of the summons and complaint. If you file in small claims court, the filing fee is usually less than $5, and you can pay the sheriff about the same amount to have the summons and complaint served. Getting your writ of execution after you have obtained judgment costs a couple of dollars, and the fee is about the same to have the judgment recorded. The clerk will supply you with the proper forms if you ask for them.

3. Collection Agencies [7.92]

As indicated in the previous section, collection agencies usually work on a contingent fee basis. There is another type of collection agency which will offer to try to collect for you by sending tough or threatening letters and/or telegrams, but will not file suit if these fail to produce results. This type of collection agency generally charges a fee in advance for this "service." There are always exceptions where such an approach works, but for the most part it does not, and you will be better off to send your own letters and telegrams and if that fails, to take it to a regular collection agency or to an attorney.

4. Bad Collection Practices [7.93]

There are always a few bill collectors who overstep the bounds of propriety. Extortion or blackmail is one thing that is not permitted by law. A collection agent who threatens to call your employer or do something else similar to that if you don't pay, is definitely out of line. Telephone calls or letters that threaten dire consequences such as physical harm, or that are intended to or do inflict mental or emotional stress, are also out of line. In such cases the court provides a remedy. Bill collectors who use threatening or abusive language or tactics can be sued for their actions and the court will award damages to the injured party.

[7.94]   5.   How to Deal with Your Creditors

If you are threatened by creditors or bill collectors, don't ignore them. That will only cause them to get tougher. Most creditors (and there are always some exceptions) will be reasonable with you if you will cooperate with them. If you have just one creditor bothering you, try to pay him off by offering him a cash settlement for less than the full amount that is owed, even if you have to borrow it somewhere else. If you can't do that, offer to make regular monthly payments to him. Most creditors will settle for this. If you have several creditors, offer to make small regular monthly payments to all of them. Be sure that you don't offer to pay more than you can afford, because if you promise to make monthly payments and then can't meet the payments, they probably won't give you a second chance. Most creditors will leave you alone as long as they hear from you regularly, even though the amount you may send them each month is quite small. If you just can't make the monthly payment but think you'll be able to make it the next month, let your creditor know this and then make every effort to do so if he agrees to give you additional time. If you can't afford to make the payment or your creditor won't accept anything less than full payment, consider what exemptions you have (see Section 5.16) and decide whether or not you are *judgment-proof* (what assets you have are all exempt from attachment). As a last resort, you can threaten to file bankruptcy (see Section 7.80) if the creditor doesn't give you time to pay off the debt on the schedule you propose. Usually the threat to file bankruptcy will cause the creditor to accept whatever arrangement you propose, as long as it means he will get some money each month (see Section 7.89).

If your creditor files suit and attaches your assets, again consider your exemptions (see Section 5.16). If your wages are attached, call the Clerk of the Court or see an attorney about getting your wages exempt or having the attachment released on constitutional grounds (see Section 5.4).

O. CREDIT AND THE CREDIT BUREAU [7.95]

Credit bureaus exist for the convenience of businesses and businessmen, primarily retail establishments. If you seldom borrow money and always pay your bills on time, you won't have a record at the credit bureau. However, if you repeatedly fail to pay your debts on time or have judgment taken against you, you probably will have a record at the local credit bureau. If your application for credit is denied by a merchant, he must reveal to you the name of the credit bureau that made an unfavorable report about you. The law allows you to see your file there any time you want to look at it. Some credit bureaus charge a nominal service charge of about a dollar for letting you look at your file. They can do this unless you have been denied credit by someone, in which case you are entitled to see your file without having to pay. By properly identifying yourself you may receive information over the telephone concerning your file at the credit bureau. If your file contains false information, you may require the credit bureau to correct it and send notice to any stores, banks, insurance companies, etc. that received the false information, as well as to any employers or prospective employers that received that information. The credit bureau has to tell you who provided most of the information that is in your file. If you feel the information is incorrect, you can require the credit bureau to investigate it. If after investigation they claim the information which is adverse to you is accurate, then you have the right to write out your own one hundred-word statement and have a copy of it put into your file. If you so desire, the credit bureau must mail your statement to everyone who received the bad report about you.

P. LABOR LAWS

1. Obligation of Employer [7.96]

The employer must provide his employees with a safe place to work. This includes tools and equipment that are safe, and proper training. Irresponsible or negligent co-workers who make working conditions hazardous must be controlled, transferred to another job, or fired.

2. Workmen's Compensation [7.97]

Most states have workmen's compensation laws. Such laws provide compensation for an employee injured on the job, unless the employee caused the injury deliberately. The employer is usually required to carry insurance to pay claims. The amounts awarded for injuries are set by formulas adopted by an administrative agency. An injured employee can appear before such an agency with his lawyer and ask for more money if he is not satisfied with the amount awarded. The amount of the award is based on the size of his medical bills, the amount of his wages, the nature and extent of his injuries, the duration of his disability, and, in the case of death or permanent disability, the number of his dependents.

An injured employee would do well to hire an attorney to represent him. The attorney should be experienced in workmen's compensation cases. The fee is normally set by the administrative agency and is typically between 10 and 25 percent of the amount (if any) awarded. Most states require that the employee give notice (usually in writing) to his employer within a few days after he is injured. Failure to do so may prevent the employee from receiving compensation.

Normally only regular employees are covered by workmen's compensation. Part-time employees, occasional employees, and independent contractors (see Section 4.31) are not usually covered.

An employer whose injury on the job is caused by the negligence of someone who is neither his employer nor a co-worker may be able to collect damages from the negligent person. For example, a delivery truck driver injured by the carelessness of another motorist could sue the other motorist and collect damages. However he probably could not keep both the money received from the motorist and from the workmen's compensation insurance company. He would probably have to pay back to the workmen's compensation carrier the amount he received from it, keeping the rest himself.

[7.98]   3.   Duties of Employee

An employee must be diligent. He should be on time for work, and should not waste time on the job. He should be reasonably careful in the performance of his duties. The orders of his superiors should be obeyed. He must be loyal to his employer and avoid hurting the employer's business or helping competitors at the expense of his employer.

[7.99]   4.   Wages

Minimum wages for most workers (but not all) have been established by federal and state laws. Extra pay for overtime is not required unless local laws so provide or the employer is required by contract with his employees or with a union to pay overtime. Wages can be withheld by an employer if the employee refuses to work (without justification) or if the employee is caught stealing from his employer or engaging in other serious misconduct.

When an employer wrongfully withholds wages, the employee may sue to collect, or get the labor commissioner to help.

5. Trade Secrets and Customer Lists [7.100]

Laws regulate the extent to which an employee can make use of secrets he learned from his employer after termination. Certain *trade secrets* of the employer are protected by law against disclosure by the ex-employee to his later employers. If an employee had access to a secret list of customers, he could not take this list to a competitor after he went to work for it.

6. Rights to Inventions [7.101]

Who is entitled to an employee's inventions? If there is no agreement, inventions made on company time or at company expense belong to both. The employer has *shop rights* (the right to use the invention in his business). Sometimes employees must sign an agreement stating that all their inventions belong to the employer. Inventions belong to the employee alone if made strictly on his time and at his expense.

7. Unions [7.102]

When must an employee join a union in order to get or keep a job? When the majority of workers have voted to belong to a union in accordance with rules and regulations of the National Labor Relations Board and similar agencies. An employee cannot refuse to join a union that is legally authorized to represent his co-workers except in those states which have *right-to-work* laws.

Both employers and unions are prohibited from coercing employees in the selection of a union to represent them. Labor relations are subject to many laws and regulations. Strikes are legal (except in the case of some government employees who may be limited in their right to strike) but are also subject to many rules. The law sometimes requires a certain period of notice, followed by negotiations before a strike can begin. Strikes can be halted by courts or by the government under certain conditions.

Both employers and employees have the right of free speech in discussing union-management problems, but threats are not permitted to be made.

The law regulates who can hold union office, how union dues are collected, and requires unions to keep books and account for dues collected and money spent.

VIII. Criminal Law and Procedure

A. INTRODUCTION

1. Nature and Purpose [8.1]

Criminal law is as old as organized society. The purpose of criminal law is to prohibit that activity which is, by contemporary standards, considered "wrong," or which tends to interfere with the rights of other citizens.

2. Broad Classification of Crimes [8.2]

a. CRIMES AGAINST THE STATE

These constitute making war against our government or giving aid and comfort to an enemy of the government.

b. FELONIES

Felonies are crimes serious enough to be punishable by imprisonment in a state prison for a term exceeding one year.

c. MISDEMEANORS

Crimes for which the maximum punishment is less than imprisonment for one year are considered misdemeanors.

d. PETTY OFFENSES

Petty offenses are minor violations of the law.

[8.3]   3.   Elements of Crime

A crime requires a *criminal intent* coupled with an *act.* It may also involve negligence or failure to do something which the law requires.

[8.4]   4.   Crimes and Torts

The terms *crime* and *tort* are sometimes confused. A *crime* is a violation of criminal law. A *tort* is a violation of a legal duty toward another person which may result in that person having a cause of action for damages (see Section 9.1).

[8.5]   5.   Principals, Accomplices, and Accessories

As used in criminal law, a *principal* is a person who commits the crime, an *accomplice* may help a principal commit the crime, and an *accessory* may help plan the crime or help the criminal escape after the crime is committed.

B. CRIMES AGAINST THE PERSON

1. Abortion [8.6]

Abortion involves the terminating of an unborn human embryo or fetus. The act of abortion may or may not be criminal. An abortion performed legally during the first three months of pregnancy is not a crime. It is up to the pregnant woman and her doctor to decide whether or not to terminate the pregnancy during this period. After the first three months of pregnancy, the state may regulate the performance of abortions for reasons having to do with the health of the mother. After six months (24 to 28 weeks) the state may prohibit abortions. State laws may allow licensed physicians to perform abortions, and may require abortions to be performed in licensed hospitals in some cases. Every state has its own abortion laws and the laws differ.

2. Assault [8.7]

Assault is an unlawful threat or attempt to harm another person. *Aggravated assault* or *assault with a deadly weapon* involves an attempt to kill or seriously injure another person with a dangerous weapon (see Section 9.2).

3. Battery [8.8]

Battery is the intentional touching or harming of another person without his consent (see Section 9.3).

4. Extortion (Blackmail) [8.9]

Extortion means extracting something such as money or property from another person by threatening him with physical harm, destruction of his reputation, or criminal prosecution.

[8.10]   5. Homicide

Homicide means the killing of a human being. If it is *premeditated* (planned in advance) and *deliberate* (intentional), it is first-degree murder. Second-degree murder means that the killing was not planned in advance, but that the killer did strike with intent to kill when he performed the murderous act. *Manslaughter* refers to homicide that is committed without the specific intent to kill. It may be voluntary, as where the enraged killer suddenly strikes another person with his fist and unintentionally kills him, or it may be involuntary, as in the case of homicide resulting from careless driving of an automobile.

Under the *felony-murder rule,* the unintentional killing of a person by one who is engaged at the time in committing a felony may become first-degree murder.

[8.11]   6. Kidnapping

Kidnapping involves forcing a person to move, or moving him without his consent, from one place to another place. The distance need not be great. Kidnapping for ransom or robbery is an aggravated form of kidnapping, resulting in more severe penalties. Transporting a kidnapped person across state lines, or kidnapping a person for ransom where any harm comes to the person, could result in a death penalty for the kidnapper (see Section 8.116).

[8.12]   7. Mayhem

Mayhem is committed by cutting or mutilating a person.

8. Rape [8.13]

Rape is forcible sexual intercourse without the other person's consent. *Statutory rape* is sexual intercourse with a female below the age of consent. The age of consent is established by state law and varies from state to state. A girl below the age of consent is considered by law to be incapable of consenting to the act.

9. Robbery [8.14]

Robbery is the taking of money or property from a person by means of threat or force.

10. Crimes of Sexual Perversion [8.15]

The law defines various crimes of *sexual perversion* which include *sodomy* (anal copulation with another human being or copulation with an animal); *child molesting* (those convicted of this crime in some jurisdictions are required to register their address with the local sheriff's office every time they move); *oral copulation* or *sexual perversion* (generally associated with child molesting or rape); and *exposure, indecency, lewdness,* or *obscenity* (various crimes involving exposure of human sex organs to public view). There are some very peculiar laws relating to sex. A woman who likes to undress without pulling the curtains can have the man who stops to look arrested as a Peeping Tom. In the reverse situation, the woman who looked might be able to have the man arrested for *exposure.*

C. CRIMES AGAINST PROPERTY

[8.16]   1.   Arson

Arson is setting fire to property with the intent to damage or destroy it.

[8.17]   2.   Burglary

Burglary is entering the building or property of someone else with the intent to steal or to commit another crime.

[8.18]   3.   Embezzlement

Embezzlement is taking, for your own use, property that has been entrusted to your care by another person.

[8.19]   4.   Larceny

Larceny is taking the property of another person without his consent, or stealing. There are several forms of larceny, including *grand larceny* (more money or value involved), *petty larceny* (less money or value involved), *shoplifting, auto theft,* and *obtaining money or property by trick or device.*

[8.20]   5.   Receiving Stolen Property or
                     Possession of Stolen Property

It is a crime to receive or buy property that is known to be or should be known to be stolen (for example, a watch or automobile tire offered for sale cheap on a street corner).

6.   Party-Crashing [8.21]

Entering the home or apartment of the owner who is giving a party without his consent is a crime in some jurisdictions and is commonly referred to as *party-crashing.*

7.   Trespassing [8.22]

Entering uninvited upon private property may be a crime.

D. COMMERCIAL CRIMES

1.   Forgery [8.23]

Forgery is signing another person's name or a phony name to a check or other document, or the unauthorized alteration of a previously signed document.

2.   Bad-Check Crimes [8.24]

Signing a check drawn on an account that does not have sufficient funds to cover the check can be a crime unless it is a special account set up so the bank automatically covers overdrafts, or unless the check is postdated and the person to whom it is given is told not to cash it until a subsequent deposit has been made (see Section 7.53).

[8.25]   3.   Price-Fixing

Competing merchants may not get together and agree to fix artificially high prices. Other similar crimes involve selling certain things (like milk) that are closely regulated by the state at a lower price for the purpose of attempting to drive the competition out of the market.

[8.26]   4.   Anti-Trust Laws

Most states have anti-trust laws patterned after the federal laws which prohibit certain business practices that tend to create monopolies and to prevent free and open competition in business.

[8.27]   5.   Unfair Competition

There are federal and state laws preventing certain commercial practices which are overly competitive in an unfair way, when the purpose of such acts is to prevent competition by eliminating competitors (like stealing secret "customer lists").

[8.28]   6.   Unfair Labor Practices

Certain practices on the part of either labor unions or management can result in criminal prosecutions of the people involved or the unions or companies involved. Forcing workers to join a union or bribing them not to join are examples.

7. Fair Employment Practices [8.29]

Employers are required not to discriminate against job applicants on the grounds of race or sex. Violations of these laws can cause penalties to be imposed upon the employer as well as entitling the applicant to damages and/or a job (see Section 13.14).

8. Mail Fraud and Pornography [8.30]

Federal laws prohibit certain mail-order business practices which result in defrauding the public. The use of the mails for the sale of obscene matter (pornography) is regulated by law and subject to criminal penalties. Federal laws prohibit the mailing of any obscene, lewd, lascivious, indecent, filthy, or vile article, thing, or substance.

E. NARCOTICS AND DRUGS

[8.31]   1. Alcohol

The law of each state sets the age at which young people are allowed to buy and consume alcoholic beverages. Below that age it is illegal to buy or consume alcoholic beverages; it is also illegal to furnish or sell alcoholic beverages to minors. The fact that alcohol is a potentially dangerous drug is evidenced by the large and growing number of alcoholics in the world today. Alcohol is a *depressant,* and for certain people it is *addictive.*

[8.32]   2. Tobacco

Most states prohibit the selling or giving of tobacco to youths below a certain age. Tobacco contains nicotine, a stimulant. Heavy long-term use leads to addiction and according to some researchers can cause cancer. Smoking by students in high school (or earlier) is still prohibited in some areas.

[8.33]   3. Drugs and Narcotics

The preparation, possession, sale, transportation, use, and growth of narcotics and potentially dangerous drugs are regulated and restricted by laws in every state and by federal law. These laws are based on the concept that society must protect itself from the influences of undesirable elements. As frequency of use of drugs expands, enforcement becomes more difficult. Eventually laws change to conform to current moral standards. Existing laws deal with drug violators on three levels: mere users are treated leniently in most cases; persons acting illegally while under the influence of drugs are given moderate punishment; those involved in pushing drugs are severely punished. As in the case of other crimes, repeated offenders face harsh penalties.

Some states allow those charged with use of a drug to commit themselves to a state drug center for treatment as an alternative to criminal prosecution. Penalties range from probation, fine, or short jail term for possession (first offense) to fifteen years to life for sale to a minor. Convicted drug abusers face strict probation requirements, as well as difficulty in getting work, obtaining passports, holding public office, etc. (see chart on pages 286-91).

MIND-AFFECTING DRUGS

	Name	Common Names	Description	Common Use
STIMULANTS	Amphetamine	Uppers Pep pills Whites	Pills in various shapes, sizes, & colors Powder	Oral Intravenous
	Benzedrine	Bennies Wake-ups	"	"
	Dexedrine Dexoxyn	Dexies	"	"
	Methedrine	Cartwheels Speed Crank	"	"
	Methamphetamine	Speed Meth Crystal	"	"
	Cocaine	Coke Leaf Snow	Extract from cocoa bush leaves	Inhalation Oral
DEPRESSANTS	Barbiturates	Downers Goofballs Reds Yellows Blues	Pills in various shapes, sizes, & colors Powder	Inhalation Oral
	Sedatives	Barbs	"	"
	Seconal	Seccy Red	"	"
	Equanil		"	"
	Miltown	Rainbows	"	"
	Doriden	Pink ladies	"	"
	Librium		"	"
	Nembutal	Yellow jackets	"	"
	Phenobarbital	Phennies	"	"

Physical Effects	Psychological Effects	Dangers
Tremor Enlarged pupils Heavy perspiration High blood pressure Abnormal heart rhythms	Excitability Talkativeness Restlessness Sleeplessness Delusions	Psychic dependence Psychosis
"	"	"
"	"	"
"	"	"
Similar to amphetamine, but faster, more marked	Violence Paranoid behavior	Psychic dependence Psychosis Death
Dilated pupils Muscular twitching	Exhilaration Relief of fatigue	Convulsions Physical dependence Death
Drowsiness Sluggishness Staggering Thick speech	Calmness Gloominess Release Quarrelsomeness	Respiratory failure Coma Psychic dependence Death
"	"	"
"	"	"
"	"	"
"	"	"
"	"	"
"	"	"
"	"	"
"	"	"

	Name	Common Names	Description	Common Us
OPIATES & NARCOTICS	Opium	Black	Dried juice or seeds of opium poppies	Smoking
	Morphine	Dreamer White stuff	Derived from opium White crystalline powder	Intravenous
	Codeine	Schoolboy	Derived from opium	Cough medicine Oral
	Heroin	"H" Horse Stuff Junk Smack	Derived from morphine Off-white or brown crystalline powder	Intravenous
	Demerol	Snow	Synthetic opiate	Oral
	Methadone	Dolly	Chemical Synthetic opiate	Intravenous
HALLUCINOGENICS	LSD	Acid Sugar Big "D" The Cube The Beast	Colorless, odorless, tasteless chemical Lysergic acid derivative Liquid or crystalline form In capsules	Oral Intravenous
	Mescaline	Cactus Mesc	Chemical taken from peyote cactus Crystalline powder	"
	Psilocybin	Mushrooms	Synthesized from Mexican mushrooms Powder or liquid	Oral
	Peyote	"P" The Button	Cactus buttons	"
	DMT	Businessman's high	Whitish chemical substance	Smoking in tobacco Intravenous
	STP		Tablets or powder	Oral

288

Physical Effects	Psychological Effects	Dangers
Relief of pain	Euphoria	Physical dependence
Constricted pupils Slow pulse & respiration	Calmness Euphoria	Physical dependence Withdrawal symptoms
"	"	"
Like morphine, but faster	"	Physical dependence Withdrawal symptoms Death
Relief of pain	Drowsiness	Physical dependence Withdrawal symptoms
"	Used in treatment of heroin addicts	Mild addiction

Dilated pupils
Increased blood pressure
Increased heart beat
Increased blood sugar
Nausea
Chills
Flushes
Irregular breathing
Trembling
Sweating hands
Chromosome alteration
	Hallucinations
	Panic
	Distortion
	Intensification of
	   visual and auditory
	   perception
	Psychosis
	Personality changes
	Mystical experiences
		Unpredictable results
		Reoccurrence of effects
		   later without reuse
		Brain damage
		Birth defects
		Psychic dependence

Similar to LSD, but
   less potent
	Similar to LSD, but
	   less potent
		Similar to LSD, but
		   less potent

Like mescaline, but
   less potent
	Like mescaline, but
	   less potent
		Like mescaline, but
		   less potent

"	"	"
"	"	"

Similar to LSD, but
   stronger
	Similar to LSD, but
	   stronger
		Similar to LSD, but
		   worse

	Name	Common Names	Description	Common Use
CANNABIS	Marijuana	Pot Grass Tea Weed Reefers Joints Sticks	Dried flowering top of cannabis sativa plant (Indian Hemp)	Smoking Oral
	Hashish	Hash	Powdered & sifted form of resin from cannabis plant	"
ALCOHOL	Liquor Wine Beer	Booze Spirits Drink Pick-me-up Nightcap	Liquid distilled or fermented from grain, hops, grapes, etc.	Oral
TOBACCO	Cigarettes Cigars Pipe tobacco Chewing tobacco	Smoke	Cured leaves of tobacco plant	Smoking Chewing
MISCELLANEOUS	Glue		Quick-drying plastic cement	Inhalation of fumes
	Hair spray			"
	Gasoline			"

Physical Effects	*Psychological Effects*	*Dangers*
Lower blood sugar Inflammation of mucous membranes Increased appetite Lower body temperature Ataxia	Distortion of sensation & perception Distortion of time & space Feeling of exhilaration Mystical experiences	Clear medical evidence of danger from occasional use presently lacking Possible psychic dependence Experts disagree on possible dangers of heavy or long-term use
Like marijuana, but stronger	Like marijuana, but stronger	Physical deterioration with long-term use
Depressing of brain control centers Unsteady gait Slurred speech Slow reactions Blurred vision	Confusion Disorientation Euphoria Quarrelsome or aggressive behavior Melancholia	Physical dependence Psychic dependence Withdrawal symptoms Liver disease Delirium tremens Death
Shortness of breath Brown teeth Deposits on lungs	Calmness	Respiratory disease Physical dependence Psychic dependence Cancer
Kidney, liver, bone, & brain damage	Exhilaration Hallucinations	Psychic dependence Death
"	"	"
"	"	"

[8.34] F. MOTOR VEHICLE LAWS

All states have extensive vehicle codes regulating the ownership and operation of motor vehicles. The most serious prohibited offenses include driving while under the influence of alcohol, drugs, or narcotics, and hit-and-run driving. *Felony drunk driving* involves injuring another while driving under the influence of alcohol or drugs (see Part XII).

G. PUBLIC CRIMES OR CRIMES AGAINST THE STATE

[8.35] 1. Anarchy

Anarchy is defined as teaching, advocating, or aiding the commission of unlawful acts which are intended to overthrow or destroy the government or governmental authority.

[8.36] 2. Attempted Crimes

Any attempt to commit a crime is itself a crime, the punishment for which will be related to the seriousness of the crime that was attempted.

3.   Bribery [8.37]

Bribery involves attempting to influence the action or opinion of a public official.

4.   Conspiracy [8.38]

A *conspiracy* occurs when two or more persons agree to commit a crime and take some step toward carrying out the plan.

5.   Contempt of Court [8.39]

Contempt of court means disorderly conduct in the court-room or disobeying an order of the court. A judge has authority to give jail sentences and fines to persons guilty of contempt of court.

6.   Curfew [8.40]

Most states and cities have *curfew* laws regulating the presence of juveniles on city streets after certain hours at night. The laws generally permit the presence of young people if they are working at a job, have a lawful excuse, or are going from one place to another (as opposed to loitering).

7.   Disorderly Conduct [8.41]

Disorderly conduct usually involves physical disruption of community order. Examples would be fighting or making loud noises in public or creating a disturbance in a public area.

[8.42]   8.   Defacing Property

Defacing property refers to vandalism or the malicious or willful destruction of public or private property.

[8.43]   9.   Disturbing the Peace

This crime involves making too much noise or performing any act which disturbs the peace and quiet of the neighborhood.

[8.44]   10.   Interfering with an Officer

Interrupting or obstructing a police officer in the performance of his duty is a crime. The law requires citizens to cooperate with, and not resist or obstruct officers in performance of their duty. In some states a person who refuses to cooperate with or even assist a sheriff or police officer in making an arrest or preventing the escape of a criminal is guilty of the crime of refusing to aid a policeman.

[8.45]   11.   Littering

There are many laws which make *littering* of streets, highways, or public property a criminal offense punishable by fine and/or imprisonment. Frequently those found guilty of *trashing* public highways are sentenced to several hours of labor, cleaning up along the edges of highways or freeways.

[8.46]   12.   Loitering

Loitering or *vagrancy* means just standing around in a public place for a period of time without any apparent reason, or without anything to do. It can also mean hanging around the streets at unusual hours of the night without any visible or lawful business. The law may apply to a person who loiters or prowls or wanders upon private property at night without any lawful business with the owner. Typical statutes define such conduct as vagrancy or loitering and make it punishable by fine and/or imprisonment. Some cases cast doubt on the constitutionality of antiloitering statutes. These cases hold that it is not right to prohibit a person from spending his time just sitting in a public place. The Supreme Court has ruled that cities cannot make it a crime for small groups of citizens to loiter in public places "in an annoying manner." The word "annoying" is open to too many interpretations and such a law is therefore too vague to be enforceable.

13. Malicious Mischief [8.47]

Malicious mischief is similar to *defacing property* and means or includes injuring or destroying someone else's property; poisoning animals illegally, or otherwise mutilating or abusing animals; burning of grass or timber; injuring street signs or fences; tampering with signals, markers, monuments, or posted legal notices; tampering with fire alarms or turning in false alarms. Many other similar acts can come under the category of malicious mischief.

14. Obscenity [8.48]

Some states have laws prohibiting the use of profane language or obscene gestures in public where other people may be offended. There are also laws that prohibit sale or distribution of pornographic writing, photographs, or motion pictures. To be obscene, the material must be found to appeal to prurient interest in sex; to depict or describe sexual conduct in a patently offensive way as specifically defined by state law, and to lack serious literary, artistic, political, or scientific value, taken as a whole. Local community standards may be used in determining whether or not material is obscene (see Section 11.13).

[8.49]   **15. Perjury**

Perjury is lying under oath. It is usually a felony.

[8.50]   **16. Resisting Arrest**

A person who resists the arrest by an officer or by a citizen making a citizen's arrest commits the additional crime of *resisting arrest* (see Section 8.69).

[8.51]   **17. Solicitation**

Asking another person to commit a crime is itself a crime called *solicitation.*

[8.52]   **18. Treason and Sedition**

Treason is making war against the government of your country or aiding an enemy of your country. A related crime is *sedition*, which involves conspiring against your government.

[8.53]   **19. Unlawful Assembly**

Unlawful assembly is the gathering of a large group of people in a public area in violation of a local ordinance or of a court order. A related crime, *failure to disperse,* occurs when a mob fails to break up when asked by police to do so.

20. Vandalism [8.54]

Vandalism is the malicious and willful destruction or defacement of property.

H. SOCIAL CRIMES

1. Adultery [8.55]

A married person who cohabits and sleeps with someone other than his or her spouse is guilty of the crime of *adultery* in states having such laws. Prosecution for such a crime is quite rare.

2. Bigamy [8.56]

Marrying or being married to more than one person at a time constitutes the crime of *bigamy.*

[8.57]   3.   Civil Rights Violations

Discrimination against a person because of race, religion, or sex may constitute a violation of federal or state law. The act of discrimination may prevent the person from getting a job, obtaining housing, or entering or making use of certain public or semipublic (privately owned but open to the public) facilities. Violation of such laws can result in criminal penalties against the violators, and sometimes provide a civil remedy in the form of the right of the person discriminated against to sue for and collect damages (see Part XIII).

[8.58]   4.   Homosexuality

It is not illegal to be a homosexual. Laws that regulate conduct of homosexuals are usually aimed at acts defined as *oral sex perversion,* or at sexual conduct between members of the same sex in public view, which is considered distasteful to most people. Generally these laws are enforced only when the act occurs in public or in the presence of someone who is offended and complains, or where one of the parties is a minor, or where the act is committed without consent of one of the parties. *Homosexuals* are people who have sexual desires primarily for those of the same sex; a lesbian is a female homosexual.

[8.59]   5.   Incest

Persons who are related by blood so closely that laws forbid their marriage to each other, who have sexual intercourse, have committed the crime of *incest.*

6. Lotteries or Gaming [8.60]

Lotteries are schemes for the distribution of money or property by chance among persons who have paid something of value to obtain the chance to receive it. Most states prohibit lotteries that are not licensed. *Gaming* includes certain card games, bingo games, roulette games, or slot machines which involve putting in or paying money on the chance to get more money back. These are generally illegal. The laws are not uniformly enforced.

7. Pandering [8.61]

Pandering means procuring a woman for a house of prostitution or encouraging a woman to become a prostitute.

8. Pimping [8.62]

A person who derives his support or maintenance from the earnings of a prostitute, or who solicits for her, is guilty of *pimping.*

9. Prostitution [8.63]

A woman who works in a house of prostitution or who peddles her sexual wares in public may be prosecuted in some states for the crime of *prostitution* and in other states as a prostitute under the vagrancy statutes.

10. Seduction [8.64]

A person who seduces an unmarried virgin by making a false promise of marriage to get her consent commits the crime of *seduction.* This crime is rarely prosecuted.

I. ARREST

[8.65]   1.   General

Arrest is the act of taking a person into legal custody. An arrest may be made by an officer of the law with or without a warrant, or it may be made by a citizen.

[8.66]   2.   Arrest by Officer with Warrant

A warrant is obtained before arrest except in cases where the officer making the arrest has actually witnessed the crime. An officer with a warrant must state that he is acting under the authority of a warrant, must show the warrant, and give the person being arrested an opportunity to read it. The warrant must be in writing, must state the law violated, name the accused, state the date and place of issuance, order the accused to be brought before a judge, and be signed by a judge or judicial official.

[8.67]   3.   Arrest by Officer without Warrant

An arrest without a warrant may be made by an officer if a crime has been committed or attempted in his presence, or if he has *probable* cause to so believe, or if he believes a citizen's arrest was lawfully made.

[8.68]   4.   Arrest by Citizen

In making a *citizen's arrest,* you simply inform the person that you wish to arrest that you are arresting him, specify the offense (in some states a citizen's arrest is only proper for felonies) that you believe he has committed in your presence, and request that he submit to your arrest and accompany you to the nearest police station or police officer. It is perfectly appropriate for a citizen who wishes to make an arrest to call upon others to assist him in making the arrest and in detaining the suspected criminal.

A citizen who refuses to respond to an officer's request for aid in making an arrest may be guilty of a misdemeanor (see Section 8.44). Because most crimes are committed out of the presence of the police, society has to rely upon the willingness of its citizens to make arrests when they have witnessed crimes. If a citizen mistakenly arrests an innocent person, he may be liable in a civil suit for false imprisonment (see Section 9.5).

5.   Resisting Arrest [8.69]

If the person being arrested refuses to submit to arrest or refuses to accompany the arresting officer or citizen, he may be guilty of *resisting arrest,* a separate crime. In most states it is the responsibility of a person arrested to submit to the arrest, even though it may be, in his opinion, unlawful. He may make his complaint about the arrest at the proper time in a proper manner. If it turns out the arrest was wrong, he may have an action for *false arrest* (also called *false imprisonment*—see Section 9.5) against the officer or citizen arresting him. *Passive resistance* ("going limp") constitutes a form of resisting arrest and can subject the person engaging in such conduct to the additional charge of resisting arrest.

6.   Use of Force [8.70]

The arresting officer or citizen may use that force which is reasonably necessary to cause the person arrested to submit to custody. Use of excessive force may turn out to be *battery* or *homicide.* Wrongful arrest may turn out to be *false imprisonment,* (sometimes called false arrest—see Section 9.5). Ordinarily it is not advisable for private citizens to resort to physical force to bring about the arrest of a person who is resisting, unless the person attempting to make the arrest is clearly able to do so without endangering himself or any innocent bystanders.

[8.71]   **7.   Arrest Based on Complaint, Indictment, or Information**

A citizen wishing to have someone arrested for a crime may go to the local law-enforcement office, usually the district attorney's (or equivalent) office, and initiate a *complaint* against the person whom he believes guilty of some illegal act. He will be required to sign a formal complaint under oath, describe the alleged offense, and request the arrest. He must be prepared to offer testimony to back up his assertions. If he acts maliciously or without *probable cause,* he may be liable for false arrest (see Section 8.69). If, on the other hand, he acts with probable cause, then he has performed a civic duty. Probable cause means reasonable grounds for believing a crime was committed by the person arrested.

An *indictment* is an accusation of a crime presented to a court by a grand jury based on secret testimony at a grand jury investigation. The court issues a warrant for arrest based on the indictment.

An *information* is an accusation of a crime filed by the district attorney or public prosecutor based on a police investigation. A court will also issue a warrant for arrest based on an information.

8.   Booking   [8.72]

After the arrest is made, the person arrested is taken to the nearest police station where the fact of his arrest is recorded in official records (*booked*), and then he is fingerprinted (*printed*) and photographed (*mugged*). A permanent record is made of the arrest. (In some states a person who is released or acquitted has the right to have the record of his arrest destroyed or turned over to him.) Money and personal belongings (except for clothing) are taken, in exchange for a receipt, if he is not going to be released on bail.

9.   Interrogation   [8.73]

Interrogation (questioning) may occur either before or after arrest. Interrogation consists of asking factual questions of a person to ascertain who he is, where he lives, what he is or was doing at the scene of the arrest, and what he knows about or what his connection may be with the alleged crime. Recent cases have limited the power of the police to interrogate suspects. A suspect should be warned of his rights at the time he becomes suspected of a crime. Just when this occurs depends upon the circumstances. Interrogation can be a delicate situation. If police warn you of your rights before asking you any questions, even when you have not yet become a suspect, you may refuse further answers to their questions. If they wait until they have obtained what amounts to a confession from you before warning you of your rights, they will not be able to use your answers to the questions, or information obtained from your answers to the questions, to convict you. A proper warning consists of the officer telling you that you are a suspect, that you have the right to remain silent, that you do not have to answer any further questions, that you have the right to an attorney, and that if you cannot afford an attorney the state (or other governmental body) will furnish one for you (see Section 11.29). After booking you are entitled to make a phone call to a lawyer, or anyone else you wish to call. If you don't reach a lawyer right away, you are not limited to just one phone call.

J. BETWEEN ARREST AND PROSECUTION

[8.74]   1.   Bail

If you are charged with a misdemeanor you are entitled to be released on *bail* (unless you are a fugitive or are wanted in connection with some other crime). People arrested for misdemeanors for the first time are most often released on their *own recognizance* ("O.R."). Whether you are released O.R. or on bail, you are required to return at a specified time to the appropriate court for *arraignment*. Bail is the security that is posted as a guarantee of your showing up at that arraignment. The bail can be cash or it can be in the form of a bail bond. Bail bondsmen are listed in the telephone directory and are available near the courthouse, twenty-four hours a day. Bail bondsmen charge a percentage of the amount of the bail bond as a premium for the bond. Once bail has been posted, if you fail to show up for the arraignment, the cash or the bond is forfeited to the court, and a warrant will be issued for your arrest for *jumping bail.* Bail bond premiums generally run between 3 and 10 percent of the amount of the bail. If you have cash available and intend to show up at the arraignment, you are better off to post cash. However, it may be difficult to get a friend, relative, or lawyer to get the cash together and bring it to the jail if you have been arrested at night or on a weekend, and in such cases the bail bondsman offers you a convenient service to enable you to get out of jail.

The bail must be *reasonable.* The amount depends on the nature of the offense, your prior record (if any), and the chance that you may commit a further crime or may flee the jurisdiction of the court if you are released. Where the custom is not to release O.R., the amount of bail for routine offenses is established by a standard schedule. If the bail is set unreasonably high, a constitutional right has been violated and a motion may be made to the court to reduce the amount of bail (see Section 11.4).

In the case of some misdemeanors (for example, traffic tickets), the arresting officer need not take you to jail. You are given the chance to sign a ticket. By signing it, you acknowledge the fact of the arrest and agree to appear for arraignment within a certain period of time. You then have the choice of appearing at that time and entering a plea, or mailing a check or delivering cash to the clerk of the court in a certain amount. This amounts to a plea of *guilty,* and is usually referred to as *forfeiting bail,* on the theory that the amount of money that you are required to send in constitutes bail. By established procedures to which the court consents, you are permitted in such a case to forfeit that bail in lieu of coming to court, entering a plea of guilty, and paying a fine.

[8.75]   2.   Arraignment and Plea

If you are arrested and not released on bail, the law requires that you be taken before a judicial officer, usually withing twenty-four hours. If you are released on bail or O.R., or sign a ticket and agree to appear (and elect not to forfeit bail), then when you appear at the arraignment the clerk reads the charges against you to the court and you are asked to enter a plea. There are generally three pleas available: *guilty, not guilty,* and *nolo contendere* (*nolo* is the equivalent of the guilty plea but simply means you do not contest the charges made against you). After your plea of *guilty* or *nolo* is entered, the court will either decide the fine and/or sentence at that time or set a hearing at a later date to determine the fine and/or sentence.

If you enter a plea of *not guilty,* then the judge will ask whether or not you waive your right to a jury trial and your right to be tried within a certain period of days. You have a right to both, and you may request either one or both, or you may waive either one or both. If you do not waive your rights, then you must have a jury trial and it must occur within the minimum period of time (generally thirty days). At an arraignment you may appear alone, without your lawyer, if you desire (a procedure that is not recommended) or you may appear with your lawyer, or your lawyer may (in some jurisdictions) appear alone, without you, and enter a plea of *not guilty* and have a date set for trial.

There are other special pleas that may be entered, such as *not guilty by reason of insanity,* or *former jeopardy* (see Section 8.105).

Plea-bargaining refers to the custom of negotiating with the prosecutor for dismissal of a serious charge in return for agreeing to plead guilty to a lesser charge. It avoids a trial, and affords one who may be guilty the chance to get a lighter sentence.

3. Habeas Corpus [8.76]

Habeas corpus means "you have the body," or "you may have the body." A *writ of habeas corpus* may be obtained from a judge to order the officer having custody of a prisoner to bring him before a court or judge in order to determine whether or not the prisoner has been improperly detained. Some uses of the writ of habeas corpus include getting bail reduced or proving that the arrest was in some way illegal (see Section 11.11).

4. Public Defender [8.77]

Most jurisdictions provide the services of a *public defender* to those unable to afford counsel of their own. The public defender is a public official, just like the public prosecutor, only his job is to defend those charged with a crime. The court may assign a public defender to represent a defendant who does not have enough money to hire a lawyer.

5. Private Defender [8.78]

In some jurisdictions local bar associations, together with public service agencies, provide legal help for those who are unable to afford a lawyer. In such cases the lawyer provided would not be on the public payroll, but would either be donating his time or would receive pay from the agency administering the private defender program. In some cases persons charged with crime can qualify for representation under the *legal aid* program, which is a program set up in some jurisdictions by the local bar association for the purpose of providing lawyers for those who cannot afford them. Contact your local bar association, or call any lawyer for details.

[8.79]   6.   Minority Rights

In some jurisdictions a legalized system of injustice may exist which benefits a majority and works against the interests of an unprotected minority. In such cases a group such as the American Civil Liberties Union may be called upon to furnish an experienced lawyer to represent the defendant because of the public issue involved, such as discrimination against a minority or some other similar problem that may result in a deprivation of rights. The Supreme Court held in one case that where a court usually imposes fines but not jail sentences for traffic violations, it cannot jail people who are too poor to pay the fines.

K. PROSECUTION

1. Criminal Courts [8.80]

When a criminal case comes to trial, the case may be heard either by a judge or by a jury, if the defendant desires a jury. There are usually some preliminary matters that are discussed between the judge and the attorneys, out of the presence of the jury. When the trial starts, the prosecutor is entitled to make an opening statement, telling the judge or jury what he expects to prove and how he will prove it (see Section 5.28). The defense attorney will then make his opening statement, or he may waive it or he may wait and make it after the prosecution has completed its part of the case. The prosecution presents its case first, calling its witnesses and introducing its documentary evidence. Each witness presented by the prosecution is cross-examined by the defense, if desired. After the prosecution has completed its case, the defense presents its witnesses and documentary evidence. The prosecution may cross-examine the defense witnesses. The prosecution may put on *rebuttal testimony* after the defense has completed its case. Such testimony is limited to rebutting arguments made or defenses raised by the defendant, and the prosecution is not supposed to use its rebuttal to present new evidence. After the completion of the case for prosecution and defense, the attorneys make their closing arguments to the jury, the prosecutor opening and closing the argument, with the defense making a single argument in between the opening and closing arguments of the prosecutor. The jury is then instructed as to the law in the case by the judge (see Section 5.41), and retires to the jury room to deliberate and to decide on its verdict. While in the jury room, the jury may ask for any of the evidence to be sent in to the jury room, or it may request further instructions from the judge, or it may have portions read from the testimony that were transcribed during the trial by the court reporter.

Normally juries are kept "locked up" until they have reached a verdict or are unable to reach a verdict (see Section 5.42). If the case is heard by a judge without a jury, he may either rule from the bench upon conclusion of the arguments or he may take the case "under submission," which means he will study the notes he has made of the trial, and the exhibits, and will perhaps clarify some points of law about which he may have some questions, and will give his decision later.

2. Jury

[8.81]

a. NUMBER OF JURORS

A jury traditionally numbers twelve. However, the Supreme Court has ruled that twelve is not mandatory. Juries will probably become smaller, although it is doubtful they will be fewer than six in number (see Section 5.27).

[8.82]

b. SELECTION

Prospective jurors are selected at random from among registered voters. If chosen for jury duty they are entitled to reimbursement for their traveling expenses according to a set scale, and to a small per diem "salary" (see Section 5.27). Selection is accomplished by questioning prospective jurors and attempting to eliminate any who may be unfit to serve for one reason or another, or who may have prejudices for or against the defendant, or who may be acquainted with any of the parties involved in the case. Where questioning by attorneys is permitted, the prosecutor and the defense attorney may also question the jurors in more detail and attempt to categorize them in their minds as being favorable, unfavorable, or neutral to their client or their side of the case. Attorneys are permitted a certain number of *peremptory challenges* (see Section 5.27). In addition, an attorney may challenge any juror for *cause.* By challenging a juror, the attorney so doing is requesting that that juror be excused from the jury and be replaced by another prospective juror. If he exercises a peremptory challenge, the attorney need not state his reasons. If he challenges the juror for *cause,* he must state his reasons (if they are not obvious to the court) and the judge will then either allow the challenge and excuse the juror or will disallow the challenge, in which case the attorney may then exercise a *peremptory challenge* (provided he has not used up all of his peremptory challenges beforehand). Sometimes the selection of a jury can take many days. Eventually both sides agree on twelve jurors (or whatever number the jury consists of), and the trial can proceed. The jury panel is then *sworn in,* which means that they take the oath to carry out their duties as jurors in the manner instructed by the judge and according to the law.

c.   CONDUCT OF JURORS   [8.83]

Jurors, of course, must remain alert while testimony is being given, and must be able to hear and see everything that goes on in the courtroom that is part of the trial. They are instructed by the court to refrain from discussing the case with anyone. The attorneys, the parties to the case, and the witnesses are instructed not to discuss the case in front of or within the hearing of any jurors in the hallway, the elevator, etc. Jurors are instructed not to make any investigations on their own or to report to the other jurors anything that they learned about the case outside of the trial. When the evidence has been presented and the arguments have been made, the judge will deliver instructions to the jurors, instructing them as to their duties and as to the law they are to apply to that particular case (see Section 5.41). The jurors are instructed to discuss the testimony and the evidence and, after due deliberation, to attempt to reach a verdict (see Section 5.42). When they have reached a verdict they inform the bailiff, who informs the judge, who requests the defendant, his attorney, and the prosecutor to return to the courtroom; when everyone is ready, the jury is brought back in to deliver its verdict. Misconduct on the part of the jury such as tossing a coin for a decision or pressuring to "force" a verdict can result in a *mistrial* (which gives the defendant the right to be tried over again).

[8.84]

d. GRAND JURY

The *grand jury* is a throwback to the old English common law. The English have since abandoned the grand jury, but it remains in many states today. Some say it is useful for taking testimony from undercover agents without exposing them and for getting testimony from children in child-molesting cases. The indictment by a grand jury is an essential step in a criminal prosecution for serious crimes in such jurisdictions. The grand jury consists of persons selected by various means, numbering from five to twenty-three, depending upon the state. It can investigate matters, can act upon its own knowledge gained from its own investigation, or it can act upon information received from the district attorney or prosecutor's office. An *indictment* is a formal accusation presented by a grand jury in order to initiate a criminal prosecution. In order to obtain an indictment, the prosecutor presents evidence to the grand jury, usually in a secret hearing not open to the public.

3. Publicity [8.85]

The Constitution of the United States guarantees the right to due process (see Section 11.8). One element of due process is a fair and impartial trial. It is possible for a case to receive enough publicity within a community so that a fair and impartial trial cannot be held in that community. It may be difficult or impossible to find jurors who have not read about the case or seen something about it on television and thereby formed an opinion. This happened some years ago in the Dr. *Sam Sheppard* case. Sheppard's conviction for murder of his wife was reversed and a new trial was granted by the Supreme Court on the ground that the extraordinary publicity in the local news media prejudiced or could have prejudiced the jurors against the defendant. To avoid the prejudice, he should have been tried in some other jurisdiction. Imagine the difficulty of the prosecutor and the defense counsel in the trial of Sirhan Sirhan for the murder of Senator Robert Kennedy in trying to find jurors who had not seen or heard of the episode on television or read about it in the local papers.

4. Extradition [8.86]

The Constitution of the United States provides that a person charged with a crime in one state, who flees to another state, may be removed from that state back to the state having jurisdiction of the crime upon demand of the governor of the state seeking the accused person. The demand must be accompanied by appropriate extradition papers, and the state authorities relinquishing a person on a request for extradition must be convinced that the alleged crime has been committed by the person being extradited. Extradition between nations is based on treaties. James Earl Ray, who was convicted of the murder of Dr. Martin Luther King, was extradited from England (where he was captured) back to the United States for trial in accordance with an agreement between the two nations.

[8.87]   5.   Courtroom Decorum

The courtroom is a place for good manners, proper dress, and neat grooming. This applies especially to the participants in the trial. Jurors can easily become prejudiced against a person by his actions, mannerisms, speech, or even his dress and personal appearance. Judges, too, are human enough to be affected by such things. Any person involved in a lawsuit who does not put his best foot forward in the courtroom is giving himself an unnecessary handicap. Intentionally disruptive tactics are unfortunately sometimes engaged in by some defense counsel and their clients. In the *Chicago Eight* trial, Bobby Seale, one of the defendants, made so much noise that the judge ordered him bound to his chair and gagged. Even in this position he was still able to create enough disturbance to cause the judge to order him removed from the courtroom. Similar events occurred in the Manson family trial in Los Angeles. Other judges in such situations have simply recessed the court and ordered the defendant held in jail until he and his attorney agree to stop disrupting the proceedings. In the future, courts may use closed-circuit television or other similar means in order to conduct orderly trials (see Section 11.36).

[8.88]   6.   Defending Yourself

There is an old saying that a lawyer who handles his own case has a fool for a client. A person lacking legal training who attempts to handle his own case is in an even more awkward position. Nevertheless there are times a person of limited financial means and considerable verbal skill and confidence in his own ability can do a fairly good job in presenting his own case. It is not advisable for the average person to try it. Anyone planning to handle his own case should take time to sit in on several complete trials involving the same or similar charges, in the same courthouse where he will be tried. Another good idea would be to see a good lawyer, even if only for a couple of hours, to ask his advice on how to prepare for trial, how to conduct the trial, how to present the case, and how to cross-examine witnesses presented by the prosecution.

Those without sufficient funds to be able to afford a lawyer in a criminal case are entitled to one furnished by the state. If you don't like the lawyer furnished to you, you have the right to ask for another one (but you can't afford to be *too* choosy). You'll have to find one you like from the available supply.

If your income is such that you don't qualify for a public defender or for legal aid but still feel you can't afford or don't absolutely have to have a lawyer, and you feel you have the ability to present your own case, this is possible. Nevertheless, you should have some help from a lawyer and do an adequate amount of investigation and reading to learn about the criminal process and be generally familiar with the way trials are conducted, as well as with the principles of evidence and general trial procedures.

7.   Trial Strategy and Tactics   [8.89]

At trial, each side tries to present its case in the best possible light. The prosecutor has to prove each fact that he needs to establish in order to "make his case," by evidence that tends to prove his point "beyond a reasonable doubt." Every fact that the prosecutor attempts to establish, and every fact that a defendant intends to establish, must be backed up by evidence, either physical evidence (objects such as a bloody knife), documents (a forged check), or testimony (statement of a witness). The overall strategy of the defense may be to cloud and confuse the issues so that the jury (or judge) will not be convinced beyond a reasonable doubt. On the other hand, the defendant may have a clear-cut defense, which only requires certain evidence to be presented that is itself believable. An example would be an alibi ("I wasn't there and can prove it by testimony of friends").

[8.90]   8.   Direct Examination

Direct examination describes the questioning of a witness by the side that called the witness to the stand initially (see Section 5.31).

[8.91]   9.   Cross-Examination

After the completion of direct examination, the other side may examine that witness, and this is called *cross-examination* (see Section 5.32).

[8.92]   10. Prior Statements

Prior statements of witnesses, in the form of statements to police officers or depositions taken prior to trial, or in the form of written documents such as letters, may be used at trial for certain purposes. One such purpose would be *impeachment.* To impeach a witness means to discredit his testimony by showing that he made another inconsistent statement, which means he must either have lied or become confused.

11. Evidence [8.93]

The law requires that evidence be presented in a certain manner. The rules of evidence are quite complex and difficult for the layman to understand. The purpose of the rules is to provide a routine and orderly method of presenting evidence in such a way that truth will emerge. Evidence includes such things as testimony of witnesses, documents, photographs, objects, records, tapes, and moving pictures. Some of the rules of evidence are discussed in Sections 5.34 through 5.38.

12. Motions [8.94]

There are numerous motions that can be made before, during, and after trial. They are technical in nature and varied in purpose. Space does not permit even summarizing all of the available motions. A legal treatise on *procedure* will give you a listing and a description of each motion.

13. Exclusion of Jury [8.95]

During a jury trial it may be necessary to discuss certain evidence out of the presence of the jury. Either side can move to exclude the jury if it feels the court should hear such evidence first before it is presented to the jury.

14. Exhibits [8.96]

Exhibits constitute the physical evidence introduced into the trial. Exhibits are generally marked with a number so that they can be properly identified. They are not marked for evidence until they have been properly introduced in accordance with the rules of evidence.

[8.97]   ## 15. To Testify or Not

One question every defendant faces is whether or not to testify in his own behalf. If he does not take the stand, the prosecutor may not question him. If he does testify, he may be cross-examined thoroughly. In minor misdemeanor cases, where the defendant has no previous convictions and makes a good witness, he probably should testify. The defendent should not testify if the prosecutor can prove his case on cross-examination by getting him to admit facts proving guilt.

[8.98]   ## 16. The Burden of Proof and Reasonable Doubt

The prosecutor must prove the defendant guilty beyond a reasonable doubt. He has the burden of presenting a case that is clear and convincing. If there is reasonable doubt about the defendant's guilt, then the finding must be *not guilty*.

L. DEFENSES

1. Accident   [8.99]

Accidents can happen. If a hunter accidentally discharges his gun and kills someone else in his party, the death may be ruled accidental, and not a crime.

2. Alibi   [8.100]

An accused person may be able to prove that he could not have committed the crime because he was somewhere else at the time. He will need another witness to back up his story (*corroboration*).

3. Lack of Capacity   [8.101]

A person may not have the requisite mental capacity to commit a crime. The law says that children under a certain age (which varies from state to state) or mentally retarded persons are presumed to be incapable of committing certain crimes. A five-year-old boy who strangles his two-year-old sister lacks the legally required mental capacity to commit the crime of homicide. *Insanity* is a defense to a charge of homicide. The defense of insanity generally requires that the accused criminal lacked the mental capacity to understand the wrongfulness of his act and to conform his conduct to the law, or, to put it another way, he either did not know that what he was doing was wrong or was unable to control himself sufficiently to avoid committing the act. The application of these rules varies from state to state. *Physical incapacity* such as that brought about by an overdose of drugs or alcohol is generally not a defense to crime unless it was administered forcibly or without the knowledge and consent of the accused. Where a particular state of mind is an element of the crime charged, intoxication of the accused may be taken into consideration.

[8.102]   4.   Civil Disobedience

Some people erroneously believe that they should not be punished for violating a law "in good conscience" because they believed it to be a bad law. Such conduct is sometimes called *civil disobedience.* Anyone who violates the law should be prepared to pay the penalty, if he is convicted, regardless of his moral reasons for violating that law. If he is correct in believing the law is unconstitutional, his conviction can be reversed on successful appeal, and he will then be vindicated.

[8.103]   5.   Consent

In certain cases, consent of the *victim* is a defense. An example would be in rape trials; if the victim consents to sexual intercourse, then there is no rape (unless she is below the *age of consent*).

[8.104]   6.   Entrapment

Entrapment occurs when a person is tricked into committing a crime by the police. In such a case he may plead entrapment if the crime was planned by the police and he was somehow persuaded to commit it.

[8.105]   7.   Former Jeopardy

You can't be tried more than once for the same crime, by the same court. That would constitute *double jeopardy,* and a plea of *former jeopardy* could be entered to the charges brought in the second trial (see Section 11.7).

8. Immunity

[8.106]

Where there are no witnesses to a crime other than the participants, there may be no way to get a conviction unless one of the participants can be persuaded to testify against the others in return for immunity from prosecution. For example, Linda Kasabian was granted immunity from prosecution for murder and other crimes in return for her testimony against the other members of the *Manson family* in the *Tate* murder case. Foreign diplomatic agents are immune from arrest and prosecution.

9. Moral Purpose

[8.107]

Moral purpose or *benevolent motives* are no defense. A sympathetic doctor who gives in to his patient's pleas for an overdose of a pain-killing drug to put him permanently out of his misery is guilty of murder.

10. Reasonable Doubt

[8.108]

The accused can successfully defend himself by creating just a reasonable doubt within the minds of the jurors on the question of whether or not he did in fact commit the crime.

11. Self-Defense

[8.109]

You have the right to defend yourself if attacked by another. You also have the right to defend a third person who is being criminally attacked. You may use reasonable force to protect your property. What is reasonable depends upon the circumstances (see Section 9.36). In other words, although you may commit a technical *battery* by physically preventing another person from committing a criminal act, your conduct is excused or justified because you may have a legitimate claim for self-defense, defense of others, or defense of property, depending upon the circumstances.

[8.110]   **12. Statute of Limitations**

A *statute of limitations* within a defense context is a law that requires that an accused person be prosecuted within a certain period of time after he has committed the crime. Depending upon the crime, or circumstances, and the jurisdiction involved, the statute of limitations may be available as a defense (see Section 5.8).

[8.111]   **13. Unequal Protection of the Law**

The constitution requires *equal protection of the law* for all persons (see Section 11.10). A possible defense to a criminal charge would be proof of the fact that the particular law was enforced only against members of a minority group.

[8.112]   **14. Violation of Due Process**

The Constitution of the United States requires *due process* in all proceedings. An accused person who can prove that his rights were violated by an improper interrogation, that he was apprehended by means of an unlawful arrest, or that he was convicted by means of evidence that was unlawfully seized can secure his release from an appellate court after having the trial court decision reversed for a violation of due process of law (see Section 11.8).

M. CONVICTION [8.113]

The judge or jury *convicts* the defendant by finding him guilty. If several charges have been brought, the defendant may be convicted or *acquitted* of all or any of the charges.

After conviction, a criminal can be put on probation, *fined* or *sentenced* to prison. He may also be ordered confined to a mental institution if he is found to be insane. After serving a portion of his sentence he may be released on *parole*. Criminal statutes generally set minimum and maximum penalties for each crime. The exact punishment is determined by the judge, in most cases, sometimes based on recommendations of official boards or departments whose job it is to determine the most appropriate punishment for the convicted criminal. Things of importance in determining the nature of the punishment include the type of crime, the age, sex, intelligence, and past record of the criminal, his motivation for the crime, his attitude toward the court and toward himself and society, and, unfortunately, at times *political considerations*. Political considerations include a lot of things such as how much money, power, or social influence the defendant or his family may have (example, the *Kennedy-Kopeckne* case), or to what extent public opinion has been aroused (example, the *Lindbergh* kidnapping case), or to what extent some particular group is able to bring pressure to bear (example, the *Bobby Seale* trial), or to what extent special interests or national security may be involved (example, the *Sirhan* case).

Misdemeanor sentences are served in the county jail. Felony sentences are served in the state prison or in the federal penitentiary. Minors or those subject to juvenile court proceedings may be sentenced to youth correctional facilities, work camps, or specialized institutions for rehabilitating youth.

Conviction can result in loss of driver's license, loss of professional license, loss of the right to vote, loss of right to serve as a commissioned officer in the armed forces or to hold a civil service job in the government, and in some cases, forfeiture of property.

After the punishment has been set and the criminal

sentenced for a specified term, he may be eligible for parole, which means he can be released early, on good behavior, and must report to a parole officer until he has served his parole. Naturally, first-time offenders get off easier than second- or third-time losers. Habitual criminals may be sentenced to life in prison.

If the sentence is for either a fine or confinement but the sentence is suspended and the person is put on probation, that means he must not commit any other criminal act within the period of probation. If he does, then the original fine and/or sentence can be reimposed as well as a new fine or sentence for the later crime.

Taking the laws of all of the fifty states together, there is a tremendous amount of difference in minimum and maximum penalties prescribed by statute for the various criminal offenses. Perhaps someday the laws may be standardized throughout the states so that the same act will constitute a crime in all states, and the policy for fine and sentence will be the same in all states.

Most misdemeanors result in sentences of up to six months in jail, and fines of up to $500. In a great many cases there is only a fine, or only a sentence, with the sentence being suspended and the person being placed on probation. Punishment of criminals is based upon the principles of *retribution* against the convicted criminal for the wrong done to society, and *deterrence*. The punishment is supposed to deter the convicted criminal from repeating his crime, and to deter the rest of society by making an example of him.

O. AFTER THE TRIAL

A defendant who has been convicted can file a *motion for new trial*. In his motion he (or his attorney) alleges that errors have been committed during the trial by the judge or by the prosecuting attorney, or that irregularities occurred in the jury's deliberations. This is no field for amateurs, and anyone who has gone so far as to handle his own defense and lost should certainly seek the aid of a lawyer before attempting to file a motion for a new trial. The same would be true of the filing of an appeal (see Section 5.44). There are strict time limits and definite formal requirements for filing an appeal and it should only be done by someone familiar with the process. The appellate court will review the briefs filed by both sides, and may listen to oral arguments. The appellate judges try to determine whether or not the trial was fair and the result justified by the evidence presented. The result of an appeal may be that the judgment is *affirmed*, or it may be *reversed* with the conviction set aside, or the punishment reduced, or a new trial granted.

P. DEATH PENALTY

The death penalty (*capital punishment*) was pronounced unconstitutional by the United States Supreme Court in 1972 by a 5 to 4 split vote. The Justices decided that the way the penalty was applied ("freakishly," according to one) was its major defect. The decision left open the possibility of a mandatory death penalty in certain cases (such as the killing of a prison guard by an inmate.) Since then some states have passed new death penalty laws which provide for mandatory death sentences for persons convicted of certain crimes, such as mass murders, killing a policeman or prison guard, or killing during the commission of another crime like robbery or burglary (see Section 11.6).

Q. VICTIMS OF CRIME

Some states provide compensation for the direct victims of criminal activity. This is on the theory that if we can't succeed in stopping crime or in protecting the victims of crime, the least we can do is to compensate the victims who have suffered from criminal activity.

Other laws have been adopted for the purpose of rewarding or aiding those who have helped victims or potential victims of crime. The Good Samaritan who goes to the aid of his neighbor should be compensated for any injury he receives as a result of his good acts. By helping to prevent a crime, he is doing a service to the rest of society, and society should be willing to pay for that service.

IX. Civil Wrongs (Torts)

A. HOW ARE TORTS AND CRIMES RELATED? [9.1]

A *tort* is a wrongful act which results in injury to another's person, property, business, emotional well-being or reputation, and for which the injured person is entitled to be paid by the wrongdoer. The law imposes a duty to refrain from such injuries to other persons, and requires the wrongdoer to compensate the injured party. A single act can constitute both a crime and a tort. A person throwing a Molotov cocktail into a building could be prosecuted for the crime of arson, and could also be sued by the property owner for damage done to the building.

B. PERSONAL TORTS

[9.2]   1.   Assault

Assault is an unlawful attempt to harm another person, resulting in making that person afraid that he will be hurt, or at least physically offended. A threat with a loaded gun would constitute an assault. Even if the gun were unloaded but the person being threatened did not know that it was empty, it could be an assault. Similarly, a threat to kick or hit a person, or to stab him or strike him with some object, or to throw something at him, or to turn a hose on him, or to unleash a dog on him, or a threat to hit him with a moving automobile or some other vehicle—all of these and any similar acts would constitute assaults (see Section 8.7).

[9.3]   2.   Battery

Battery goes beyond assault and means the actual touching or striking of another person's body without his consent. The battery does not have to be physically harmful. It is sufficient if the mere touching is offensive to the person who has not consented to be touched (see Section 8.8).

[9.4]   3.   Defamation

Defamation is an unprivileged (see Section 9.30) attack upon the reputation of another person. It is *slander* if it is oral, *libel* if it is written. To be *defamatory*, the attack must tend to harm the reputation of the person being defamed by holding him up to the hatred, contempt, or ridicule of others. Defenses to a defamation action such as *truth* and *privilege* will be discussed in sections 9.29 and 9.30. In order for a statement to be defamatory, it must be *published*, which means *communi-*

cated to some third party. For example, if a boss unjustifiably accuses one of his employees of being a thief within earshot of another employee, the slander has been published and the employee whose reputation has been damaged can sue his boss. If the employee who overheard the accusation repeats it to another employee, that constitutes a separate act of slander for which the gossiping employee can also be sued. If the defamatory remark tends to injure a person in his trade, business, or profession, it is called *slander per se.* In such a case the person who has been defamed does not have to prove that the defamation has actually damaged him dollarwise in order to be awarded money damages by the court.

4. False Imprisonment [9.5]

False imprisonment does not mean being tossed in jail improperly (although it can include false arrest—see Section 8.69). It does mean unlawful restriction of a person's freedom of movement—for example, locking a person in a room or inside a car against his will. The person confined must be aware of the confinement, he must not consent to it, and the confinement must be intended by the party responsible for it. An accidental confinement is not false imprisonment, as for example the accidental locking of a customer inside a store. The confinement need not last very long, and physical force need not be used. Mere threats are enough. A gas station attendant committed false imprisonment when he drained the water from the radiator of a customer's car to prevent her from leaving until the police could come to settle their dispute. The restaurant manager who prevents a patron from leaving because he mistakenly believes the patron has not paid his bill can be sued for false imprisonment. Store managers who want to detain suspected shoplifters for questioning have to be very careful.

Some jurisdictions permit them to do this, others do not. The problem for the store owner arises only if he detains an innocent person, because no one actually guilty of shoplifting is going to recover for false imprisonment because he was detained for questioning. In most states, if the store manager had *reasonable cause* to believe a person had pocketed some merchandise without paying for it, he would be within his rights to use reasonable force to detain that person until the police arrived. Such detention, for a brief period, would not be false imprisonment.

[9.6]   5.   Fraud

Fraud is sometimes called *misrepresentation*. When someone makes a false statement to you, intending you to rely upon it, and you rely upon it and are consequently damaged, fraud has occurred. To collect for fraud you must prove that a statement of fact was made to you, that the statement was false, that the person making it knew the statement was false (or had no reasonable basis for believing that it was true), that you relied upon the statement, that the person making it intended you to rely upon it, and that you were damaged because you relied on it. For example, if you bought a house without obtaining a termite inspection report (which would not be very smart), and you did so because the seller told you the property was inspected recently and there were no termites (and you were foolish enough to believe him and not ask for a copy of the report), and you relied upon that statement to go ahead and buy the house and it turned out later that the statement was false (that the house was not inspected, or that it was inspected and found to be infested with termites), you could sue him for fraud. (You might also have an action against him in contract, which is covered in Part IV). In such a case you

could return the house and get back your money, or you could
collect the difference between what you paid for the house and
what it was really worth, with termites.

6. Insults   [9.7]

In some states you may find *insult statutes* which were
originally passed to keep the peace and to cut down on the
number of duels. Such statutes enable you to sue those who
insult you by vicious and obscene language. In some cases the
law also permits the suing of an employee of a railroad, ocean
liner, or airline who uses abusive language, or a hotel clerk or
motel clerk who mistakenly accuses a couple trying to register
of not being married. The law also protects you from over
aggressive bill collectors representing collection agencies who
specialize in high-pressure tactics and make use of insulting
language (see Section 7.93).

7. Negligence

a.   REASONABLE MAN STANDARD   [9.8]

Negligence is doing something that a reasonably careful and prudent person would not do, or failing to do
something such a person would do under the circumstances. The person who should have foreseen that an
accident, damage, or injury could result from his carelessness can be held liable to those who have been damaged as
a result. The law sets up a standard of conduct, sometimes
called the *reasonably prudent man standard*. In the case of
a child, the standard is sometimes modified to mean *a
reasonably prudent child of similar age, intelligence, and
experience.* What this means is that each person must act

in accordance with that standard. If you allow your conduct to fall below that standard and commit a careless act or forget to do something you should do out of carelessness, you are then said to be negligent. For example, you back your car out of the driveway without looking first. Or you park your car on a hill and walk away without setting the parking brake first. In the one case you have a negligent *act* and in the other case you have a negligent *omission* (failure to set the brake).

[9.9]

b. PROXIMATE CAUSE

In order to be liable for negligence, the negligent act must cause some damage to someone—the damage must be *proximately caused* by the negligence. For example, backing the car out of the driveway without looking would be the *proximate cause* of an accident involving a vehicle that happened to be passing your driveway at that moment. Suppose, because of the negligence of the railroad, the warning signals at a grade crossing are not working, but while a train is approaching a vehicle is stalled upon the tracks, so that when the train comes along it cannot avoid hitting the vehicle. In this case the negligence of the railroad in not maintaining the warning signals is not the proximate cause of the accident; the proximate cause is the stalling of the vehicle on the tracks.

A more common example would be the wearing of seat belts. In some states it is now the law that passengers must wear seat belts in automobiles. If they do not have their seat belts on and as a result are thrown through the windshield in a head-on collision, their recovery for their injuries may be greatly reduced or entirely eliminated when they attempt to sue the negligent driver of the other car who violated their right of way. In such a case the court would say that they were *contributorily negligent* in not wearing their seat belts (see Section 9.11). The belts, if used properly, would prevent passengers from being thrown through the windshield. However, if they were not hit head-on, but were struck from the rear and suffered whiplash injuries to their necks, the fact that they were not wearing seat belts would not be a proximate cause of any injury to them (wearing the belts would not prevent the whiplash) so they would be able to recover from the negligent driver of the vehicle that struck them.

What is the amount of harm for which a negligent person is responsible? The answer is that he is responsible in most cases for whatever harm is *reasonably foreseeable* at the time of his careless act. For example, a worker who carelessly drops a large metal object into the hold of a ship full of inflammable materials could be liable for the destruction of the ship if the metal object strikes a spark that causes an explosion and fire.

c. *LAST CLEAR CHANCE* [9.10]

The law of negligence is complex. The doctrine of *last clear chance* is a complicating factor that occasionally changes the outcome of a case. Suppose you are backing your car out of the driveway without looking. Having done that, your car stalls in the middle of the street. Half a block away a cement truck is lumbering toward you. The driver watches you back out of the driveway, notices the car stopping in the middle of the road, but for some reason does not immediately apply his brakes but waits until it is too late to stop, and then hits you. Under the law of *last clear chance* he would be liable to you, even though you were negligent, because he had the last clear chance to avoid the accident (by timely application of his brakes) and he failed to do so.

[9.11]

d. CONTRIBUTORY NEGLIGENCE

Some states allow *contributory negligence* as a defense in a negligence case. Where this law is enforced, a person is held responsible for his own safety. If he fails to be reasonably prudent about it, it may prevent him from recovering for injuries proximately caused by the negligence of another person. An example would be a person who crosses the street without looking. His negligence in so doing would be called contributory negligence, and this would stop him from recovering from the motorist who was negligently inattentive in running into him with his car. The classic example of negligence and contributory negligence is the case of two automobiles colliding at an intersection, where, had either one of the drivers observed a reasonable degree of caution, there would not have been an accident. In such a case neither driver can recover from the other in states following this doctrine.

[9.12]

e. COMPARATIVE NEGLIGENCE

Some jurisdictions do not follow the contributory negligence rule, but follow the *comparative negligence* rule. Under that rule the judge or jury compares the negligence of both parties and may make a partial award of damages to the party who was *less* responsible for the accident, even though he was not entirely free from fault.

[9.13]

f. GROSS NEGLIGENCE

Gross negligence means conduct that is not merely *plain* negligent but is *very* negligent. Is the difference important? The answer is yes, under certain conditions. One such condition would be in a jurisdiction having a *guest statute.*

g.   GUEST LAWS   [9.14]

In states having *guest statutes,* if you are a passenger in an automobile and the driver negligently involves the vehicle in an accident, you cannot recover damages from him if he was only *ordinarily negligent.* (This would not be true if you were a *paying passenger* as opposed to a guest.) However, if he were guilty of *gross negligence,* you could recover in that state, even though you were a guest. Determining whether you are a guest or a paying passenger is not always simple. You may be buying gas and sharing expenses and still be a guest, in some cases. Guest statutes may be unconstitutional because they deny equal protection of the law (see Section 11.10).

h.   ASSUMPTION OF RISK   [9.15]

If you go to a hockey game and sit in an area where you could get hit by a flying puck, under the law you have assumed the risk of being so struck. This *assumption of the risk* would prevent you from being able to recover for a loss of teeth or other injuries. In order to assume the risk, you must be aware of the nature of the risk. Thus, although you may assume the risk of getting hit by a flying puck, you would not necessarily assume the risk of getting hit by a hockey stick that one of the players threw at another player in the middle of a fight. If you go to an amusement park and ride on the ferris wheel, or go to a ski resort and ride the chair lift, you may see signs saying that you use this equipment at your own risk. This does not mean you cannot recover from the management if you are injured because the equipment is negligently maintained. It means you assume the risk of obvious hazards such as falling out of the chair if you are not careful. It does not mean that you assume the risk that the equipment will break down and you will suffer frostbite while suspended in the air, or that you will get a whiplash injury because of a sudden jolt in the cable or mechanism. A close question would be accepting a ride as a passenger in a car driven by a drunk. If you knew he was drunk, you probably assumed the risk of getting involved in an accident by agreeing to ride with him. If you knew he had had a drink or two but did not think he was intoxicated to the point that his ability to drive was impaired, then you have perhaps not assumed the risk. If you ride with a drunk but, through no fault of his, you are injured when the car is struck by another vehicle, you have not assumed that risk, and could recover from the driver of the other vehicle. In such a case you could also say that the negligence of the driver of your car in attempting to drive while intoxicated (which might also be gross negligence) was not a *proximate cause* of being struck by another carelessly driven vehicle (provided the intoxicated driver of your car did nothing to contribute to the collision).

[9.16]

i. DUTY TO OTHERS

In order for you to be liable for negligent conduct, you must have failed to perform a duty to some other person who was injured as a result. If you had no legal duty to that person, then there is no negligence. To put it another way, you don't have a duty to avoid carelessly injuring a trespasser on your property whose presence is unknown to you. If you drop some junk out of your attic window in the middle of spring cleaning and it hits somebody walking below who is, unknown to you, trespassing upon your property, you should not be liable to him for negligence because you had no duty to watch out for such an unknown trespasser (see Section 10.33). In most states the law does not place the duty upon you to help other people who are injured or in trouble. There may be a moral duty to be a Good Samaritan, but there is no legal duty. Thus you have no legal duty to go to the aid of a drowning swimmer. However if you do go to his aid and accidentally amputate his foot with your outboard motor while trying to save him, you might be held liable for negligence. In that case, the jury would no doubt take into consideration your actions in trying to save him, and might even figure that he is better off out of the grave with one foot than in the grave with both feet.

8. Res Ipsa Loquitur [9.17]

These words, translated from the Latin, mean "the thing speaks for itself." The classic example of a *res ipsa loquitur* case is the man walking along the sidewalk who is hit on the head by a barrel of flour that rolls out the window of a factory. He can't prove that any certain person is responsible for his injuries, but the court would say that "the thing speaks for itself," meaning that under ordinary circumstances a barrel of flour does not roll out of a window unless somebody has been damned careless. Another example is the patient who finds out a month after his operation that somebody left a surgical instrument in his stomach. He doesn't know who did it, but *somebody* must have been careless. Generally he sues the surgeon, the hospital, the anesthesiologist, the nurses, and everyone else he can think of. When it comes to trial, he merely proves the fact that the instrument was left in his stomach, and it is up to the defendants to prove that they didn't do it. (These cases are usually settled without going to trial.) Where the doctrine applies, the injured party merely proves that he was injured, and it is up to each defendant to prove that it was not his fault. If he can't do so, he is liable. There are other requirements for *res ipsa*—the instrument that caused the injury must have been under the exclusive control of the defendants, and the injury must not have been due to any act of the plaintiff.

[9.18]   9.   Malicious Prosecution

This involves an action for damages against a person who maliciously brings a criminal or civil action against another. If your business competitor sued you, not because he had a legitimate claim but because he wanted to harass you, and you succeeded in defending yourself from his suit, then you could sue him for malicious prosecution. To be successful, you would have to prove that he did not have reasonable or probable cause to sue you in the first place and that he acted maliciously. If you were able to prove this, you could probably get *punitive damages* (in addition to compensatory damages).

[9.19]   10.   Invasion of Privacy

A good recent example of this type of suit is Ralph Nader's suit against General Motors and others. Nader claimed that General Motors had hired detective agencies to poke into his private life, to hound him with ceaseless investigations and surveillances, and to write reports about him in order to try to discredit his consumer crusade. He sued General Motors, and the other defendants, for *invasion of privacy* (among other things). The case was settled for a very large amount of money. Mr. Average Citizen has a right to privacy, which means that other people do not have the right to expose his private life to public view. Unfortunately for the public servant, the well-known entertainer, or the big-name politician, the right is not quite the same. By becoming public figures, they subject themselves to a certain amount of invasion of privacy which the ordinary citizen would not have to put up with. Thus Elizabeth Taylor is forced to put up with a constant "invasion" of her private life which exceeds what the ordinary citizen would have to put up with.

11. Infliction of Emotional Distress [9.20]

The crank who calls to tell the lady that her husband has been killed in an automobile accident or that her son has been killed in Vietnam, or the obscene telephone caller who repeatedly picks on one victim, can be sued for *intentional infliction of emotional distress*. In such an action the *victim* can recover compensatory damages for injuries to his mental or emotional state, and can also probably recover punitive damages where it is clear that the other person acted maliciously. In some cases negligent infliction of emotional distress may permit recovery of damages. One example would be where a funeral parlor negligently mixes up bodies and has the wrong body on display at a funeral when the bereaved and the guests arrive to view the remains.

12. Inducing Breach of Contract [9.21]

The law protects contractual relationships between parties. Suppose you have a written contract with your gardener that has a year to run. Your neighbor, knowing that you have this contract, convinces the gardener to stop working for you and to come to work for him instead, at a higher rate of pay. If he was motivated by the intent to interfere with your contractual relationship with your gardener, you could sue him for damages for inducing breach of contract. Of course you would have to prove that you had been damaged. Under similar circumstances, if your neighbor had no idea that the gardener worked for you but merely offered to hire him at a rate of pay that turned out to be higher than what you were paying him, and the gardener broke the contract with you on his own volition and went to work for your neighbor, you would have an action against your gardener for breach of contract, but not against your neighbor for inducing breach of contract.

[9.22] ### 13. Conversion

Conversion means the unlawful use or disposal of property belonging to another. If you loaned your lawn mower to your neighbor and he sold it to someone else, you could sue your neighbor for conversion. If you found something that someone else had lost and made no effort to find its owner, but used it yourself, that could be conversion (see Section 14.3).

C. TRESPASS

1. Trespass to Personal Property [9.23]

This is sometimes called *trespass to chattel,* chattel meaning *personal,* as opposed to *real* property. If someone slashed your tires with a knife, threw a rock through your windshield, or poisoned your dog, you could sue him for trespass to chattel and recover damages.

2. Trespass to Real Property [9.24]

Under ordinary circumstances (unless some kind of legal privilege exists), one does not have legal right to intrude upon the private property of another. You have a right to keep people off your private property, and if they or their children or pets intrude upon your property, you can sue for trespass and collect any damages that may have resulted from the act of trespass. Farm and ranch owners can sue hunters, fishermen, motorcycle and jeep riders, and similar types who come on their property without permission (see Section 10.33).

D. STRICT LIABILITY

In some cases the law allows recovery against a person for the damages he caused even though he did not act intentionally and was not guilty of any negligent conduct. It is said that when a person engages in the type of conduct or activity which is *ultrahazardous*, or which imposes an extraordinarily high risk of harm to others, that he will be liable for any harm that results, whether or not he was at fault. If a man stores dynamite in his tool shed in a residential area and, through no fault of his, it blows up and injures his neighbor, the neighbor can sue him. The same would be true if he kept a pet mountain lion on his property and it escaped and injured a neighbor's child. A man who builds a swimming pool which later, through no fault of his, collapses and floods out his neighbor living on the next lower lot, will be liable for the damage in some states.

In the area of food and drugs, or any substances used on or taken into the human body, the law is especially strict. If you get food poisoning from eating or drinking something you bought, you can sue and collect damages without having to prove that the food or drink was contaminated because of someone's negligence or carelessness. The same is true in the case of products such as automobiles or airplanes, which are potentially hazardous if not properly constructed. If your defective steering gear breaks and you run into a tree, the automobile manufacturer is going to be liable to you even if he carefully manufactured and carefully inspected the vehicle before it was sold (provided there was a flaw in it when it left his hands) (see Section 7.43).

E. MALPRACTICE

It will probably come as no surprise to you to know that doctors and hospitals can be sued for *malpractice*. You should know that lawyers, accountants, dentists, engineers, architects, and indeed any professional person from whom you obtain professional services or advice can be liable to you if the service is substandard or the advice is incorrect. An obvious case would be the doctor who amputates the wrong limb, a dentist who pulls the wrong tooth, an accountant who makes a mistake in the figures, a lawyer who allows a statute of limitations to run on your action without filing suit, or an architect whose house collapses. By what standards are these men judged as to the performance of their professional duties? The answer is that they are judged by their own professional standards. Malpractice means the negligent or careless or substandard practice of one's profession. Whether conduct in a given case is malpractice or not is determined by the judge or the jury. In deciding this question, they will listen to the testimony of other men or women within the same profession who will say whether or not they think malpractice occurred. The big problem in malpractice is getting other professionals to testify against their colleague. Sometimes you may have to go to a medical association or bar association, etc., for assistance in finding help. In a small town you may have to go out of town in order to find a professional who will testify against a colleague, because no one who lives and works in the same town and who is associated professionally from time to time with a person, wants to appear against him in court as a witness.

F. DEFENSES

There are many possible defenses to a suit in tort, including those that follow.

[9.27]   1.   Lack of Specific Intent

Battery involves intentional physical contact with another person. If you accidentally stumbled and fell against another person, this would not constitute battery.

[9.28]   2.   Consent

Certain torts require a lack of consent in order to create a cause of action. If you consent to someone borrowing your car, you cannot sue him for trespass to chattel. A girl who requested a doctor to give her a physical examination could not later sue the doctor for battery for touching her private parts. In order to be a defense, consent must be freely given; it must be given by a person old enough or having the mental capacity to understand the nature and significance of the consent; and it must be given with proper understanding of the circumstances. A girl might consent to have sexual intercourse with a boy, but not with his three friends. In some cases the law does not allow the defense of consent. Statutory rape is such a case (see section 8.13).

[9.29]   3.   Truth

Truth is one of several defenses against a defamation action. An employee may sue his boss for calling him a thief in the presence of other employees, but if the boss proves the charge was true, then the employee cannot collect.

4. Privilege [9.30]

In the area of defamation, there are several privileges which constitute defenses against actions for slander or libel. For example, a newspaper reporter is allowed to make *fair comment* about your actions if they are newsworthy. To successfully sue a newspaper, magazine, or radio or television station for what was said about your involvement in a public event, you would have to prove actual malice or calculated falsehood on the part of the defendants. Similarly, a literary or film critic is permitted to make fair comment about a book or a movie. The law permits defamatory statements to be made in a courtroom by lawyers, judges, and witnesses. Such statements are *privileged*. Congressmen can make statements on the floor, as congressmen, that they would not have immunity for if they made them as private citizens. A boss can tell his bookkeeper that he thinks one of the employees is stealing petty cash, and ask him to check up on it. You may be privileged to go on another person's property to retrieve a hub cap that has fallen off your car and not be liable for trespass. In any tort action it is not enough to ask whether a wrongful act has been committed. You must also ask whether there exists some privilege which would excuse the conduct under the circumstances.

5. Lack of Proximate Cause [9.31]

In section (9.9), *proximate cause* was discussed as an essential element of a negligence action. An obvious defense to a negligence action is proof that the alleged negligence was not the proximate cause of the injury. If you were driving without a license, and a child darted out from between two parked cars into the path of your automobile, and was injured as a result, your negligence in driving without a license would not be the proximate cause of injury to that child.

[9.32]   6.   Contributory Negligence of the Plaintiff

As discussed previously (Section 9.11), contributory negligence is, in some jurisdictions, a defense in any action for negligence. If you are sued by another motorist, you can defend yourself by proving that he was *contributorily negligent.*

[9.33]   7.   Assumption of Risk by the Plaintiff

As discussed earlier (Section 9.15), certain activities involve risks, and therein lies a possible defense. If your friend invites himself along on your canoeing trip, and you point out the obvious hazards of canoeing to him, and he loses some valuable camera equipment when the canoe capsizes, you might defend the claim that he makes by pointing out that he assumed the risk that the canoe would capsize.

[9.34]   8.   Lack of Capacity

A very young child may not be capable of committing an intentional tort, such as battery, or may lack the intelligence and experience to be guilty of negligent conduct.

[9.35]   9.   No Damage or Nominal Damage

Even if you are found liable for a tort, if you can prevent the plaintiff from proving he was really damaged or injured, the damages awarded might be very little (*nominal*) or even nothing at all.

10. Self-Defense   [9.36]

As discussed in Section 8.109, you may defend yourself
with the use of reasonable force against an attack by another
person. The amount of force must be reasonable under the
circumstances, and must not exceed that which is necessary to
stop the attack.

11. Defense of Others   [9.37]

You also may use reasonable force to protect members of
your family from an attack. This includes friends and even
strangers. Be sure you saw the beginning of the fight that you
are attempting to stop, or you may assume that the wrong
person started it. You should also be sure that the people
fighting want your help, or at least that one of them does—
otherwise you may find yourself outnumbered in the fight and
outflanked in the courtroom if any charges are brought against
you.

12. Defense of Property   [9.38]

If you have property, either real property or personal
property, you can use a reasonable amount of force to stop
someone from taking it from you or damaging it. What is
reasonable will depend upon the circumstances. If you blast a
boy stealing your son's bike with your shotgun, that could be
manslaughter. If you use just enough force to stop him and hold
him until the police arrive, you are not liable for battery even if
he suffered some bruises as a result. Defense of property can
turn into self-defense very quickly if the thief or burglar you
surprise in your home threatens you with a weapon. In such a

case you may assume your life is in danger and act accordingly. Unless he runs before you have a chance to do anything, you may use whatever force or weapon you have handy. Of course, if you "have the drop" on him and have some experience in these matters, you could disarm him and call the police. However, a woman who is alone at home when an intruder breaks in will probably not have more than one chance to protect herself and the chance should not be wasted by worrying about legal consequences.

[9.39] **G.** INSURANCE AGAINST TORT LIABILITY

The best defense against a tort action is a good insurance policy. An automobile public liability, property damage and medical pay insurance policy is a *must* for everyone who owns and/or drives an automobile. The public liability limits should not be less than $100,000. It costs very little more to increase the limits from $100,000 to $500,000, and if you kill or critically injure a "breadwinner," the case may be worth more than $1,000,000 (see Section 9.45). The insurance company is liable for the total cost of defending you and for the amount of any judgment up to the policy limits (and even beyond, if the company refused to accept an offer to settle that was within the policy limits). Your policy should include *uninsured motor-*

ist coverage (some states require this). This will insure you for damages or injuries caused by the operator of an uninsured motor vehicle.

You should also be covered (under your homeowner's policy) for accidents that may happen to other people while they are on your property or in your home. In addition, as a *rider* to that type of policy, you should have some personal public liability insurance that covers you for such things as hitting someone with a golf ball, accidentally shooting someone on a hunting trip, etc. Most insurance policies say that the insurance company will provide a lawyer, pay for the defense, and pay any judgments against you for matters covered by the policy, up to the limits of the policy. You owe it to the rest of the world, as well as to yourself, to carry adequate insurance (see Section 3.86).

H. DAMAGES

[9.40]   ## 1.   Physical Damage

Physical damage may include physical harm to your body or damage to your property. You can collect for both. The amount of property damage is determined by estimates of what it costs to repair the damaged item, or by the actual repair bills. Physical damage to the body is not so easily measured. How do you put a value on a lost leg? It is tough to do, but the judge or jury has to try.

[9.41]   ## 2.   Loss of Money

If a gas station must close down for two weeks for repairs because a negligent motorist wiped out three gas pumps with his pickup truck, the income lost by the owner of the gas station can be determined from a look at his books. That amount in dollars can easily be figured by the judge or jury and can be awarded to the station owner.

[9.42]   ## 3.   General Damages

This is a term used to describe the amount that a judge or jury awards for the pain, suffering, anxiety, and inconvenience endured by a plaintiff who is wrongfully injured by a negligent defendant. In a typical automobile accident case, the *general damages* will normally be the largest single item of damages awarded to the plaintiff.

[9.43]   ## 4.   Special Damages

Special damages means the items that are known exactly, such as hospital and doctor bills, ambulance bill, towing bill, automobile repair bill, prescription drug bill, etc.

5.   Mental and Emotional Distress   [9.44]

The law permits recovery of damages for *mental and emotional distress.* A mother seeing her two-year-old child being run down by a truck is entitled, in some states, to be paid by the negligent driver for her mental and emotional distress for having to see such a thing. If you suffered a great deal of pain as a result of injuries you received in an accident that was the other fellow's fault, you would be entitled to an award for pain and suffering. If scars or other disfigurement were a permanent result, you would be able to recover damages for the mental and emotional distress that you would feel by having to appear in public, in front of friends, etc. with such scars or disfigurement.

6.   Harm to Others or Wrongful Death   [9.45]

Some states allow a wife or husband to recover damages for *loss of consortium* from the party who was negligently responsible for injuring their spouse. *Consortium* covers anything from companionship to sexual satisfaction. Where death is caused by negligence, the decedent's estate can recover for his medical bills, and in some cases for his funeral bills and for his pain and suffering. A widow or children may recover what the decedent would have been expected to earn during his working lifetime, had he lived his normal life expectancy. A widower may recover the cost of hiring a housekeeper to take the place of a wife who was killed. Some states put a top limit on the amount that can be recovered for wrongful death. Parents can recover for the death of their children and vice versa. Until recent years the loss of a child, particularly a younger child, was not worth much, or so juries seemed to think. A defendant was entitled to have the jury instructed that the cost of raising a child would have to be deducted from any amount awarded for loss of the companionship or awarded for loss of potential earnings of the child. Also potential earnings are hard to prove where the child is only five years old at the time he is killed. However, in recent years the trend has been to increase the size of judgments and verdicts for wrongful death of a child. There is a realization of the fact that in spite of the expense of raising them, and in spite of the family turmoil they sometimes cause while growing up, children are, after all, worth something to their parents, and the irreplaceable loss of a child should receive more than a token award of a few thousand dollars.

[9.46]   **7.   Loss of Earnings**

This is generally the second largest item of damages in a case where a person is seriously injured and can't work for a long time. In the case of an employee who worked before the accident, it is easy to figure the amount of his wage loss if you know his time out of work and rate of pay. If he will be permanently prevented from working, you can figure the amount that he would earn over his lifetime, complete with cost of living increases, and fringe benefits, etc.

It gets tougher when the person is self-employed. Then you have to prove a reduction in his future earning capacity by showing what it would have been had he not been injured, and what it is likely to be as a result of the injuries received.

[9.47]   **8.   Loss of Reputation**

In a defamation action, the successful plaintiff is entitled to the amount reasonably calculated to compensate him for his loss of reputation. Loss of reputation damages are difficult to prove. If they can be tied in with loss of income or job opportunities, then it is easier. A professional wrestler would have a tough time convincing a jury he has been damaged by someone calling him a faker. On the other hand a surgeon who was accused of being a "butcher" would easily get an award for substantial damages if he won his case. Mr. Average Citizen who is falsely accused of some small sin in a local social club meeting wouldn't get much in a defamation action.

9. Size of Damage Awards [9.48]

The trend in damage awards has been up, to keep pace with the increase in the cost of living and to reflect greater degree of sophistication among judges and jurors. Juries in cities or metropolitan areas seem to award more than juries in small towns or in rural communities. In many states today, juries do not award as much in civil damage actions (such as automobile accident litigation) as do judges. In such states the insurance company defense lawyers are the ones who demand juries, and not the plaintiff's lawyers. The insurance company defense lawyers feel that they have a better chance of keeping the verdict down with a jury than they do with a judge, or perhaps even getting a defense verdict. This is particularly true in those states having the contributory negligence rule (see Section 9.11). Here the defense is frequently able to convince the jury that the plaintiff was in some small way partially responsible for the accident and therefore should not be entitled to recover anything at all. Jurors are not supposed to know that there is any insurance in the case, but most automobile accident cases that come to trial do involve insurance, whether the jury is told this or not. Most courts prohibit mentioning the fact that insurance is involved in the case on the theory that this will cause the jurors to award more money (see Section 5.27). If one of the witnesses in an automobile accident trial says that the defendant has insurance, then the defense attorney will ask the judge to instruct the jury that "no insurance company is a party to this action." This is supposed to tell the jurors that they should not take into consideration the fact that the defendant is insured in awarding damages to the plaintiff. (However, what it usually does is to confuse the jurors, because it makes them think that the defendant is not insured, when in fact he is.)

In this day and age it is probably unrealistic to assume that jurors are not aware of the fact that there is insurance in automobile accident cases, anyway. Furthermore, the insurance companies do such a good job of propagandizing people into thinking that they are constantly being hit with staggering damage awards in civil cases that a lot of prospective jurors have been brainwashed to one degree or another into believing that the only way they can help to keep their own insurance premiums down is to penalize some poor plaintiff by giving him something less than an adequate award of damages.

There are of course cases where clever plaintiff's lawyers have succeeded in hoodwinking juries into awarding fantastic sums to plaintiffs who really didn't deserve that much money. However, even though these cases always grab the spotlight, they are relatively few and far between, and the average plaintiff is very lucky to get an adequate award out of a jury after paying his attorneys' fees and other expenses of litigation. Judges can and frequently do reduce the size of a jury's verdict where the jury was influenced by an emotional appeal or prejudice to award a fantastically large amount.

Most experienced plaintiff and defense lawyers can very accurately evaluate an accident case for you, once all the facts are known. For this reason 90 percent of these cases never come to trial but are settled beforehand. It is only the ones that are difficult to evaluate, or the ones where liability is not clear, that come to trial. Some cases also come to trial because the plaintiff is overreaching, or because the insurance company is too cheap to make a decent offer.

10. Punitive Damages

[9.49]

Punitive damages (also called *exemplary damages*) can be obtained in a case in which the defendant acted willfully or maliciously. Punitive damages are in effect a penalty to punish the defendant for bad conduct. If your neighbor deliberately and without cause punches you in the nose, you could get punitive damages in addition to your general and special damages. The largest punitive damage awards are usually found in defamation cases where some big publishing company, magazine, or newspaper has published libelous material about a person in order to sell more copies.

11. Costs

[9.50]

The winning party in a lawsuit is entitled to recover his *costs.* Costs do not include attorneys' fees, but include such things as the fee charged by the court for filing a complaint and for issuing other legal documents, fees paid to the sheriff or a private process server for serving summons and complaint, and the cost of depositions. Costs do not include expert witness fees, unless the expert is appointed by the court. In the typical automobile accident or personal injury case, the largest item of expense will be what the plaintiff and the defendant pay their doctors for expert testimony. Doctor's fees run anywhere from $250 to $500 a day for testimony; that does not include the doctor's examinations of the patient or the time the doctor spends talking to the lawyer prior to trial. In a serious injury case in which the plaintiff may have an orthopedist, a neurologist, and an internist testify in his behalf, he may have expert witness fees of over $1000 to pay. These are not recoverable as *costs,* and the jury is usually unaware of the fact that he has to pay these out of his own pocket after he has paid his lawyer. The same, of course, is true of the defendant, but these costs are paid by the insurance company, and if the company has refused to settle a good claim and it gets hit for a large damage award, it should have no complaint about expert witness fees which it might have saved if it had made a reasonable settlement offer.

[9.51]   12. Improving the System

A lot of abuses occur on both sides (plaintiff and defendant) in the civil litigation field. Most of the abuses on the defendant's side are traceable to a few insurance companies and the unscrupulous investigators and claims agents they hire to settle good claims with injured plaintiffs for very small amounts, and by calloused defense counsel who do nothing but try cases for insurance companies and who stake their reputations on how many defense verdicts they get, regardless of whether the plaintiff in a given case has a good case or not. These lawyers are aided by some unethical professional witness doctors who make lots of money by specializing in examining plaintiffs for insurance companies and then appearing in court to testify against the plaintiff for the purpose of minimizing his injuries. Of course, there are other doctors on the plaintiff's side who do the same thing (see Section 5.24). Most of the abuses on the plaintiff's side occur at the hands of a few personal injury lawyers whose firms tend to specialize in handling that type of case and who use unethical methods to obtain that type of business. This type of lawyer is called an "ambulance chaser," but today the methods they use to corner the local market in such cases are much more sophisticated than merely chasing after ambulances (see Section 5.24). Some of these lawyers try to build small injuries into big claims because they increase the size of their fee by getting a big verdict.

13. No-Fault Auto Insurance [9.52]

Partly because of the excesses on both sides of this *adversary system of justice,* some states have considered going to a workmen's compensation or administrative tribunal type of hearing for cases involving injuries resulting from automobile accidents. Others have adopted *no-fault auto insurance systems.* Under such a system (Massachusetts was the first state to adopt one), insurance companies are required to pay actual amounts of their own policy holders' medical bills, wage loss, and other special damages up to a certain limit, regardless of who was at fault in the accident. For damages in larger amounts, litigation is still required. The idea of this is to eliminate the excesses that occur on both sides in small cases and to prevent them from clogging the court calendars, leaving room for the larger cases that are more difficult to settle and perhaps have to be tried.

14. Attorneys' Fees [9.53]

Attorneys' fees are not costs, and are not ordinarily recoverable by either party in an action (see Section 4.37). There are exceptions to this. One exception is in the case of a written agreement providing for payment of attorneys' fees by the loser to the winner of a lawsuit. You will see this provision in a promissory note, a loan agreement, an installment sale contract, or a lease. Attorneys' fees may also be recovered when a statute so provides. Antidiscrimination statutes, anti-trust laws, and truth-in-lending laws are examples of laws that permit the injured party to recover attorneys' fees in addition to damages.

[9.54]   **15. Suing the Government**

If you are injured by a government vehicle or government employee, you should seek legal advice at once. You may sue the government—local, state, or federal—but first you must file a claim. The claim must be in the proper form, and you must file within a short period of time.

X. Real Property

A. PURCHASE AND SALE OF PROPERTY

1. Use of Purchase Agreements [10.1]

Never buy or sell a piece of real property without having an agreement in writing (see Section 4.7). If you are buying a home from a builder or subdivider, he will present you with his contract form and you should review it carefully or have it reviewed by an attorney.

If you are buying a home from another individual and a real estate broker is involved, he will have a form contract which he will present to you for your signature, and he will then take it to the seller for approval.

If you are dealing directly with the buyer or seller of a home, you should be certain that the purchase agreement you use covers at least the following points:

- *Names*: The names of both parties and the date (husbands and wives should both sign) must be included.

- *Description of Property*: The street address, city, and county is used, but it is a good idea to include the legal description if you have it available.

- *Purchase price and deposit*: How much deposit

will be paid down, and to whom will it be paid? Ten percent of the purchase price is an average figure to use; $250 should be a minimum. A deposit ought to be held by a third party such as a title company or a real estate broker's office.

• *Payment of Balance:* How and when will the balance of the purchase price be paid? Will it be in cash, or a combination of cash and a note?

• *Financing*: Will buyer assume seller's loan? Will seller loan money to buyer? Is FHA or VA financing involved (see Sections 10.4 and 10.22)?

• *Escrow*: Where and when will escrow be opened? When will escrow close? Who will pay the costs of escrow (see Section 10.19)?

• *Possession*: Will possession be given at close of escrow? If before or after, will buyer or seller pay rent in the interim?

• *Personal Property*: Personal property included in the sale should be specifically described.

• *Inspections*: Sales should be subject to termite inspection and in some cases plumbing, heating, roof, and appliance inspection.

• *Title*: What type of deed will seller give buyer (see Section 10.16)? What conditions, easements, restrictions, etc. will title be subject to? Are there any assessments? Will buyer obtain a title insurance policy, or an abstract? Will a survey be involved (see Section 10.15)?

• *Taxes and Insurance*: Will real estate taxes be prorated to the close of escrow? Is buyer assuming seller's insurance, and if so, will premiums be prorated to the close of escrow?

- *Commission*: If a commission is involved, who pays and what is the rate?

- *Escrow Deposits and Impounds*: Does the seller have any *impounds* or *deposits* in connection with a loan, and will the buyer pay the seller for these in cash, or will they be included in the buyer's note for the balance of the purchase price (see Section 10.19)?

- *Conditions*: Does the buyer wish to make the purchase subject to obtaining a particular loan such as an FHA loan or a VA loan, or a conventional loan with a maximum interest rate and in a minimum amount? Does the buyer wish to make the purchase contingent on the sale of some other property he owns?

- *Loss in Event of Destruction:* If the premises are destroyed by fire, or otherwise, before close of escrow, who should bear the loss?

- *Changes in agreement*: All changes in any agreement, whether a typewritten agreement, printed form agreement, or handwritten agreement, should be initialed by both parties.

2.   Real Estate Agents [10.2]

A real estate broker is a person whose job it is to bring together the buyer and seller. In return for compensation he will act as a middleman to buy or sell a piece of property for a client. A real estate salesman is employed by a broker to perform the same job. Both a broker and a salesman must be licensed (see Section 4.29). The activities of a broker and salesman are regulated by state law. Violation of any laws or regulations pertaining to a broker or salesman can result in loss of license. A salesman can only earn a commission by working for a broker. He cannot sell property on his own. The commission is paid to the broker who shares it with the salesman who is licensed through the broker.

Real estate agents are not allowed to make *secret profits.* This means they have to disclose the fact that they are acting as principals when they are buying or selling for their own account. It also means that they must disclose to the party who is paying them a commission, any other commission or profit they will make on the deal. Some states require real estate brokers to contribute to a fund which can be used to pay money to persons who are damaged by fraudulent or illegal acts of real estate agents in the event that those agents are unable to pay the damages.

The job of the agent is to handle the advertising and sale of the property if he is requested to do so by the seller. The agent is usually paid by the seller. This doesn't mean that he gives his full allegiance to the seller, however; most brokers consider themselves as middlemen without allegiance to either buyer or seller. If pressed, they will admit that their primary concern is to make the deal on terms acceptable to both parties, and not necessarily to try to get the best possible deal for either the buyer or seller.

If you agree to pay a commission, know exactly what it will be. The average or customary fee on residential property runs between 5 and 7 percent of the total gross sales price. The commission is always negotiable, and if the agent wants your business badly enough, or wants to close the deal badly enough, he will cut his commission.

[10.3]   3.   Commission Agreements

To be enforceable, the agent's commission agreement must be in writing. Don't be reluctant to negotiate the amount of the commission with the agent.

The listing agreement should state how long it lasts. Ninety days or less would be reasonable. You may wish to be able to terminate on ten days' written notice. There are various kinds of listing:

- If you are counting on realizing a certain *net* after commission and sales expenses on the sale of your property, you might consider a *net listing,* which means that the agent can keep as his commission everything that he gets above the *net price.*

- An *open listing* means if you sell the house yourself you don't have to pay a commission, and if some agent other than the listing agent brings in a buyer, he will get the commission.

- *Multiple listing* means that your house will be listed by all brokers. This gives you the widest exposure. A broker producing a buyer will usually split the commission with the *listing broker* (the one who first gets the listing from you).

- In some states it is possible to become liable for a commission even without a written agreement. An example would be where a broker got your permission in a casual conversation to find a buyer for your house, and he did in fact introduce you to a person who bought your house. It is therefore best to have all agreements with brokers in writing and know exactly what you are getting into. Be sure you keep a copy of the agreement.

- An *exclusive agency listing* means that the broker is entitled to a commission even if the property is sold by another broker. However the owner may sell the property himself and will not have to pay a commission.

- An *exclusive right to sell* listing not only makes the broker the sole agent but provides that the broker gets a commission even if the owner sells the property himself without the broker's help. Try to avoid this.

Exactly when the commission is payable depends upon the agreement. If it says payable only upon sale, the broker doesn't get his commission until the deal closes. If it doesn't say that, the broker may be entitled to his commission when he produces a buyer who is willing and able to buy the property on the terms of the listing agreement, even though the sale doesn't go through. If the deal doesn't go through because you (the seller) prevent it, the broker may be entitled to his commission anyway.

Most standard agreements provide for forfeiture of the deposit in the event the buyer doesn't go through with the deal. They also provide that the real estate agent is entitled to some proportion (usually half) of the deposit (but not to exceed the full amount of the commission) in the event of a default by the buyer.

[10.4]   4.   Check List for Buyer

The following are some of the more important items that the buyer of any real property should check out before buying:

- *Purchase Price*: Is it reasonable? Is it negotiable?

- *Title*: Obtain a preliminary title report or an abstract of title and examine it carefully and check out any questionable items.

- *Zoning*: If you plan some use for the property other than its present use, you will have to check on the zoning. If its present use is a *nonconforming use* (see Section 10.48) you will also want to know that.

- *Assessment*: Check with representatives of local municipalities and districts to see whether any bonded improvements are contemplated and whether any assessments are expected to be placed on the property.

- *Liens*: By checking title you will find out if any recent liens have been recorded. Also see whether any recent improvements have been made on the property and whether there might be lien rights that have not yet been filed.

- *Competency of Sellers*: Be sure sellers have the legal capacity (age and mental capacity) as well as legal title to convey.

- *Financing*: Be sure to check on the balances due on any mortgages to be assumed. Check the provisions of the same to see whether they can be assumed without penalty or without increase in interest rate or payment of *points*. Also check to see whether they contain an *acceleration clause* (see Section 10.22). In the event of an FHA mortgage or conventional loan with an *impound,* check on the amount of the impound or reserve account.

- *Possession*: Make sure the seller is in possession of the property, that there are no tenants or other persons living on the property, and that possession can be delivered to you.

- *Insurance:* Make sure insurance will be in effect after close, whether you assume the existing policy or purchase your own.

- *Deposit*: Have deposit held by a title company or a broker or attorney, not by the seller.

- *Personal Property*: Inventory of all personal property and applicances included with the property should be made. Be sure there are no *chattel mortgages* on any of the property.

● *Inspections*: Have termite inspection made, seller to pay for any damage, buyer to pay for any preventative measures. Consider plumbing, heating, and roofing inspection.

● *Title Insurance and Escrow*: Try to get seller to pay for title insurance policy or abstract. Negotiate on who will pay for escrow costs, recording costs, and transfer taxes. Specify date escrow will close. Specify how title will be taken by the buyers (see Section 10.19).

[10.5]   5.   Check List for Seller

● *Commission Agreement*: If you use an agent, do you have a written *commission agreement* that is complete?

● *Mortgage*: Does your *mortgage* contain an acceleration clause or a prepayment penalty (see Section 10.22)?

● *Appraisal*: Have you obtained an *appraisal* of your house? You will need this to get an FHA loan.

● *Impound or Reserve Account*: What is the status of your *impound* or *reserve account* with your lender? Provide for buyer to reimburse seller for the amount of the account in addition to the purchase price of the property.

● *Deposit*: Get an adequate deposit from the buyer and be sure the agreement provides that he forfeits the deposit if he backs out of the deal. Try to get 5 to

10 percent of the purchase price. If the buyer gives you a personal check, don't hold it, but cash it immediately.

• *Title insurance and Escrow Costs*: Try to get the buyer to pay these or to split them (see Section 10.19).

• *Financing Costs*: Try to get the buyer to pay for these, because they are for his benefit (if he is not paying all cash).

• *Insurance*: Try to get the buyer to assume your insurance policies and pay you the prorated amount for the remaining period of the policy. You get more money this way than you will if you have to cancel the policy and ask the company for a rebate.

• *Secondary Financing*: If you take back secondary financing, make sure you have a note that does not have an illegal interest rate (see Section 7.77) and that it is secured by a mortgage or deed of trust that is recorded (see Sections 10.69 and 10.70).

• *Personal Property Included in Sale*: Be sure to specify what is included so that you can take everything else with you. If FHA financing is involved, you may have to list the property separately and have it paid for separately by the buyer.

• *Possession*: Don't give the buyer possession of the premises until escrow has closed, you have received your money, or the down payment and the note for the balance secured by a mortgage or a deed of trust, and you have removed all of your personal property from the premises.

• *Utilities*: Be sure to notify all utility companies to cancel the contract for services in your name so you won't be billed for any utilities furnished after the close of escrow. Also be sure to notify all cleaning services, spray services, gardeners, delivery services, and the post office of the sale.

[10.6]   6.   Options and Contracts of Sale

An *option* is one kind of contract. When used in connection with real property it describes the situation in which the owner of the property (*optionor*) gives to a potential purchaser (*optionee*) the right to purchase the property. The optionee pays something to obtain this right. The term of the option is specified in the agreement. The option agreement itself must contain all the details of the complete purchase agreement, including the price to be paid, how it is to be paid, and the details on close of escrow (see Section 10.19). When would you use an option agreement instead of a purchase contract? One time would be when you wanted to buy a house but didn't want to get committed until you'd found a buyer for your own house. It is awkward sometimes to have to close escrow on the house you are buying when you haven't yet sold your present house, and you find yourself carrying two houses for a while. One way to avoid this would be to buy an option to purchase the second house. Under these conditions you would try to get the option payment to apply to the purchase price in the event you exercised your option. However an option is hard to get on residential property. A more common or more likely example would be a farmer or rancher who has property in the path of development. The buyer is willing to purchase the property, but wants to have a long time to study it, get engineering done, etc., before closing escrow. An owner doesn't want to tie up his property for such a long period of time unless he gets some cash for it right now. Under an option agreement the developer can study the property without any strings attached and he doesn't have to go ahead with the purchase if it turns out the development would be too expensive, or is premature, for example. At the same time the owner gets a reasonable amount of cash to pay for the option and he gets to keep the money even if the deal isn't closed. The option price can be anything at all that the parties agree upon, but generally is equivalent to the *reasonable rental value* of the property over the term of the option. If the property could be rented at $500 a month and the option is for three months, a reasonable option price would be $1500. Buyers like to have option agreements recorded because this protects their right to purchase the property and insures that the seller will be able to deliver title when the option is exercised. Sellers don't like to have options recorded because if the buyer doesn't exercise his option, it still remains on record and unless the buyer executed a quitclaim deed and authorized seller to record it when the option expired, a title search will disclose the option and raise questions until it can be determined that the option has expired.

A *contract of sale* is a particular type of purchase agreement. There is no special form for this agreement. What distinguishes it from an ordinary purchase is that seller hangs on to the title of the property until the buyer has paid the full purchase price. The purchase price is paid in a series of installments which may take many years to complete. All during this time the seller retains title, and if the buyer ever defaults in his payments, he can lose all of his rights under the contract. The purchaser does not have legal title, but he has *equitable* ownership of the property. The seller of the property who still owns it is free to sell his interest to any third party, subject to the contract of sale. The buyer, to protect his interests, should have his contract of sale recorded. The seller, in order to avoid a cloud on his title, should get a *quitclaim deed* (see Section 10.16) from the buyer and have the buyer agree that the quitclaim deed may be recorded in the event the buyer defaults on his contract. If the seller can't get a quitclaim deed from the buyer, after the buyer defaults the seller may have to bring a *quiet title action* (lawsuit to settle a title dispute) in order to clear the cloud from his title which is caused by the recorded contract of sale. The purchaser under a contract of sale may also transfer his interest under the contract to a third party. The third party would then presumably finish making the installment payments. When the final payment is made, the purchaser is entitled to have title transferred into his name.

Supposedly, the advantage to a seller of a contract of sale over a standard purchase agreement is that if the buyer defaults, the seller doesn't have to go through a mortgage foreclosure or deed of trust foreclosure proceeding to get his title back. Because most states have antideficiency judgment statutes (see Section 10.73), there doesn't seem to be much advantage to a buyer in having a contract of sale as opposed to a standard purchase agreement, with the seller taking back a mortgage or deed of trust. Land contracts are usually used to make a sale to a buyer who can only afford to make a very small down payment plus very small monthly payments over a long period of time.

Anyone contemplating buying or selling land under a contract of sale, or anyone involved in a situation where a default in a land contract has occurred, should consult a lawyer. The rules that apply in these situations are tricky and they are not uniform.

[10.7]   7.   Purchase or Sale of Acreage

Anyone buying acreage should have a specific purpose in mind for it. If he intends to use it as farm land, or a tree farm, orchard, or vineyard, then it should be evaluated on that basis by experts in those areas. If he plans to develop it or to hold it for investment purposes, he should check on such things as access, traffic circulation, availability of water, gas and electricity, telephone service, sanitary sewers, storm drains, etc. Some thought should be given to the nature of the soil and any potential problems that may arise in connection with putting septic tanks or drainage fields on the property. Earthquake hazards, annexation (see Section 10.52), and zoning (see Section 10.48) should also be considered. If the property has been subdivided, or the purchaser intends to subdivide it in the future, considerable thought should be given to the applicable subdivision laws and regulations. Many states have laws restricting the splitting up of property into smaller parcels. A typical state statute, for example, would regulate a division of property into five or more parcels of forty acres or less in size. Division into four or less parcels, or division into parcels of more than forty acres might be exempt from state regulation but might be regulated by local ordinances. In addition to state laws, counties and cities may have ordinances regulating the division of property. Where such laws exist it is a criminal offense to violate them. It also means the buyer has questionable title when he purchases an illegally subdivided piece of property.

8.   Subdivision Lots [10.8]

Most states now closely regulate the sale of subdivision lots. The federal government also now regulates the interstate sale of land. Before buying a subdivision lot either in your state or in another state or a foreign country, you should ask for and receive a copy of a *public report* which is issued either by a state government (real estate division) or by the federal government (Office of Interstate Land Sales). This report will describe the property in detail and tell you most of the things you need to know before deciding whether to buy a lot or not. Some of these laws require a developer to give you a copy of this report, and have you sign a receipt for it, following which he has to wait a certain period of time (usually two or three days) before the deal can be closed. During that period of time you have the absolute right to pull out and get all of your money back. If the developer fails to give you a copy of the report before you buy, you also have an absolute right to get your money back. You should read the report very carefully. Before buying be sure you understand how and when streets, water, gas and electricity, and either sewers or septic tanks will be provided. If there are no sewers and lots are to have individual septic tanks, you can't be positive that the lot you've picked out will be suitable for a septic tank until you actually apply for a building permit and submit a design to the local building department. Just because the subdivision in general has been approved for septic tanks does not always mean that every single lot in that subdivision has been approved for septic tanks by the local building inspection department. If, however, you buy a lot that turns out not to be suitable for a septic tank, and therefore you can't build anything on it, you have a right to rescind the contract and get your money back (see Section 4.45).

If you are buying or considering buying a recreational subdivision lot, a good rule to follow is to buy if you plan to build on the lot or put a trailer on it and get some immediate use of it, or plan to hold it for a long-term investment. People who buy solely for the purpose of making a quick profit by selling a lot in a few months are generally disappointed (see Section 10.68). Particularly in connection with recreational subdivisions, consider only the *recreational amenities* that are present and usable, or which the *public report* indicates have been bonded by the developer. Even then, you have to be somewhat careful because the subdivider-developer may have agreed to build amenities that are far less grandiose than the ones the overeager salesman may describe to you. Even though amenities are bonded, that doesn't mean that they will be completed in the time and in the manner that the buyer has been led to expect, in every case.

9.   Apartments [10.9]

Many people today are buying duplexes, triplexes, and apartment houses for investment purposes. There are many books written on the subject of such investments and anyone contemplating entering this field should read one or two of them. The main things to consider in investing in any apartment are listed in Section 10.65.

In addition to the items listed in Section 10.1, an agreement for purchase and sale of an apartment house should contain provisions for the handling of advance rental payments and security deposits of tenants. Rents are prorated to the date of close of escrow and the adjustments are made in the purchase price to take into consideration the rentals and the security deposits.

If you are planning to buy an old apartment and fix it up, you should check with the local building department and find out what the building code will require when you start to remodel. You may find that you are in for a very expensive replumbing and rewiring.

10.   Condominiums and Townhouses [10.10]

Most condominium laws are designed so that the owner of a condominium unit owns everything within the airspace bounded by the interior surfaces of the walls, floors, ceilings, windows, and doors of his unit. The rest of the building, referred to as *common area*—which includes the land itself, walkways, entryways, garages, patios, swimming pools, storage areas, etc.—is owned in *common* by all of the unit owners. Usually the condominium unit owners form an association, which maintains the common areas. A condominium can exist on leased land that is owned by a third party, who leases it to the condominium owners' association. Condominiums are becoming popular because they cost less than single-family homes, yet give most of the advantages of living in a single-family residence. There is less privacy, it is true, but money can be saved on utilities and maintenance, and exterior maintenance such as gardening and painting, etc., is usually taken care of by the association (using dues or assessments collected from the members). One of the nice things about owning a condominium is that you can take a trip for a couple of months somewhere and not worry about what is going to happen to your property while you are away. It is not like renting an apartment because a tenant pays rent to a landlord and doesn't have the tax advantages (deductibility of interest and taxes) that the owner of a condominium has.

Before buying a condominium be sure you carefully read the *declaration of restrictions.* This is a recorded document which describes the property and sets forth certain restrictions on the property that apply to every owner. You should also read the *articles* and *bylaws* of the association (if there is an association) to see what provisions, rules, and regulations they contain that apply to every unit owner.

Townhouses are similar to condominiums, but not quite the same. When you buy a townhouse you actually own the ground on which your dwelling stands. In addition, you may own the exterior walls of your dwelling. However you may have one or two walls in common with adjoining owners. All of the townhouse owners will also usually own in common the open area around the townhouse units, which may include landscaped areas, a swimming pool, etc. The townhouse owners may form an association (similar to a condominium owners' association) that will establish certain rules and regulations for the use of the common areas. Townhouses offer the same advantages as condominiums except that there is a little more privacy, as well as a little more responsibility in maintenance.

11. Stock Cooperatives   [10.11]

Stock cooperatives have been mainly popular in the East. They offer many advantages over rented apartments. In a stock cooperative situation you don't own the apartment and you don't own the interior airspace; instead you own stock in a corporation. The corporation owns the apartment house. As a stockholder you are entitled to occupy a certain apartment within the apartment building. The stockholders are subject to annual assessments for maintenance and operation costs which are paid to the corporation like rent. The cost of the stock is roughly equivalent to the value of the apartment that you will have the right to occupy, plus your share of the remaining facilities of the building such as garage, elevators, etc. By buying stock in a stock cooperative you can get out of the cycle of continually paying rent to a landlord and never having anything to show for it when your lease runs out. If you desire to move you may be able to sell your stock to another individual who then gets the right to occupy your apartment. Some cooperatives, particularly those that are FHA-financed, require the stock to be sold back to the corporation at the same price for which it was purchased. In some cases (particularly in New York City), people have made large profits on the sale of stock in stock cooperatives after living in a stock cooperative apartment for a few years. Of course it is not quite as easy to sell the stock as it would be to sell a single residence, but it is probably just as easy to sell the stock as it would be to sell a condominium or a town house, particularly if you live in an area where stock cooperatives have been around for a number of years and are understood and accepted by the people. The owner of stock in a stock cooperative has many tax advantages over one who merely rents an apartment.

[10.12]   **12. Commercial Property**

If you are thinking about buying commercial property as an investment, you should seek the advice of a qualified realtor specializing in commercial property. There are many great values in commercial property, especially in the so-called "net-net leases," or "triple-net leases." There are many different phrases used and many different meanings attached to those phrases, but most commonly accepted definitions of these terms are as follows: "net" means *taxes,* "net-net" means *taxes and insurance,* "net, net, net" (triple net) means *taxes, insurance, and maintenance.* In other words, with a triple-net lease, the tenant pays, in addition to rent, all the taxes, all the insurance costs, and all the maintenance costs. The best possible investment in commercial property would be commercial property in a good location with a *prime* tenant on a long-term triple-net lease. A *prime tenant* means something like a chain grocery store, a bank, or a large insurance company or title company. In other words, it means someone who is going to be in business for a long time. In investing in commercial property, *location* is extremely important, as are the type and quality of construction. The type of tenant and the type of lease are the other two things to consider. Commercial leases are different from residential leases and anyone unsophisticated in this area should have a lease either prepared or reviewed by a lawyer experienced in this area before investing in commercial property.

13.   Farm and Ranch Property   [10.13]

The buying and selling of farm and ranch property is a very specialized area. Because in most cases large sums of money are involved, it is best to get the property appraised by a qualified appraiser. The purchase will not only include the land, which has to be valued as land, but also farm buildings, farm machinery, growing crops, and perhaps livestock. Each of these items should be valued separately and the purchase price should be allocated among the various items, rather than simply lumping everything together and paying one total price. The land, of course, is not depreciable, but the farm buildings and machinery are, and so may be the livestock. The farm machinery and equipment are depreciable over a shorter period of time than the buildings (see Section 10.17).

Some attention should be given to the question of who has the right to the crop that is on the property at the time an agreement is signed. Does the crop belong to the buyer, or does the seller have the right to remove the crop within a certain period of time? If livestock is involved, care should be taken to fully describe the livestock, including any offspring that may not be in existence at the time the agreement is signed but may appear before the escrow is closed. Particular attention should be given to any easements and to the matter of water rights. As in the case of any sale of acreage, mineral rights are also of importance and the buyer should know whether he is getting all of the mineral rights, or whether they are reserved by the seller or have been reserved by a previous owner or transferred to some third party. Also be sure not to overlook any payments due from the Department of Agriculture or other similar governmental agencies.

14. Discrimination in Sale or Lease of Property

There are many laws now on the books, both at state and federal level, which prohibit discrimination based on race, religion, etc. in the sale or lease of property. There are also investigating agencies and protective bodies to help enforce the laws. Any individual who feels that he has been discriminated against in this area should see a lawyer. He can also contact the nearest HUD regional office (Assistant Regional Administrator for Equal Opportunity), or visit the local office of the United States Attorney General. Any one of these should be able to advise him after hearing the facts of the case as to what his rights are and what course of action he should follow (see Section 13.4). Persons who own property and are tempted for personal reasons to discriminate against potential purchasers or potential tenants on the grounds of race, etc., should know that these laws provide substantial penalties for such actions. The penalties include fines, punitive damages, and sometimes give the person discriminated against the right not only to collect damages but also to collect attorney's fees incurred in any suit brought to enforce his rights. The law prohibits discrimination in lease of apartments in multiple units (except rentals of rooms or units in dwellings having four or fewer units, with the owner living in one of them). Typical acts of discrimination include: quoting higher rent; claiming manager is not home; requirement of longer lease; claim of a waiting list for apartments; claim of no unit available; later date for occupancy given; credit check required; etc.

What about the sale or lease of single-family privately owned housing? Discrimination is prohibited if a broker or sales agent is used; discriminatory advertising is used; the home is not owned by a person (is owned by a corporation, partnership, etc.); the owner owns more than three houses; the owner sells more than one house in which he was not the most recent resident in any two-year period; FHA or VA financing exists on the house. In the case where discrimination is not prohibited by law (it can be argued that the 1866 Civil Rights Act may apply to discrimination in *all* cases), a member of a minority race wishing to purchase a house from a seller who discriminates should consider using a white agent to make the deal for him. The white agent can contract to buy the house, in his name, but the agreement should state that the property can be purchased either by the buyer "or his nominee." The deal should be made for cash so that the seller can't try to get out of it by "rejecting the credit" of the minority race buyer after he finds out who the true buyer is.

15. Title [10.15]

If you are buying property, you should make sure that you have *clear title.* In some states extensive use is made of title insurance policies issued by title insurance companies. In such states the title insurance company will search the title and will give the buyer a title insurance policy insuring his title in the full amount of the purchase price. A standard title insurance policy will insure the title of the buyer against defects in title resulting from other documents of record such as deeds, easements, liens, mortgages, deeds of trust, etc. However if you read the fine print in such a title policy you will find that it does not insure title against *off-record risks.* That means it does not insure against such things as easements (see Section 10.35) or claims based upon adverse possession (see Section 10.36). You can get a special title policy generally referred to as an ALTA (American Land Title Association) policy, which costs a little more. If you have that kind of a policy the title company will inspect the property to find out whether there are any apparent easements, adverse possessors, power lines, pipe lines, roadways or pathways, etc. When you have an ALTA policy you are insured against *off*-record risks as well as the risks insured against by standard policies. The cost of a title insurance policy for a typical house may be a couple of hundred dollars. In some counties the seller customarily pays, and in some counties the buyer customarily pays. In spite of custom, however, it is always a matter that can be negotiated.

Where title insurance is not available, the buyer can obtain an *abstract*. This is usually provided by an attorney who goes to the recorder's office and searches the record himself and then issues a written opinion regarding the title. An abstract is really a summary of the previously recorded documents affecting the title to property. Abstracts are difficult to understand and they don't necessarily protect you the way a title insurance policy does.

In some states there are different kinds of title insurance policies, some of which will protect your title but will not protect you against liens or encumbrances. Make sure that the title policy you get is the kind that insures your title so that it is marketable, and also insures it against liens or encumbrances. A title company will issue you a *preliminary title insurance report* before the close of escrow. This will show you exactly what the status of title will be after your insurance policy is issued. You should carefully read all exceptions and ask for details if you don't understand any of them. Most properties are subject to public utility easements for power lines (either overhead or underground) and possibly for water or gas lines. These may be standard in the particular neighborhood and should not concern you (there is nothing that can be done about them anyway). However (particularly in the case of larger properties) there may be some easements of record for road purposes that may be many years old. These should be checked out carefully to find out whether they have been used recently, and if not you should persuade the title company to eliminate them as exceptions and give you clear title not subject to such items. Although title insurance may be expensive, it is a good investment and is only a small percentage of the total you are paying for the property.

16. Deeds [10.16]

A deed is a written instrument by which title to real property is transferred by the *grantor* to the *grantee.* The deed must be dated and signed by the grantor. Some states require one or more witnesses. Because the deed has to be recorded, it also must be notarized. The property must be accurately described in the deed, using the official legal description, which can be obtained from the official county records.

A *grant deed* simply states that the grantor *grants* the property described in the deed. By statute the use of the word *grant* implies that the grantor has title to the property, that he has not previously conveyed it to someone else, and that the title is free from undisclosed encumbrances made by the grantor.

A *warranty deed* guarantees that the grantor does own the property, has the right to convey it, and that no one else has any interest in the property. In other words, it goes beyond a grant deed and gives more protection to the grantee. A grantee who gets a title insurance policy along with his deed doesn't need a warranty deed. However if title insurance is unavailable, the grantee should ask for a warranty deed.

A *quitclaim deed* is a deed that merely transfers all of the grantor's interest in the property, whatever it may be. There are no warranties that the title is any good. Whatever rights the grantor has are passed to the grantee by such a deed. Quitclaim deeds are not used in ordinary property transfers. One situation in which a quitclaim deed would be used is when a seller had deeded property to a buyer and immediately afterwards the buyer defaults in a payment and agrees to deed the property back to the seller.

Once the deed has been duly executed and notarized, some states require that tax stamps be affixed to it; others require simply that a transfer tax be paid at the time the deed is recorded. After the deed has been recorded it should be returned to the grantee. However, once the deed has been recorded, it doesn't matter if it is lost, destroyed, or stolen. The important thing is that the grantee has title recorded in his name. Once that is done, only he or someone acting for him (with proper legal authority) can convey title.

[10.17]   **17. Income Tax Factors**

The application of income tax laws to the purchase and sale of property is far too complex a subject for coverage in this book (see Section 6.40). A few simple points that often come up can be mentioned.

Any time you sell property for more than you paid for it, you have a tax problem. If you held the property for longer than six months, you may be able to have the gain taxed at *capital gain* rates, which are less than ordinary income rates. If you are selling your residence, there is a special exemption which permits you to postpone tax if you reinvest the proceeds in another residence withing a certain period of time. Upon sale of property other than your residence, you will be taxed on the gain unless you exchange the property (see Section 10.23). If the property was held for investment, you may qualify for a capital gain treatment of the gain. However if you are classified by Internal Revenue as a *dealer,* then you may be subject to *ordinary income tax.* A dealer is a person who buys and sells many properties or who buys property intending to improve and sell it for a profit. The question of dealership status is a complicated one and requires the advice of a CPA or a tax attorney.

It is possible to postpone payment of tax by electing to have the sale treated as an *installment sale*. To qualify, seller must not receive more than 29 percent of the total purchase price in the calendar year (tax year) of the sale. If he does receive more than 29 percent, he has to pay the full tax on the entire gain even though he doesn't receive the total purchase price in that year. If he receives no more than 29 percent of the purchase price in the year of sale, and gets the rest later, he only pays part of the tax now, and the rest later.

Depreciation is another important tax factor in real estate investments. Land is not depreciable. That means if you buy raw land, you can't deduct anything each year from your income tax except the taxes you pay on the property and the interest on the money you borrowed to purchase it. Buildings are depreciable over a period of time which is calculated as the *useful life* of the building. This might be anywhere from ten to forty years, depending upon the type of construction, age of the building, etc. The rate of depreciation may vary depending upon whether it is a new building or one that was purchased from the previous owner. In a case where *accelerated depreciation* is permitted by law, the owner of such property can increase the rate of his annual depreciation deductions. (This results in large depreciation in the beginning, slowing down later on.) To learn what kinds of property are depreciable at accelerated rates, and what the rates are, you should consult an expert. The furniture and furnishings in an apartment house purchased as an investment can also be depreciated over a period of time equivalent to the useful life of such items. The more rapid the rate of depreciation and the larger the depreciation is in relationship to the total investment, the less will be the taxable income each year.

Interest on loans is deductible, and so are property taxes. These two deductions help to produce *tax shelter* (see Section 10.55) for the real estate investor.

18. Real Property Taxes

The taxation of real property can only be discussed in very general terms because of the variations in the law of different states. State law establishes the basis for property taxes and also sets forth certain exemptions. Exemptions, such as veterans' exemptions and exemptions for property used for religious or charitable purposes, must be claimed by the filing of a proper form.

Real property taxes are normally assessed and levied by the counties. Valuation is determined annually on a particular date. The assessment roll is prepared based on the name of the record owner of property on a certain date each year. The law requires that all taxable property must be treated alike if it is of like kind. That is, each parcel must be assessed on the same basis as every other parcel.

The law normally provides procedures for requesting adjustment of taxes. This is sometimes referred to as *equalization.* A taxpayer who feels that his property has been assessed higher than his neighbor's property of comparable value can petition the county for equalization. He can have his taxes lowered only if he can prove that other similar properties are taxed lower because they have been appraised or assessed at lower values.

Taxes may be made payable either in one annual installment or in two semiannual installments. Penalties and interest attach to late payments. Where taxes are delinquent for a certain period of time, the property will be sold to the state for nonpayment of taxes after publication of notice. Once assessed, taxes become a lien on the property and are prior to all other liens.

When property is *sold to the state* for nonpayment of taxes, which normally occurs at the end of the first year in which the taxes have been delinquent, the law normally provides for a *statutory period of redemption* which may be several years in duration. That means you can "buy back" your property by paying the delinquent taxes, plus penalties and interest. After the redemption period has passed, an actual sale occurs as opposed to the first sale, which was merely a notation on the tax rolls that the property was sold to the state. The property would be sold to the public at a public auction by the tax collector after proper notice has been given. Any person, including the former owner of the property, may buy the property at such a tax sale. A tax deed is issued to the highest bidder and the proceeds of sale go to the taxing agencies. It is possible in some cases, where the property has not yet been sold to the public after the statutory redemption period has passed, but is still owned by the state, that the former owner may be able to redeem it by paying all delinquent taxes and penalties.

Once again, these rules can only be generally stated, and they vary greatly among the different states.

19. Escrows   [10.19]

An *escrow* is a means of providing a custodian for holding funds or documents, handling clerical tasks, making prorations and adjustments, and providing a clearing house for exchange of money and documents. The *escrow holder* serves as a kind of *dual agent* (representing both sides). Most states require escrow agents to be licensed, although there may be exceptions for banks, attorneys, title companies, etc.

Once an agreement for sale of property has been reached,

an escrow is set up, and the money and the deed and other documents to be exchanged are deposited into escrow. Both parties sign escrow instructions directing the escrow holder to handle the money and the documents in accordance with the agreement. If a title insurance company is involved, the title company will search the title and prepare a preliminary title report. If an existing loan is being assumed by the buyer or is being paid off by the buyer, a statement must be obtained from the lender showing the unpaid balance including principal and interest.

If a new loan is being placed on the property, the lending documents have to be prepared, approved by the lender and the buyer, and the escrow statement must include loan fees, appraisal fees, etc.

If the preliminary title report shows certain conditions of title which are questionable or which are not acceptable to the buyer, these questions must be resolved and an attempt must be made to remove the objectionable items from the title prior to close of escrow.

When all documents have been prepared and are in the hands of the escrow holder, such things as interest on outstanding loans, insurance premiums on insurance to be assumed by the buyer, real property and personal property taxes, rents, etc. must be prorated. That means the portion due up to the date of close is charged to seller, and the portion due thereafter is charged to buyer.

Just prior to recording of the deed, a final search is made of the title to be sure that no recent items have been recorded which would show up against the title following recording of the deed. The deed is then recorded and at the same time or immediately thereafter the escrow holder pays the money and delivers the documents to the people entitled to them.

The buyer should obtain at closing: a copy of any insurance policy which was in effect prior to the sale and which he has assumed; a copy of any mortgage he is assuming; a bill of sale for any personal property involved in the transaction; keys to the premises; and a *closing statement* indicating all charges and prorations. Shortly after the close of escrow he should receive the original copy of the recorded deed, together with his title insurance policy (if the deal involves title insurance).

The seller receives a closing statement, a check for the balance due him, and a note and deed of trust if he is financing a portion of the purchase price. If he is the beneficiary of a mortgage or deed of trust on the property for the balance of the purchase price which he is financing, he should also receive a copy of the title insurance policy (if title insurance is involved) and may be entitled to a copy of an insurance policy showing him as a co-insured.

Where termite reports are used, a copy of a report by a licensed pest control operator is furnished to each party as part of the escrow documents. Although it is a matter of agreement, usually the seller pays for any corrective measures and is charged in the escrow for the amount estimated for these repairs in the pest control operator's report, while the buyer pays for any preventive work which needs to be done to minimize possibility of termite damage in the future.

If the agreement itself does not spell out who pays the costs of the escrow, the escrow instructions should then cover the matter.

Where an existing loan is being assumed, if it is the type of loan where, in addition to principal and interest payments, monthly payments are required to build up a fund to pay annual insurance premiums and real property taxes, problems can arise if prior payments have been insufficient and additional money is due. If this isn't taken care of at the close of escrow, the buyer may have to put up the additional amounts after the close. If there should happen to be an excess in the fund, the seller should be entitled to a refund or to a credit in the escrow.

20. Recording of Documents

Recording laws have been adopted in all states which provide a system of recording title to property so that property can be safely transferable. The recording statutes prevent the owner of a piece of property from being able to sell that same piece of property to several different buyers. The recording statutes require that all conveyances of real property may be recorded in the office of the county recorder of the county where the property is located. When a conveyance is recorded, that means that anyone dealing with the property after that time has been put on notice that the recorded conveyance exists. The recording statutes also provide that if the owner of property sells it to Mr. X first, but the deed to Mr. X is not recorded and the owner thereafter sells the property again to Mr. Y, and Mr. Y records his deed, Mr. Y becomes the owner of the property, even though Mr. X got his deed first—that is, assuming Mr. Y did not actually know of the prior deed to Mr. X before he recorded his deed.

In order to be recorded a document must be *acknowledged,* or in some way duly and legally certified in accordance with the legal requirements of the state. Generally this means that it must be notarized by a notary public.

Documents are recorded by the county recorder's office. This is done by entering or recording the document in the official records of the county. Entries are made in the order in which documents are received, and numbers are assigned to each document to indicate which one was recorded first when two or more were recorded on the same day or at the same time on the same day. These records are open to public inspection. Once a document has been recorded, everyone has *constructive notice* of the fact. That means everyone is presumed to know that the document has been recorded in the same way that everyone is presumed to know the law.

21. Estates (Interests) in Real Property

[10.21]

There are many different types of *estates* (interests) in real property. *Fee simple,* or *fee simple absolute,* are the terms used to describe complete legal title to real property.

A *life estate,* or an *estate for years,* refers to interests in property that last only for the lifetime of a particular person, or for a certain period of years.

A *remainder* is an interest in property after the termination of a life estate or an estate for years.

Title may be held in many different ways. This includes joint tenancy (see Section 6.45), tenancy in common (see Section 6.51), tenancy by the entireties (see Section 6.52), and community property (see Section 6.49). Title can also be held in trust or by a custodian or a conservator, or it can be held by a title company under a *holding agreement.*

22. Financing

[10.22]

The sale of property may be financed by the seller when he takes back a note secured by mortgage (see Section 10.69) or deed of trust (see Section 10.70) on the property. It may be financed by *conventional* means where the buyer borrows from a bank, savings and loan, or other financial institution. If the purchase is financed through Federal Housing Administration (FHA) it means that FHA insures the loan, and the interest rates are lower than for conventional financing. The down payment may also be somewhat lower. However the seller may have to pay *points* to the lender, which means a kind of loan fee. This is to offset the lower interest rate charged to the buyer. An FHA loan may be for a longer term than a conventional loan. However there are limits on the total amount of financing that can be obtained under an FHA loan.

A Veterans Administration (VA) loan is a loan guaranteed by the Veterans Administration, and is available only to qualified veterans. The interest rate is even lower than the FHA rate, and the amount of the down payment is either very small or may be nothing at all.

Anyone seeking conventional financing should shop around. Banks may at times give slightly lower interest rates than savings and loan institutions, but they may not loan as large an amount, and it may be for a shorter term. Financial institutions have their own appraisers and sometimes the amount of the appraisal (and therefore the amount of the loan) varies considerably. Usually where property is being sold, the appraisal is the same as the purchase price unless for some reason the property is greatly overpriced.

A *second mortgage* is a mortgage or deed of trust taken back by the seller when the buyer doesn't have enough money to pay the difference between the amount of the loan and the purchase price. Second mortgages are generally for higher interest rates and for shorter terms than first mortgages. Some banks or financial institutions will not permit second loans to be on the property if they have the first loan. Most banks are prohibited from making second loans on property.

In considering a first or second loan on the property, the following points should be noted: the interest rate, the term, the frequency and the amount of the installment payments, whether the loan is fully amortized or contains a *balloon payment* at the end (see Section 7.67), *acceleration clause* (clause providing that the loan becomes due on sale of the property), and *prepayment penalty* (clause providing that additional interest must be paid if the loan is paid off early).

Where an FHA loan is involved, the seller should be sure he understands the *premium* or *discount* charged by the lender under an FHA-insured loan. The discount is a percentage of the total amount and is often referred to as *points,* with each point equaling 1 percent of the total. The points must be paid by the seller under FHA regulations (not by the borrower), except that in some cases the buyer may pay one point, while the seller pays the rest.

Most lenders require you to have your house appraised before they will agree to make a loan. What if the appraisal is for less than the agreed-upon purchase price? You may then be forced to choose between lowering your sale price or letting the buyer back out of the deal if it was dependent on getting that loan. Once in a while you can get the appraiser to reconsider his appraisal and raise it slightly if you can show that other comparable properties were appraised at higher values. Or you may be able to get another appraisal at a higher figure.

If you are selling a house subject to an existing loan, you should try to get released from the loan by having the new buyer substituted in your place. The alternative to this, and one which most lenders require, is that the new buyer simply assumes the loan, which means that the seller remains liable in the event that the new buyer defaults and that the property does not produce enough money at a foreclosure sale to pay off the loan.

If a seller owns property which is free and clear and he doesn't need the funds from the sale in order to buy other property, he might consider financing the sale himself by taking back a first mortgage or first deed of trust on the property. In that event the seller should get a fairly sizable down payment out of the buyer (at least 10 percent and possibly as much as 29 percent (see Section 10.17).

23. Exchange of Property [10.23]

One way to postpone having to pay income tax on the sale of appreciated property (see Section 10.17) is to trade it for another piece of property. The Internal Revenue Code permits the owner of property to exchange it for similar property without having to pay any income tax. The tax catches up with him when he sells the exchanged property later on. His *cost* or *basis* for the exchanged property is the same as the *cost* or *basis* for the property which he originally owned and which he exchanged for the other property. The tax that he eventually pays is based on the difference between the cost of his original property and the sale price of the property acquired in exchange. It is not always easy to find a suitable exchange property. What frequently happens when a seller is willing to exchange but is not willing to sell is that the buyer will find a suitable piece of exchange property and will arrange to buy it and then exchange it for the property that he wants. These three way exchanges involve some tricky tax rules and the advice of a tax attorney should be obtained.

B. LEASES

1. Unwritten Leases [10.24]

The statute of frauds (see Section 4.6) generally provides that leases for more than a year must be in writing. Leases for less than a year can be either written or oral. If they are oral they of course will have to be very simple and will normally include only the fact that a certain amount of rental is to be paid each month. There may also be a requirement of a security or cleanup deposit (see Section 10.25). The law of each state contains many statutes and many decisions that govern the relationship of landlord and tenant that are by law included in any unwritten lease.

2. Written Leases [10.25]

There are many different types of written leases. There are residential leases, commercial leases, industrial leases, etc. There are also leases that are strongly in favor of the landlord and leases that are more or less "neutral"—that is, they don't particularly favor either party. Leases slanted in favor of tenants are very rare. Lease forms are quite common and can be obtained at any stationery store. Most real estate offices carry several different versions of leases, as do banks. Attorneys also have form leases, but usually they prefer to use a lease that is custom-made to fit the situation because they recognize that form leases do not always contain all of the provisions required in a particular situation, and sometimes many of the provisions in a form lease are unnecessary or undesirable in a particular situation. Because of the great differences among various kinds of leases, the landlord should choose a written lease form with great care, and a tenant should read it with great care. A landlord planning to use the same lease over and over again should have it examined first by his attorney to make sure that the form cannot be improved upon in any way for his benefit. A tenant who is signing anything other than a month-to-month lease should have it reviewed by an attorney unless it is a fairly simple and straightforward document that he can easily understand.

A lease of course should include the names of the landlord and tenant, the location of the premises, and should state when the term begins and when it ends. It should also state the amount of the monthly rental and the date on which the rental is due. It should cover the amount of the security deposit. Any agreements concerning occupancy should be spelled out. This should include the number of persons entitled to occupy the premises, whether any pets or children are permitted, and what the premises may be used for. The question of subleases and assignments should also be covered. Will they be permitted, or will the consent of the landlord be required? Most written leases cover maintenance and repairs and indicate who has the responsibility for these items and what happens if these responsibilities are not met by the party having them. In some states the tenant is permitted to apply his monthly rental to the cost of making repairs if the landlord, upon reasonable request, does not make certain repairs or perform certain maintenance that he is required to do under the lease. Some leases contain a provision requiring the tenant to waive this right. Whether or not the right exists in the first place, and, if it does exist, whether or not it can be waived, is a matter that varies from state to state. Some courts have imposed upon landlords a duty to keep their tenants' dwelling safe, clean, and habitable and have excused the tenant from the obligation to pay rent where the landlord has failed to fulfill that duty.

The written lease should provide that the tenant is liable for damage or destruction of the premises (reasonable wear and tear excepted) and that he must leave the premises in a state of cleanliness comparable to that in which it was received by him. The landlord is authorized to apply the security or cleaning deposit to the cost of repairs or cleanup following termination of the lease. The cautious tenant will make a careful inspection of the premises in the beginning to make sure that the landlord doesn't attempt to charge him for repairs of items which were already damaged at the beginning of the lease.

3.   Month-to-Month Tenancy [10.26]

A *month-to-month tenancy* means a tenancy that lasts only for one month at a time and that can be terminated by either the landlord or the tenant by giving one month's notice in advance. Such a lease can either be oral or written. It differs from a lease for a term in that only one month's notice is required to terminate it. Neither party has to give a reason for terminating the lease. Under a written lease, neither party can terminate the lease until it expires· unless they mutually agree on earlier termination. Of course any lease can be terminated by either party at any time if the other party has breached the lease. The terms *tenancy at will* and *tenancy by sufferance* are used in some states to describe tenancies that can be terminated by either landlord or tenant at the end of any period of time, such as thirty days, sixty days, etc.

4.   How to Handle Tenants [10.27]

Successful landlords are those who handle their tenants gently but firmly. If a tenant breaches his lease in any way, he should immediately be informed of this by the landlord and be asked to correct it. If the breach involves not paying his rent, he should be given a *notice to pay rent or quit.* This is sometimes referred to as a *three-day notice*, or similar name. It must be in writing, should be addressed to the tenant, and should be delivered to him. It should state that he is in breach of the lease for not paying his rent (or other breach) and should direct him to pay the rent (or cure the breach) or leave the premises within three days (or whatever time is required by law). If the tenant fails to cure the breach within that time period, the landlord can file an *unlawful detainer action*. To do this he files a complaint in the local court having jurisdiction over the matter, alleging the existence of the lease and the default by the tenant. He asks that the premises be restored to him, that the tenant be forced to vacate, and that the rental be paid. When the summons and complaint are served on the tenant (see Section 5.3) he is given a short period of time to file an answer. If he has some defense to the matter (maybe he hasn't paid his rent because the landlord hasn't fixed the leaky roof) he should file an answer. If an answer is not filed, the landlord will be permitted to take the default of the tenant and get an unlawful detainer judgment. Based on that judgment he can obtain a writ, take it to the sheriff, and ask the sheriff to have the tenant removed. There are different ways to handle this event. The best is to ask the sheriff to serve some sort of a *scare notice* on the tenant first, informing him of the fact that he and his personal belongings will be removed from the premises if he does not leave voluntarily. In most cases that will work. If it does not, then the sheriff should be asked to remove the tenant and his possessions and place the possessions in storage or whatever is permitted by law. Unfortunately, unlawful detainer proceedings are expensive from the landlord's standpoint. In addition to attorneys' fees and costs involved in filing and serving the action, he may also have to post a sizable amount of money with the sheriff to get the sheriff to serve papers and to remove the tenant from the premises. True, these amounts are recoverable from the tenant, but very often tenants who can't pay rent are *judgment-proof* (no assets) and a larger judgment is of little practical value. For this reason many landlords are reluctant to bring unlawful detainer proceedings. However in many cases a landlord simply must do this in order to impress upon not only this tenant, but all other tenants in the building (if it is a multiple residential unit) that late payments or other breaches of the lease will not be tolerated. Once the word gets around that the landlord is soft on tenants, it may act as encouragement to other tenants to be late in the payment of their rent, etc.

Landlords should also make an attempt to get out in front of their tenants far enough so that they have time to bring unlawful detainer proceedings without in the meantime losing rental. This means getting an adequate security deposit in advance, and getting the first and last month's rental in advance on a term lease. For example, a tenant on a one-year lease should be required to pay the first month's rental in advance and the last month's rental at the same time. Thereafter he pays each succeeding month, on the first of the month, so the landlord is always a full month ahead of him. If the tenant decides to leave one month early, the landlord has his last month's rental and has a whole month to look for a new tenant.

5.   How to Handle Your Landlord   [10.28]

If you are asked to sign a written lease, read it carefully and if you find any really objectionable provisions in it, try to get the landlord to agree to change them (all changes should be initialed by both parties at the time the agreement is signed).

If for any reason you find it difficult to pay your monthly rental, speak to the landlord about it. Let him know in advance that you will not be able to make your payment on time, and tell him specifically when you will make it. If you can't agree to pay the whole amount within a few days after the date it is due, offer to pay him part of it at that time and agree to pay the balance within a reasonable period of time. Most landlords will be reasonable about it if you communicate with them and appear to be making a reasonable effort to pay the rent.

If you feel the landlord is not living up to his obligations under the lease, don't hesitate to mention it. If it is a fairly serious breach, and you are a tenant under a written lease for a long term, send him a written notice and keep a copy of it. In the notice tell him exactly what provisions of the lease you feel he has not lived up to and if you desire, indicate that you will consider the lease broken and will leave if he does not correct the situation within a certain period of time.

If you have differences with your neighbors such as arguments over noise levels or who has the right to use what part of the property, refer these matters to your landlord rather than arguing with fellow tenants. It is his job to take care of things like that. If you think that the place needs repair, ask the landlord to do it. If he refuses, you might consider volunteering to do it yourself and ask if you can do this and either have him reimburse you for the repairs or allow you to deduct the amount thereof from your rental (see Section 10.25).

If you are unable to pay the rent and the landlord threatens to file an unlawful detainer action against you, you can make him aware of the fact that you know how expensive an unlawful detainer action can be for a landlord, and how much time and difficulty it takes to actually get rid of a tenant. You can probably arrive at some sort of a compromise which will allow you a reasonably short period of time within which to find another place to move, which will prevent him from having to bring an unlawful detainer proceeding.

6. Discrimination

[10.29]

Discrimination in the lease of housing is against the law. The laws provide remedies for prospective tenants who are denied access to rental apartments because of the landlord's discrimination based on race, religion, etc. (see Section 10.14).

7. Deposits

[10.30]

A landlord who thinks ahead will always get a deposit from his tenant. The deposit should be at least 25 percent of the amount of the monthly rental. The deposit should be held until after the tenant has vacated the premises and the landlord has made his inspection. Many arguments arise over the failure of the landlord to refund the deposit after the tenant has left. If the tenant has reason to doubt the good faith of his landlord, he should have some reliable person witness the fact that he has cleaned the premises and left them in a state of good repair following termination of the lease. Laws in many states require landlords to strictly account for deposits and to refund them promptly after termination of the lease where the property has been left in good condition.

8. Termination

[10.31]

A lease may terminate of its own accord, or it may be terminated by either party in the event of a material breach of the lease. Destruction or condemnation of the premises will terminate the lease. Upon termination, the landlord may require the tenant to leave. In some cases the tenant may be entitled to part of the money from the condemnation.

[10.32]   9.   Rent Subsidies and Rent Controls

Certain governmental programs provide for the subsidizing of certain low-rental dwellings. The dwelling unit must be of a type that qualifies and must be in an area which is approved for subsidization. The tenant must also qualify as a person entitled to such aid. For details consult your local county welfare agency or your local HUD office. During certain periods of time rent controls may be in effect which limit the amount and frequency of rent increases. In such cases the landlord must notify the tenant in advance of the rent increase, and the increase must not exceed what the law allows. Normally there are no rent control laws, and the controls, if any, are put on in emergency situations by presidental decree.

C. RIGHTS AND DUTIES

1. Trespass

[10.33]

Trespass is the unauthorized entry on property belonging to someone else (see Section 9.24). The trespasser is subject to a civil suit and may also be subject to criminal prosecution. Trespassers who are requested to leave private property should do so promptly and peacefully. The property owner is entitled to use reasonable force to remove trespassers; what is reasonable depends upon the circumstances (see Section 9.38). Most states have a number of statutes that discuss trespass and give the property owner various remedies. It is important for owners of large acreage to protect themselves against trespass. Courts in some states have held that trespass by the general public across property over a period of several years leads to a right of easement in favor of the general public. The only way for a property owner to prevent this from happening (where that is the law) is to either fence his property or have it properly posted with "no trespassing" signs and to regularly patrol it. As a property owner and taxpayer he is entitled to the assistance and protection of the local sheriff's office or other legal authority in keeping trespassers off of his property.

Property owners have duties toward some trespassers— especially children. If your neighbor's small child falls into your unfenced pool after entering your back yard, you may be held liable. You have a duty to keep your property free from dangerous conditions that might cause injury to "uninvited guests." A greater duty of care is owed to persons who have your permission to be on the property (see Section 9.16).

2. Nuisance

[10.34]

The law prohibits the use of private property in a manner that constitutes a *nuisance* to surrounding or adjoining property owners. A nuisance is an activity that unreasonably interferes with the rights of other people to enjoy their property. A nuisance might consist of a large number of animals, or of a particularly noisy or smelly activity. Where a nuisance exists, or where someone thinks it does, the remedy is to file a suit in a local court having jurisdiction over the matter asking that the alleged nuisance be enjoined (stopped). When the summons and complaint have been served upon the property owner who is allegedly responsible for the nuisance, he will have to come into court and show why the activity his neighbors are complaining about should not be stopped by court order.

[10.35]   3.   Easements

An *easement* is a right to use property that belongs to another. An *express* easement is created by the agreement between two parties that an easement shall exist on the property of one for the benefit of the other. An *implied* easement exists where it is obviously necessary for one party to have an easement across the property of another in order to get to and from his property. Another type of easement is one by *adverse use*. Such an easement can be created where one party openly and continuously uses the property of another (without his consent) over a period of time (usually five years). The adverse use may take the form of a footpath, riding trail, or road that is continually used. One way for the owner to prevent this is to put up a barrier periodically (once a year) with a notice that the right to pass is subject to consent of the owner.

[10.36]   4.   Adverse Possession

It is possible for one person to acquire legal title to property of another person simply by physically occupying that property for a certain period of time (usually five years). The occupation must be *continuous, open* (obvious), and *adverse* (not with permission or consent of the owner). In addition, the person claiming title by adverse possession may be required to have paid the taxes on the property during that five years that he occupied the property.

5. Encroachments [10.37]

An *encroachment* is something that protrudes from one property onto or across the property of another. The encroachment may be in the form of a wall, overhang of a roof, or a fence or driveway. The owner of property being encroached upon should take steps to eliminate the encroachment or to seek damages for it so that the encroaching party does not gain an easement for encroachment which he may do if the encroachment is obvious and continues for a period of years.

6. Covenants, Conditions, and Restrictions [10.38]

Covenants, conditions, and restrictions (CC&Rs) exist of record in the case of most modern subdivisions, town houses, and condominiums. They are usually created by the original subdivider who first divided the property into separate lots, or units. The CC&Rs were originally created for the benefit of the lot or unit owners. They restrict the activities that can be conducted on the property (as for example restrictions to single-family residential) and regulate such things as setback lines, heights of buildings, and use of the premises for certain purposes. Certain provisions in older CC&Rs, such as barring sale to nonwhites, are no longer enforceable. All people who own lots in the subdivision subject to CC&Rs are bound by them, and anyone who violates the CC&Rs can be sued by any one of the other property owners to enjoin (stop) any activity that is in violation of the CC&Rs. The CC&Rs may provide for an *architectural control committee* which has the power to review plans for any new buildings or for any remodeling jobs. They may also regulate such things as the storage of trailers, keeping of pets, and the repair or dismantling of automobiles, etc. CC&Rs are usually established for a specific term which may be ten or twenty years, and thereafter they may either expire or may be renewed (either automatically or otherwise) for an additional term. Anyone buying property subject to CC&Rs should carefully read them so that he will know what provisions they contain.

D. CONDEMNATION

1. Direct Condemnation [10.39]

Real property may be acquired by the government by exercise of the power of eminent domain upon payment of just compensation. Eminent domain or *condemnation* is the legal process by which an authorized governmental body takes private property for some public purpose. If the state wants your property for a freeway, or the local school district wants it for a school, things would begin with the filing of an action for condemnation of the property. Occasionally the condemning authority would attempt to negotiate first before filing the suit, but usually the proceedings are filed, and then the negotiations begin. Where property is needed for a freeway, the state will sometimes take the property immediately and will deposit into court the amount of money which the state appraisers say the property is worth. The property owner can take the money and settle the case or he can leave it in there, allow it to draw interest, and litigate the question of fair market value if he believes the state appraisers have not valued the property high enough.

Cities, counties, or other state governmental agencies, school districts, public utilities, and various districts have power of eminent domain. Property taken must be taken for the purpose of being put to a use that is more of a public necessity than the use to which it is already dedicated. A property owner has the right to dispute the assertion of the state that his property will be used for a public purpose.

2. Inverse Condemnation [10.40]

Occasionally a case comes along in which the state does not file an action to take property, but its actions nevertheless amount to the same thing as taking the property. An example would be the building of a dam which causes water to back up onto privately owned property, flooding it and making it useless. The owner of that property could sue for inverse condemnation. Another example would be where a freeway is built that cuts off access to a property, making it valueless. That owner could also sue for inverse condemnation. Such cases rarely occur because the condemning authority generally recognizes the rights of property owners whose property is affected by such public improvements and either offers to purchase it or files a condemnation action. However where the owner is deprived of the use of his property and the state refuses to pay for it, the law permits him to file an inverse condemnation action. In such action the property owner becomes the plaintiff and the state the defendant, although the property owner is alleging that the state has taken his property through exercise of the power of eminent domain. At a trial the issues would be the same as in a regular condemnation proceeding except the property owner would have to prove that the deprivation of the use of his property was equivalent to a taking of the property.

[10.41]   3.   Fair Market Value

In any condemnation proceeding the main issue is the *fair market value* of the property. Fair market value is defined as the price that a *willing buyer* would pay and that a *willing seller* would agree to accept, in the open market, based upon the highest and best use of the property. *Highest and best use* means the most profitable use to which the property could be put at the time the condemnation action is filed. If the property is at the time of the condemnation action being used as an orchard, but has highway frontage that is zoned commercial, the property owner is entitled to have the property considered as commercial property rather than as farm land when it comes to setting the fair market value. Fair market value is determined by appraisers (see Section 10.43). The property owner can give his opinion as to the value of his own property if the case goes to trial (see Section 10.44).

4. Negotiations [10.42]

The condemning authority will put an agent in charge of the acquisition of property needed for a public purpose. It is his job to have the property appraised, coordinate with the appraiser or appraisers, and to contact the owner of each parcel and attempt to negotiate a settlement.

The appraisals of the condemning authority and the appraisals of the property owner will generally differ in amount (see Section 10.43). The negotiating period is the time in which both parties attempt to compromise these differences and agree upon a fair market value which is acceptable to both sides. Both sides must recognize that it costs money to go to trial and that it is sometimes better to pay a little bit more, or to take a little bit less, and avoid the time and expense of trial as well as the risk of having to pay more or having to take less than you expected.

5. Appraisers [10.43]

The condemning authority will always have the property appraised by one or more appraisers. The state doesn't have to tell you what value its appraisers placed upon your property unless the matter is litigated.

You might at first obtain an appraiser whose qualifications are that he has been in the real estate business in the area for a number of years and has a good idea of the value of the property in the neighborhood. He could, for a relatively low fee, give you his opinion of the value of your property. On the basis of this you could attempt to negotiate a more favorable settlement offer.

If, however, you are faced with a trial, it will not do to have an inexperienced appraiser appear as your witness. The experienced attorney for the condemning authority will make mincemeat out of any witness who doesn't really know his business. Preferably he should have appeared in court before as an expert witness and should be experienced in resisting cross-examination as well as in presenting his own testimony on direct examination. There are several organizations or societies to which qualified appraisers belong. These include the American Institute of Real Estate Appraisers (members use the designation MAI), the Society of Real Estate Appraisers (SREA), and the American Society of Appraisers (ASA).

If you hire an appraiser, be sure you find out in advance what his fee will be. You might consider having him do a preliminary report for a smaller fee, and then do a complete report and testify at trial as a witness, for a larger fee, if you can't settle the case based on his preliminary report.

[10.44]   6.   Trial

If a condemnation case cannot be settled, it will then have to be tried. The condemning authority presents its case first. It establishes that the property is being taken for a public use, and gives its evidence of the fair market value of the property. It calls its appraisers and asks them for their opinions as to the value of the property. Thereafter the property owner gets a chance to present his witnesses and his own testimony concerning the value of his property.

Condemnation trials tend to be somewhat lengthy and

boring because they deal in a lot of technicalities. They may be heard in most places either by a judge or jury, although some states require jury trials. Most of the time at condemnation trials is taken up in considering *comparable sales*. This term refers to the sales of other similar property located reasonably close to the condemned parcel. Comparable sales are those which occurred relatively recently in time and which involved property that is quite similar to the property being condemned in all material respects. Most of the argument revolves around distinguishing various comparable sales and trying to convince the judge or jury which one should be given the greatest consideration in arriving at fair market value of the property.

7.   Severance Damages [10.45]

In addition to fair market value at the time of the *taking* (the time the government undertakes formal steps to acquire the property, such as by filing a condemnation action), you are also entitled to be compensated for damages to or loss in value of the remainder of your property when only a part of it is taken. When the remaining portion of the property is made less valuable because of the partial taking, you have what are called *severance damages*. This can occur if access to the remaining parcel is cut off, or if the remaining parcel is such in size or shape that it is difficult to develop or sell, or if you have increased expenses such as fencing, or any direct interference with light, air, view, etc. The severance damages are the difference in value of the remainder of the property before the taking and after the taking.

However, in some states where the remainder of your property has benefited by something such as a newly paved or improved access road, or the development of a lake so that you now have lakefront property, the government may be entitled to set off any *special benefits* which the remainder of your property receives against your claim for severance damages, to reduce that claim for severance damages. However the benefits, in order to reduce the claim for severance damages, must be peculiar to your particular property and not of generally equal benefit to all of the people in the community. If the latter is the case, the benefits are *general benefits*, and the government cannot offset general benefits against a claim for severance damages.

[10.46]   8.   Recovery of Costs and Expenses

Such things as moving expenses and time lost from work are not recoverable.

The appraisers' fees as well as the cost of a survey are recoverable in some states, but not in others. The same is true of attorneys' fees.

[10.47]   9.   Settlement by Owner

Should the owner of property attempt to negotiate settlement of the condemnation case without the aid of an attorney? The answer is "sometimes yes, sometimes no." If the property owner is relatively sophisticated, knows the value of his property, and has some skill at negotiating, he may be able to work out a satisfactory price with the condemning authority. If the property owner is inexperienced, doesn't really know much about property values or about negotiating prices, or if a lot of property is involved, then he should seek some professional help and not try to do the negotiating himself. To some extent this also depends upon the condemning authority. The practice varies from state to state, and within each state.

Some agencies will make one offer, based upon their highest appraisal of the property, and will not pay any more than that without going to court. Others will make an offer below their highest appraisal and will be prepared to negotiate settlement up to the amount of their highest appraisal. Still others will offer to pay the amount of their highest appraisal, and on occasion will go beyond it in order to settle without going to court.

Finally, if you are not able to negotiate a settlement that is satisfactory and you don't want to turn the case over to an attorney, if the thought of conducting your own trial is challenging to you, you might represent yourself and testify in court, giving your opinion as to the value of the property. Occasionally a property owner meets with success in such an attempt.

E. ADMINISTRATIVE PROCEDURES

1. Zoning

Local governments, using the *police power* which they have by law, regulate the use of land and buildings by enacting *zoning* laws. The purpose of zoning is to promote public health, safety, comfort, convenience, and welfare. The typical city zoning ordinance establishes different zoning categories for residential, commercial, and industrial areas. There may also be farming or agricultural zoning. Within a zone, such as residential, there will be subzones for single-family, duplex, or multiple dwelling units. Superimposed upon these will be height limitations within certain zones. Most zoning is a result of various plans which have been subjected to differing pressures over a period of time. The ideal thing would be for a city to adopt a comprehensive general plan or master plan at the time that it was first incorporated, and to see that that plan is carried out. This rarely happens, usually when a single developer acquires a large piece of property and plans and develops an entire new city. Some outstanding examples of this approach to zoning and planning exist. However most areas of the country have been developed over the decades without a great deal of long-range planning.

The average citizen runs into zoning problems when he wants to do something on his property that is prohibited by a local zoning ordinance, or when some nearby property owner wants to do something on his property that would violate the zoning regulations or require a change in the zoning.

If a property owner wants to do something the zoning forbids, he may seek a variance (see Section 10.49) or a use permit (see Section 10.50). If a property owner objects to something his neighbor is doing which is in violation of the zoning ordinance, he can ask the local authorities (city or county attorney, etc.) to stop the objectionable activity by enforcing the zoning ordinance.

Occasionally it is possible to get the zoning which has been in effect for a long time changed. To do this you must persuade the local authorities that circumstances have changed greatly since the zoning was first enacted, and that because of the changed circumstances some other zoning would be better. Neighborhoods do tend to change over a period of time and what was once a prime residential area can become an area that is better for multiple residential dwellings, or even for administrative and professional offices.

On any legal question involving zoning, the most important thing to consider is the local zoning ordinance.

Spot zoning refers to zoning that creates a sort of island of property which is zoned differently from the surrounding property. Although spot zoning is frowned upon and occasionally is ruled illegal, there are cases where it is acceptable—for instance, a neighborhood shopping center.

When a zoning ordinance is enacted, there may be certain areas within a zone that are in conflict with the zoning: for example, an apartment house located in an area zoned for single-family residences. That apartment house would be termed a *nonconforming use.* A newly adopted zoning ordinance cannot outlaw an existing property use, but it can limit it in the future. Eventually, if the zoning remained the same, the land on which the apartment house sits would become available for single-family homes when the apartment house was torn down after it became too old to be usable. Some zoning ordinances will place a time limit on a nonconforming use. For example, a warehouse in a residential neighborhood might be permitted for a period of twenty years, after which time the owner would have to remove it and devote the property to residential use.

[10.49]   2.   Variances

The typical zoning ordinance permits the authorities to grant exceptions in certain cases. The exceptions are called *variances*. For example: suppose the zoning requires 8,000-square-foot lots, and all lots in the neighborhood are 8,000 square feet except for one, which is 15,900 feet. If the owner of that lot wants to divide it into two smaller lots, one of them less than 8,000 square feet, he can apply for a variance. In such a case it would be up to the planning commission or planning director to study the matter and recommend granting or denial of the variance. The city council or other local governmental body would then consider that recommendation and grant or deny the application for a variance.

Applications for variance are filed in accordance with the provisions of the zoning ordinance. Variance requests are heard at public hearings where anyone interested in the matter can speak for or against the application. If you wish to apply for a variance, the local city or county officials will be most helpful in showing you how to do it. They can tell you what form your request for variance should take, how to prepare it, when and where to file it, and how to present the case. Many property owners are capable of filing their own application for a variance and making an appearance before the planning commission and before the city council or county board of supervisors, etc. without the aid of an attorney. Those who would like to try handling their own variance case, but are unsure of themselves, would be well-advised to consult with an attorney and get some advice from him on how to handle their own case.

[10.50]   3.   Use Permits

Although a variance deals with such things as size of lots, setback lines, and height limitations, *use permits* deal with uses of property which conflict with the zoning requirements. Most zoning ordinances have a section permitting the granting of use permits for activities that are in conflict with the zoning ordinance but that are desirable or essential for the public convenience or welfare—for example, a rest home in a residential neighborhood. A use permit, when obtained, allows a property owner to make some use of his property which would otherwise be in violation of the zoning ordinance. He is allowed to continue that use as long as the permit is effective. Such permits usually have a time limit, and have certain conditions attached to them which can result in their being terminated if the conditions are not met.

4.   Administrative Hearings   [10.51]

Hearings before governmental bodies such as planning commissions, city councils, or boards of supervisors are known as *administrative hearings*. They may take the form of an application for a use permit, an application for a change of zoning, or an application for a variance (as well as many other forms). Local ordinances spell out the procedures for such hearings. These procedures must be strictly observed by anyone who seeks to gain something from an administrative hearing.

A citizen seeking something personally from a local governmental body should be aware of the fact that there is more involved than the wording of the ordinance and his own particular viewpoint. Most applications for variances, use permits, or changes in zoning create controversy. They also have a way of becoming political issues. Therefore it behooves a citizen seeking something from an administrative hearing to first ask himself if this is going to create any problems with his neighbors. If so, he should contact these neighbors first, and try either to get them to support him or at least to be neutral.

Second, he should find out by asking around what the attitude of the city staff is, and try to get a favorable reaction from them. Finally, he should attempt to find out in advance, what the reaction of planning commissioners and/or city councilmen or county supervisors, etc., will be before he allows his matter to come before them. Most battles on such matters as controversial zoning or planning are won prior to the public hearing by a lot of good hard preparation.

There are strict time limits in local ordinances that have to be followed, and there are also procedural remedies that must be followed. Before you can seek relief from a court for what you consider to be the ill-advised or illegal action of a governmental body, you must *exhaust your administrative remedies*, which means you have to follow up on whatever remedies the local ordinance provides before you can take the matter into court (see Section 5.7).

[10.52]   5.   Annexation

As cities grow and expand, more property comes within their jurisdiction by the process of *annexation*. Annexation requires notice, a public hearing, and the approval of a majority of property owners within the area being annexed to a city. The benefits of annexation include availability of city services, water supply, sewers, road maintenance, and police and fire protection, etc. The disadvantages are higher taxes and sometimes stricter controls over the use of the property. A key question in most annexation proceedings is how the property will be zoned after annexation. Anyone thinking about developing property after annexation should be sure to discuss with the city staff what zoning will be applied to the property after annexation.

F. INVESTMENTS

1.   Basic Principles of Real Estate Investment   [10.53]

There are certain basic principles with which every real estate investor should be familar, both as to meaning and application.

a.   *APPRECIATION*   [10.54]

Appreciation refers to the increase in value of real property that occurs with the passage of time because of rising prices, increase in building costs, etc. Although all real property does not always appreciate, the long-range trend over the past few decades has been continual increase in the price of land.

b.   *TAX SHELTER*   [10.55]

Real estate investors with large incomes look for *tax shelter*. This means a place where they can put their money and get a good return, but without having to pay more income tax on that return. A good tax shelter is an investment that produces a *paper loss* which the investor can write off against his ordinary income from his earnings or from other investments. The loss is a combination of the depreciation, interest, and tax writeoff that can be applied against an income from other sources to reduce taxes.

c.   *CASH FLOW*   [10.56]

Cash flow refers to the net cash available for distribution to the investor on a periodic basis (usually an annual basis). It means the amount of cash the investor can put in his pocket after all expenses have been paid.

[10.57]
d. LEVERAGE

When investing in real estate, it is possible to pay a small down payment (10 to 30 percent) and borrow the rest. That way, with a small amount of money (comparatively speaking) you can purchase a large or valuable piece of property. Using a small amount of money to buy an expensive piece of property is using *leverage*. Leverage is important in real estate investing because even though you have only 10 percent of the purchase price invested in a project, you are getting 100 percent of the benefit of the appreciation, cash flow, and tax shelter.

[10.58]
e. EQUITY BUILD-UP

When leverage is used to purchase real property by borrowing everything except a 10 or 20 percent down payment, monthly or other periodic payments will have to be made to repay the loan. A portion of each payment is *interest* and a portion is *principal*. The portion of each payment that is principal reduces the amount of the loan and builds up the equity (interest of the owner) in the property. Over a period of time the amount of each payment that is interest decreases and the amount of each payment which is principal increases and the *equity build-up* increases. Equity build-up is important because it increases the net value of the buyer's investment in the property.

[10.59]
f. DEPRECIATION

Depreciation means the deductions that can be taken against income. Depreciation is important because it produces tax shelter (see Section 10.17).

g. COMBINATION OF FACTORS [10.60]

Any good real estate investment should combine all of the above factors. Knowledgeable investors feel that they should be able to get an annual return of between 15 and 20 percent on their investment in the form of cash flow, equity build-up, and tax shelter. Appreciation would be an additional amount on top of that which could only be estimated because the true appreciation is not known until the property is sold.

2. Types of Investment

a. FORM OF OWNERSHIP

(1) Single Ownership [10.61]

Until recently the most common form of ownership for a real estate investment has been single ownership or ownership by a husband and wife. Such investments normally consist of a small piece of land, a second home, a duplex, or a small apartment building.

(2) Group Ownership [10.62]

A popular way to increase leverage and obtain better overall investment return is for a small group of people to get together and pool their funds to purchase an apartment building or a piece of commercial property which can be leased to one or more tenants. The members of the group will take title as tenants in common (see Section 6.51) or else will form a partnership or a corporation to hold title. Generally they prefer to hold title as individuals to get the most tax advantage out of their investment. It is well to have a written agreement, in such cases, that spells out the understanding among the parties, particularly what happens in the event someone dies or wishes to sell his interest.

[10.63]   *(3) Syndicates*

In recent years real estate syndicates have captured the public's fancy. A syndicate is a group of investors who pool their funds to purchase a large piece of property, usually an apartment house complex. Most syndicates are limited partnerships (see Section 7.28). Investors tend to be *limited partners,* and the promoter is the *general partner.* The general partner puts the deal together and sells limited partnership interests to the investors. The advantage of a limited partnership interest is that an investor is protected in the event things go badly; that is, he won't lose anything more than the amount he invested. This is not true of a general partner (see Section 7.23), who is liable for the debts and obligations of the limited partnership in the event that the limited partnership funds are not sufficient to pay such debts and obligations. Naturally a general partner is compensated for taking this risk as well as for managing the property.

Syndicates can either be *closed,* as where the individuals all know each other and have had business dealings together before and simply put their money together and form a syndicate to buy property. They can also be *open,* which means that money will be solicited from the general public. In most states any solicitation of the public requires a permit from the corporation commissioner or equivalent state officer (see Section 7.30). If any sale takes place across state lines, or if a person in one state buys an interest in a syndicate in another state, a federal permit from the Securities Exchange Commission may also be required. In such cases the law protects the investor by giving him an absolute right to a return of his investment if the syndicate was required to have such a permit and did not have it before it took the investor's money. Any investor who feels he has been taken, or who is dissatisfied with his investment and would like to find a way out, should first check to see whether a permit was required and if so whether the syndicator obtained a permit before taking his money (see Section 7.30).

Most of the large real estate syndicates that offer opportunities to invest to the general public require a minimum net worth and a minimum annual income from potential investors. These standards are not always strictly adhered to, sometimes because the syndicator bends the rules a little and sometimes because an overeager investor exaggerates his income or his net worth so that he will be permitted to invest in the syndicate.

The first rule of investing in a real estate syndicate is to check on the record of the syndicator. Don't take his word for it, but find out from independent sources how long he has been in business, what his reputation is, and what kind of a return he has produced in the past for other investors.

The second rule is to take a careful look at the particular property that is being offered. The facts and figures should be carefully analyzed to determine whether the investment is a good one. For an inexperienced person this involves getting some professional help from realtors, accountants, and attorneys.

The third rule is to carefully examine the proposed deal itself. Find out what is in it for the syndicator. How was the property acquired or how is it to be acquired by the syndicate? Is a commission to be paid to the syndicator? If so, how much? What other fees will the syndicator make on the deal? Is he investing his fees in the project by taking a percentage in lieu of receiving cash outright? Has he agreed to manage the property for the life of the syndicate? If so, is the management agreement reasonable? Will any assessments be made on the investors in the event more funds are needed? You should be sure that any project is adequately financed. Usually the best way to do this is to provide for a cash reserve in the beginning that is large enough to take care of all possible contingencies. That way no one will be likely to be asked to put up more money and have his interest in the project reduced if he is unable to invest additional funds at that time.

One key question that should be asked before investing in any real estate syndication is, "How difficult is it to get my money back out?" This question is sometimes tough to answer. Some syndicators will "guarantee" to repurchase your interest at any time. Be cautious of any such blanket guarantees. If the syndicator is capable of doing that for all investors he wouldn't need your money in the first place. Some syndicators will tell you that they will attempt to sell your interest to another member or to an outsider in the event you wish to get out. They will also tell you that they have always in the past been able to find a buyer for anyone who wanted to get out. Although that may be somewhat reassuring, it is far short of an ironclad guarantee. Therefore the fourth rule of investing in real estate syndicates is: Don't invest money in a real estate syndicate if there is a reasonable probability that you may have an immediate need for those funds in the near future. The average life of a real estate syndicate is five to eight years. The reason for this is that after that period of time the benefits of accelerated depreciation (see Section 10.17) taper off and the investors are better off to sell the building and get into a new investment where they can start taking some more accelerated depreciation.

(4) Real Estate Investment Trusts [10.64]

A real estate investment trust (REIT) is like a syndicate, and is indeed a form of real estate syndicate. Instead of a limited partnership, the vehicle for investment is a trust. The investors pay their funds to the trustee of the trust who purchases the property, manages it, and distributes cash flow and allocates depreciation, etc. to the investors. Real estate investment trusts are generally quite large (over 100 members) and the typical trust will invest in many different properties. In a way the owner of an interest in an REIT is like a shareholder in a large corporation, the main difference being that he may have certain tax advantages that a shareholder would not have.

b. KIND OF PROPERTY

(1) Apartments [10.65]

Apartments are excellent investments for investors who know what they are doing or who have an experienced manager who will manage the property for them. In evaluating a potential apartment investment one must consider the location, the access, the neighborhood environment, the age of the building, the type of construction, the state of repair, the probable maintenance or replacement costs, the probable vacancy rate, the competitive rental rates in the area, and the price and terms upon which the building is available (see Section 10.9).

(2) Commercial Property [10.66]

Commercial properties make excellent long-term investments. Location is a key factor. Also important is the type of tenant and the term of the lease. It is best to invest in commercial property when there is assurance of a long-term lease with a substantial tenant—one who will be able to pay the rent (see Section 10.12).

[10.67]

(3) Land

Any investment in raw land must be looked upon as speculative. Because no depreciation will be available (see Section 10.17), the tax shelter benefits are missing (except for interest on the loan if the investor finances the purchase). Therefore the appreciation must be greater to justify the investment. A careful analysis of the appreciation potential must be made (see Section 10.7). Farm land or timber land can be an excellent investment because the farm or the forest may produce income while the property is appreciating, and there may be some tax shelter benefits in the form of depreciation of farm equipment, farm buildings, and livestock (see Section 10.13); in the case of timber there are special tax benefits which include capital gain treatment on the sale of timber.

[10.68]

(4) Recreational Land

Many opportunities exist today for investment in recreational land. Opportunities range from purchase of large acreages down to the purchase of fully developed subdivision lots (see Section 10.8). In some cases an investment in a subdivision lot pays off in the form of a large gain on the sale price when the lot is sold within a few months after it has been purchased. However this is the exception and not the rule. The price of subdivision lots is controlled by the demand. If there is enough land available of the same quality and having the same recreational possibilities so that the developers can keep an endless supply of lots coming to the market, the price is not going to go up. The only time the price goes up is when a development takes place in a unique area where there is only a limited amount of land available—after it has all been sold, the price for land in that particular area may go up. If you wish to make a large profit on an investment in recreational land, you are generally better off to buy and hold undeveloped acreage in a good area. Many people have made small fortunes by buying land in large quantities around the site of a proposed lake that is to be created as a result of a new dam being constructed at some time in the future. However the word gets around and soon the price of the land is driven up by purchasers speculating on the rising demand for the land. It always happens sooner or later that the market tapers off and many people get left holding the bag because the land was overpriced by the time they bought it. They have little hope of making a profit and will be lucky to get their money back without taking a loss on the sale.

Beware of the romance of subdivision lots or acreage for sale in far off "Paradises," especially if you happen to live in some other state. Ask yourself, "If it's really that good a deal, why would they have to come as far away as my state in order to try to sell it?" Perhaps you ought to go there and take a look at the property before you decide to buy it. Be sure to ask for a copy of the public report required by the Interstate Land Sales Act (see Section 10.8).

In recent years there has been a boom in the sale of Mexican real estate to North Americans. North Americans can own land in certain parts of Mexico, but they must agree to surrender some of their rights as U.S. citizens when it comes to ownership of the land. They have to subject themselves to Mexican law and to the jurisdiction of Mexican courts. This is fine as long as no legal problems arise, but if they do arise, a North American absentee owner of Mexican property will have an uphill battle on his hands. There is a prohibited zone which extends inland for 100 kilometers from the borders of Mexico and 50 kilometers from the coastline of Mexico. Within that zone foreigners are absolutely prohibited from owning fee title to real property. Many schemes have been cooked up by overeager subdividers to get around these laws. They include such things as selling 99-year "club memberships" and long-term leases. Until recently the only interest in land that could be legally acquired in the prohibited zone by a North American was a 10-year lease. Anything longer than that was of dubious legality. However, recently the Mexican government has apparently authorized the selling of 30-year "trust estates" to North Americans. In theory this means that a North American can acquire most of the rights of ownership of the property for a period of 30 years, and after that the property may be transferable to someone else so that perhaps at the end of 30 years it still may be possible to get some or all of the original money back out. In any event an investment in Mexican real estate calls for experienced legal advice. If the Mexican real estate is sold in the United States, in a state which has up-to-date laws and regulations, the seller will be required to give you a public report (see Section 10.8) prior to taking your money.

G. SECURITY INTERESTS

1.   Mortgages   [10.69]

A *mortgage* is a legal document that transfers an interest in real property to a person other than the owner to secure a debt. Legal title and possession of the property still belong to the owner. The owner is also called the *mortgagor*, and he mortgages his property to the *mortgagee* (lender) by executing and delivering a mortgage instrument, which is then recorded. Recording the mortgage gives the mortgagee an *equitable interest* in the property. If the debt is not paid, the mortgagee can *foreclose* on the property. The terms "first mortgage" and "second mortgage" refer to the recording dates of the instruments. The earliest mortgage recorded is the first mortgage.

2.   Deeds of Trust   [10.70]

A *trust deed* is a legal document by which title to property is conveyed to a trustee to secure a debt to a third party who is the *beneficiary* of the deed of trust. The trustee has only such title to the property as is necessary to act as a trustee, which includes the right to sell the property in the event of default in payment of the debt. In the meantime the owner of the property (trustor), like a mortgagor, can transfer title to the property or further encumber it, subject to the recorded deed of trust. Mortgages and deeds of trust are quite similar, and indeed many states regard deeds of trust as simply mortgages with a power of sale (see Section 10.72).

3.   Priorities   [10.71]

The earliest mortgage or deed of trust that is recorded (bears the earliest recording date) *usually* has priority over all subsequent mortgages or deeds of trust. As each subsequent mortgage or deed of trust is recorded (if there are more than one), its priority is in turn established. There is no limit to the number of mortgages or deeds of trust that can be placed on a piece of property, in theory. As a practical matter, the number is limited by the relationship between the fair market value of the property and the total amount of liens in the form of mortgages or deeds of trust that at any given time are of record (have been recorded).

The recording date of a mortgage or deed of trust is not *always* the deciding factor in establishing priorities. Under some circumstances a mortgage or deed of trust that was executed earlier than some other mortgage or deed of trust may take priority over the latter even though it was not recorded until later. In other words, you can't always assume that priorities are established by recording dates when you are dealing with mortgages, deeds of trust, recorded judgments, governmental tax liens, etc. When questions over priorities arise, it is necessary to get legal advice.

[10.72]   4.   Foreclosure or Sale

Under an ordinary mortgage, an action must be brought in the appropriate court to obtain a *decree of foreclosure* and *order of sale*. When judgment is obtained establishing the validity of the mortgage and the amount due, including interest, costs, attorneys' fees, and so forth the court will order the property sold in the manner provided by law, which usually means a public auction, with notice being posted and published. If the mortgage includes a *power of sale*, then the mortgagee may have the property sold without having to file an action and go to court to get a judgment. This is similar to the exercise of the power of sale by a trustee under a deed of trust.

In some states you are permitted to have *judicial foreclosure* under a deed of trust, in which case the procedures are similar to foreclosure under a mortgage. Normally a sale under a deed of trust would be conducted by the trustee, exercising his power of sale. The steps required are all spelled out in the statutes. Generally there must be a period following notice of foreclosure during which the trustor (debtor) has the right to stop the sale by paying the beneficiary of the deed or trust what he owes him to date. Following this initial period there is usually a second period of time in which the trustor can stop the sale by paying off the entire amount of the debt (not just the amount due to the date of notice of foreclosure). During this second period of time notice of the sale must be published in a newspaper. After passage of the required time the property is then sold at public auction by the trustee. In some states, under certain circumstances, even after the sale has been completed, the debtor (former owner of the property) has a period of time within which he can buy his property back (*redeem* it) by paying everything he owes plus the costs and expenses of sale, interest, attorneys' fees, etc.

5.   Deficiencies   [10.73]

In the Depression of the thirties, a lot of people were unable to pay their mortgages or deeds of trust and because property values had fallen so sharply, judicial sales or foreclosure sales did not produce enough money to pay off debts that were owed, and the creditors came after the debtors for the remainder (deficiency) of what was owed. As a result, many states passed statutes outlawing deficiency judgments following foreclosure or judicial sale of property under a mortgage or deed of trust. However the antideficiency judgment statutes are limited in their application to certain types of loans and to situations where certain conditions apply. Any debtor, therefore, who owes a debt secured by a mortgage or deed of trust on real property should find out whether or not he will be subject to a deficiency judgment if he "walks away" from his obligation and lets the mortgagee or trustee sell the property to collect the debt.

[10.74]   6.   Homesteads

The purpose of the homestead law is to provide a family with a home that cannot be taken away from them by their creditors. Under most state laws the homestead consists of a residential dwelling together with the land on which it sits. A *declaration of homestead* must be signed, notarized, and recorded. If a homestead is properly executed and recorded, it protects the homeowner from a forced sale of his property by his creditors. The statutes creating the homestead privilege set forth the maximum amount that can be claimed as a homestead. You cannot homestead a $100,000 house and expect it not to be reached by your creditors. However if you had an $80,000 mortgage against the house, and under the homestead law of your state the homestead exemption was $20,000 you could protect yourself from the creditors. But as soon as the $80,000 mortgage was paid down, the creditors could come in and have the property sold. You would get to keep the $20,000 (which presumably you would invest in some other home and place a homestead upon it) but the creditors would get whatever else was left over after the mortgage or deed of trust was paid off. Only one homestead is permitted at a time to a person or to a married couple, and the homestead property must be an actual residence. Not all claims can be barred by filing a homestead. It won't protect you against mortgages or deeds of trust or judgments or other liens recorded prior to the declaration of homestead. A homestead will not protect you against mechanic lien claims for work done on the property after the homestead was recorded. If you execute a mortgage or deed of trust on property you have previously homesteaded, the homestead is "lifted" to the extent of the mortgage or deed of trust which then takes priority over the homestead. These rules vary from state to state and local statutes should be consulted. When you sell property subject to a homestead, you generally have a certain period of time within which you can invest the proceeds of the sale in other property upon which you may declare a homestead. Forms for declaration of homestead can be purchased at most stationery stores that carry legal documents. Most attorneys make a nominal charge for preparing and filing a declaration of homestead.

The law of water rights is complex and varies from one state to another. In general the owner of property has a right to use all water that falls upon his land any way he desires.

Riparian rights are the rights to use water flowing in a stream on or bordering the property for domestic purposes. There are limits on how much water can be so used, limits on the purposes for which it may be used, and limits on the amount of water that can be stored, and how long it may be stored.

Appropriative rights are the rights to take water from a stream and store it for later use. *Appropriative* rights are exercised by filing an application for appropriation of a certain amount of water for certain purposes. Storage and use plans must be approved. The agency having jurisdiction will review applications for appropriation of water and decide which ones to approve.

A property owner who diverts or changes the course of drainage of water on his property in a way that interferes with the natural flow will be liable to an adjoining landowner whose property is flooded or otherwise damaged by the change in flow.

XI. Constitutional Law

A. RIGHT TO BEAR ARMS [11.1]

The Second Amendment to the Constitution provides that the people shall have the right to keep and bear arms. The inclusion of this amendment in the Bill of Rights was to insure the right of the people and the right of the various states to collectively arm themselves for defense. The authors and supporters of this amendment remembered that an aroused and armed citizenry had saved the Colonies at various times from the French, the Spanish, the English, and the Indians. The right to bear arms then was based on the concept of the citizen-soldier, ready at all times to spring into action with his own rifle to protect his country. This concept is no longer realistic.

Today guns of various types may be kept for such purposes as hunting, target shooting, etc., but laws exist that regulate the manufacture, sale, and possession of firearms. Laws prohibit the carrying of concealed weapons (without special permits from the police). The National Firearms Act prohibits the interstate transportation or sale of such weapons as sawed-off shotguns, machine guns, and silencer-equipped pistols. Recent state legislation requires registration of all types of guns. Such laws have been upheld as constitutional and not in violation of the Second Amendment.

Because of recent increases in violent crime, many people have armed themselves with rifles and handguns. The so-called

"Saturday Night Special" is a cheaply made small-caliber pistol, usually made in a foreign country, which until recently could be purchased anywhere for a few dollars. This type of gun accounts for a large number of homicides each year. Literally millions of such weapons are at large in this country. Before attempting to carry such a weapon in your car or on your person, you should check with your local police department to find out what state laws and local ordinances exist that might make the carrying of such a weapon illegal.

Federal and state laws prohibit certain persons such as aliens from possessing firearms, and require the seller of a gun to sell it only to a purchaser who is qualified under law to own such a weapon.

B. ARREST

The Fourth Amendment to the Constitution provides that people shall not be arrested without *probable cause*. For the circumstances under which an arrest is proper see Sections 8.65 to 8.71. If an arrest is improperly made, you may have an action against the police for false arrest (see Section 8.70); but even if you consider the arrest to be improper, do not resist (see Section 8.69). Protest politely, but cooperate—you will get your chance later if the arrest has been improper.

C. ASSEMBLY

The First Amendment guarantees the right of the people to *assemble peaceably*. The Supreme Court upheld the right of black demonstrators to march, sing, listen to speeches, and to demonstrate in South Carolina in 1961, where no violence or disruption of traffic was involved. The Court suggested that the decision might have been different if traffic had been stopped or if the demonstrators had attempted to enter a park that was closed to the public. Assemblies that are peaceful and do not cause a disturbance or violate the rights of others are constitutionally protected. Assemblies that are in violation of local ordinances, or that disrupt traffic, or disturb the peace and quiet of a neighborhood may be prohibited or controlled. The police are usually caught in the middle between demonstrators and their sympathizers, on the one hand, and people who claim the demonstration has infringed upon their rights on the other.

Assemblies or demonstrations by students in school are subject to the further limitation that such activities will not be permitted to disrupt school activities. Some courts have upheld the punishment of students who were merely present at a riot but did not participate actively.

[11.4] **D.** BAIL

The Eighth Amendment of the Constitution provides that *excessive bail* shall not be required. In a case involving twelve officials of the California Communist Party who were indicted on charges of violating the Smith Act, the Supreme Court held that it was improper for the federal district court to set bail for each of the twelve defendants at $50,000 each. The Court said that bail must be set on an individual basis, and that it is not possible to penalize one individual because someone else jumped bail. If bail can be set unreasonably high, a man who may turn out to be innocent can be kept in jail without a trial. One purpose in setting bail is to enable a person to get out of jail and start working on his defense. If bail is set too high, the law provides a remedy by way of a motion to reduce bail and an appeal to a higher court (see Section 8.74.)

The Sixth Amendment provides that in all criminal prosecutions the accused has the right to counsel for his defense. Every person accused of a crime has the right to a lawyer, and if he cannot afford one, the state must provide one through the public defender's office, or the court must appoint an attorney to handle the defense. The average defendant does not have the legal skill to protect himself in a criminal trial. Recently we have witnessed some strange cases in which defendants accused of spectacular crimes have insisted upon defending themselves and have refused to cooperate with court-appointed counsel. This puts the courts in a difficult position because if a man has a right to be defended by an attorney, he probably also has a right not to be represented by counsel, if that is his desire. However if he represents himself, and does it poorly, some higher court may order a new trial and require that defense counsel be provided.

[11.6] **F.** CRUEL AND UNUSUAL PUNISHMENT

The Eighth Amendment prohibits cruel and unusual punishment. Originally this meant no torture. In one case the Supreme Court held that a sentence of fifteen years in chains for a $300 theft was in violation of the Eighth Amendment. In another case the Supreme Court held that it was not cruel and unusual punishment to put a man through the process of being electrocuted twice when the electric chair failed to work the first time. In a 1972 Supreme Court case involving the death penalty, some of the Justices said that they believed that the death penalty constituted cruel and unusual punishment (see Section 8.116).

[11.7] **G.** DOUBLE JEOPARDY

The state should not be allowed to make repeated attempts to convict a person for a crime; once is enough. The Fifth Amendment to the Constitution provides that a person who has been tried and found innocent of a crime cannot be tried again by the same court for the same crime. However, if he is tried and found guilty and appeals, the second trial, if granted, would not constitute double jeopardy. Neither is it double jeopardy if a *mistrial* has been declared and the defendant is retried, starting all over again. It is not double jeopardy for a person to be tried by two different courts (the courts of two different states, or a federal and state court) for the same crime. A man who shot the President of the United States could be tried by the state in which the crime was committed, and could also be tried by a federal court.

H. DUE PROCESS

The Fifth Amendment provides that no person shall be deprived of life, liberty, or property without due process of law. The Fourteenth Amendment provides that no state shall deprive any person of life, liberty, or property without due process of law. There are two kinds of due process: *substantive due process* and *procedural due process*.

Substantive due process means that the particular law itself that is involved in any given case must be fair and reasonable and not arbitrary.

Procedural due process means that authorities must act reasonably in carrying out or enforcing laws. An example of a violation of procedural due process of law can be found in the trial in 1961 of a man accused of bank robbery, kidnapping, and murder in a Louisiana court. A local TV station televised from his jail cell a conversation with the sheriff during which he admitted that he had committed the crimes. Three of the twelve jurors in the original trial admitted seeing the televised confession before the trial. His conviction was set aside by the Supreme Court so that he could be retried in another city. (He was again convicted in the second trial.) The court said that the amount of publicity in the case prevented him from having a fair and impartial trial, and that constituted a violation of procedural due process of law. Other examples of lack of due process would be the deliberate and systematic exclusion of black jurors by the state when a black is on trial, or trial before a judge who is obviously prejudiced against the defendant.

[11.9] I. DEPRIVATION OF PROPERTY

The Fifth Amendment provides that private property cannot be taken for public use without just compensation. The government can take property by exercise of the power of eminent domain (see Section 10.39), but it must pay the fair value of the property to the owner. Sometimes the government can deprive someone of property without intending to do so. A North Carolina chicken farmer won a case against the Air Force when his chickens were frightened to death by repeated noise from large military airplanes flying low over his property. Even though the government had only used the airspace above his property, the Supreme Court said that the effect was that of appropriation of his property, and that the government had to pay for his chickens. With the increasing size and noise of jets and the expansion of airport runways in the direction of residential areas, the right to quiet enjoyment of private property comes increasingly into conflict with the interests of companies engaged in transporting the public. When a freeway extends through a piece of property, the case clearly calls for compensation of the owner. However when a homeowner claims to be disturbed by the noise of departing and arriving jet traffic at the local airport, he may or may not be entitled to compensation. It seems that it depends upon how close he is to the runway, and whether he or the airport was there first.

J. EQUAL PROTECTION [11.10]

The Fourteenth Amendment to the Constitution provides that no state shall deny any person the equal protection of the laws. It is based on the words in the Declaration of Independence that "all men are created equal." The Fourteenth Amendment requires all states to treat citizens equally. Thus a law cannot be enforced against one race or sex, but not against another. Neither can one race or sex be denied access to public buildings or public schools. On the basis of these principles, a Louisiana county (parish) was told by a federal court that it could not close its public schools to the public and then reopen them as private schools (segregated) while the state continued to support public schools in other parts of the state. The court said this would not only deny equal protection to the minority students, but would also deny equal protection to all students (including white students) who lived in that county.

The liquor license at Mory's, the tavern popularized by the Yale Glee Club in the "Whiffenpoof Song" had its liquor license revoked for refusing to serve women, based on a state law that prohibited any state agency from sanctioning discriminatory practices.

[11.11] **K.** HABEAS CORPUS

Article I, Section 9 of the Constitution states that the privilege of the *writ of habeas corpus* shall not be suspended unless, when in cases of rebellion or invasion, the public safety may require it. In addition to the U.S. Constitution, most state constitutions guarantee the right of habeas corpus.

The Latin words translate into "you have the body." What they really mean is that "you shall bring the prisoner into court." The idea is to provide a means of preventing a prisoner from rotting in jail without a trial or without charges being filed against him. A prisoner who has a reason to protest something, such as being held without charges, without a hearing, without a trial, or receiving brutal treatment in jail, can have a public hearing by filing a writ of habeas corpus with the court. He gets an order from the court that he be brought to the court for a hearing on the matter. When the writ is issued, the authorities to whom it is issued (usually prison or police officials) have to prove to the court that they are holding him on proper legal grounds (see Section 8.76).

During the Civil War a writ of habeas corpus was used by the parents of an underaged boy who had enlisted without their consent in the Union Army. The parents tried (unsuccessfully) to get the boy out of the army. In another famous case decided by the Supreme Court at the same time, the court stated that the army had no right to suspend habeas corpus in the State of Maryland where civilian courts were still operating. However President Lincoln persuaded Congress to approve the suspension of habeas corpus (the only time this has been done) for the duration of the Civil War. After the war the Supreme Court again ruled that neither Congress nor the president could suspend the privilege of habeas corpus in any part of the United States where civilian courts were still operating. Some other purposes for which a writ of habeas corpus has been used include claims of cruel and unusual punishment, claims that a prisoner is being held under unreasonably high bail, and claims that a prisoner was not advised of his right to counsel before answering police questions that resulted in the police obtaining information to convict him.

The Second Amendment to the Constitution states that a well-regulated militia is necessary to the security of a free state. It goes on to say that the right of the people to keep and bear arms shall not be infringed (see Section 11.1). This means Congress shall not take away the right of the *state militia* to bear arms. It does not permit people to have private armies. Thus, where state laws prohibit private military organizations, they are not in conflict with the Constitution of the United States.

The First Amendment provides that Congress shall make no law abridging freedom of the press. There have been many cases over the years involving claims of freedom of the press. Although newspapermen have the right to publish almost anything, there are certain limitations. The *clear and present danger* rule is one of the limitations imposed by the Supreme Court. That rule is simply that no one has a right to publish or print material that results in a clear and present (meaning obvious and right now) danger to the community. An example would be an editorial in a newspaper advocating that someone be lynched or a building be burned, etc.

The *libel* rules (see Section 9.4) also constitute a limitation on the right of freedom of the press. A newspaper reporter who publishes libelous material may be sued by the injured party. In a really heavy case of libel, in which the reporter acted maliciously, he might even be prosecuted by the state for criminal libel. However newspapers and other public media have certain privileges which permit them to go a long way in publishing material that borders on libel.

Obscenity laws (see Section 8.48) also put limitations on freedom of the press. Courts have continually wrestled with the problem of what is obscene and what is not obscene, and laws change in this area as morals change. There will always be some limitations based on morality. It is doubtful whether society as presently constituted would allow the publication of hard-core pornography on the front pages of daily newspapers.

Rights of students to publish and distribute written material on campus are subject to the restriction that the material and the means of distribution thereof must not materially interfere with the educational process.

The First Amendment prohibits Congress from making any law that would make any religion an *official religion*. It also prevents Congress from prohibiting the free exercise of religious beliefs. You are entitled to believe in whatever religion you wish and to practice any religious beliefs as long as you do not break any laws or interfere with the rights of other people in so doing.

The courts have interfered with parents who would not allow their children to be treated by doctors because of religious beliefs, where the children's health was endangered.

In the early days of the *Mormon Church*, polygamy (having more than one wife at the same time) was practiced. A member of the Mormon Church was charged with bigamy (see Section 8.56) for having more than one wife. He defended himself by relying on his freedom of religion as guaranteed by the First Amendment. The case went to the Supreme Court, which ruled that the conviction for bigamy should be upheld. In deciding the case the Court stated that laws should not interfere with religious *belief* and *opinion*, but that they may prevent *practices* that are dangerous or illegal. To allow religious practices to be uncontrolled would permit some citizens to take the law into their own hands.

In another case some students who belonged to Jehovah's Witnesses were expelled from school for refusing to salute the flag. When a federal court prevented the students from being sent to reform school, the board of education appealed and the case went to the Supreme Court. The court held that students cannot be forced to salute the flag if this conflicts with their religious beliefs. The Court said that no governmental official can force citizens to confess, by word or act, their faith in politics, nationalism, religion, or other similar matters of opinion. The action of the local authorities in compelling the flag salute went beyond the authority granted under the Constitution.

The Supreme Court in 1963 ruled that compulsory prayer and Bible-reading exercises in public schools were unconstitutional. However, the teaching of religious history or the use of the Bible as a reference book in the classroom is acceptable.

Other highly controversial matters involving the law and religion include the tax exemptions that are given to church-owned property, use of federal money for direct or indirect aid to church schools, and church-sponsored laws that prohibit the conducting of business on Sunday.

There has been much controversy surrounding the conflict between religious beliefs and the compulsory draft laws. The draft laws contain exemptions from the requirement of military service in cases where that service would conflict with a person's religious beliefs. In 1971 the Supreme Court ruled, in the case of Muhammed Ali (Cassius Clay), that the religious beliefs of an individual, held in good faith, (no pun intended), could justify or excuse his refusal to submit to the compulsory draft.

O. SEARCHES AND SEIZURES

The Fourth Amendment states that the right of people to be secure in their persons, houses, and personal documents and papers shall not be violated by unreasonable searches and seizures, and that search warrants shall not be issued except when there is a good reason for doing so, based upon sworn testimony (see Section 11.16).

[11.16]   1.   Search Warrant

When armed with a search warrant, an officer may legally search a house, building, or automobile, etc. A warrant is obtained by presenting a judge with a sworn affidavit or sworn testimony to the effect that *probable cause* or *reasonable cause* exists to believe that a crime has been committed, and that certain evidence, important to the case, is located in a specific place.

[11.17]   2.   Probable Cause

It is improper for a warrant to be issued based upon the mere opinion of an officer, unsupported by any facts. Something must have occurred, or some facts must exist which are known to the officer requesting a warrant, that would reasonably cause him to believe that a crime had been committed and that evidence important to that crime (consisting of material described in the affidavit upon which the warrant was based) is in fact located in a particular place he wants to search. If an officer wants to go on a "fishing expedition" to someone's house because he thinks he may find something illegal there, but he doesn't have any reasonable cause for believing this other than his own personal suspicions, reasonable or probable cause does not exist for the issuance of a warrant. Even if he obtained a warrant and searched the premises, the evidence he seized could be suppressed (see Section 11.23). The Supreme Court has ruled, however, that the police may stop and search a suspect based on an anonymous tip that the suspect is carrying a loaded pistol.

3. Use of Force   [11.18]

It is improper for a search to be conducted by means of *unreasonable force*. This means force directed against an individual. It would be proper to stop someone from swallowing some pills, flushing something down the toilet, or throwing it away. However it would not be proper, once he had swallowed the object, for the police to take him to a hospital and have his stomach pumped. Evidence seized by means of unreasonable force can be suppressed (see Section 11.23). A requirement that a suspected drunken driver submit to a test of blood, breath, or urine is not considered to be the use of unreasonable force.

4. Personal Search   [11.19]

A person who is arrested at or near the scene of a crime shortly after it was committed may be searched. However the search cannot extend beyond his person and the immediate vicinity, unless the arresting officer first obtains a search warrant. Traffic violators can be searched to ensure that they are unarmed and to prevent the destruction of evidence. If an officer arrests someone for speeding and sees evidence such as drugs sitting in plain sight on the car seat, he may seize that without having to first obtain a warrant. "Stop and frisk" actions by the police are beyond their authority unless they have probable cause (see Section 11.17) to suspect a concealed weapon. In such a case they may "pat down" suspects for weapons, but cannot search inside pockets.

[11.20]   5.   Search of Car or Locker

Ordinarily a car cannot be searched without a warrant when the driver is stopped for a minor traffic violation. If he is stopped because of suspicion of burglary or theft, or transportation of illegal drugs, etc., then the car may be searched by the arresting officer. If the officer arrests a person for speeding and finds out the driver is a wanted drug pusher, and if he thinks that drugs might be concealed somewhere in the automobile, he can then probably search the car without a warrant. But he can't search the car after stopping a speeder just because he is suspicious of the driver's dress, haircut, or conduct.

Student lockers may be searched by authorities in emergency situations, such as where a peculiar odor (marijuana), for example, is coming from a locker.

Border searches are different. Officials may search your car and question you (even without giving *Miranda warnings* (see Section 11.29) without having to show probable cause or get a warrant.

[11.21]   6.   Search of Dwelling

Police cannot search a dwelling or a building without first obtaining a search warrant. Police cannot search a house (without a search warrant) when arresting the occupant of the house. However they can pick up evidence that is lying around in plain sight during the time they are making the arrest. Controversial "no-knock" laws exist in some states and may continue in various forms in federal legislation. Such laws permit police to enter without knocking (but with a warrant) if they *reasonably* believe that knocking first would lead to injury or to destruction of evidence. If you have something illegal in your house or car, don't consent to a search. Make it clear *you will not interfere*, but that you do not give your permission to the search. Note that parents can consent to let police search their minor child's room, even over the child's objections (unless the child is "emancipated" and is paying rent while living with his parents).

7. Wiretaps and Bugs [11.22]

Tapping a telephone or installing a hidden microphone in someone's dwelling or automobile is illegal. The laws are not entirely settled in this area as yet, though, and there may be certain circumstances under which some law-enforcement agencies can get court permission to use wiretaps or bugs. However, anyone faced with evidence gathered in such a manner certainly has a good chance of getting the evidence excluded from any trial (see Section 11.23).

8. Exclusion of Evidence [11.23]

Where evidence is gathered illegally (in violation of the Constitution or in violation of federal statutes or state laws), the person against whom the evidence is being used at trial should object to the use of the evidence. If he is represented by counsel his attorney will do this. The judge will have to decide whether to admit the evidence for use at trial or to exclude it. He may exclude the evidence if he thinks it was gathered in violation of constitutional rights. If the judge permits the evidence to be used and the defendant is convicted, he can raise the question of violation of his constitutional rights in his appeal. If the appellate court, upon reviewing the case, decides that the evidence was gathered in violation of constitutional rights, the conviction would be reversed and a new trial would be ordered in which the illegal evidence could not be used (see Section 11.27).

[11.24] P. SPEECH

The First Amendment provides that Congress cannot pass laws that prevent people from speaking or voicing their views. There are of course some limitations on this freedom of speech. The law of slander (see Section 9.4) is one such limit. No one has the right to use vulgar and profane language in public which is offensive to other reasonable people and in violation of obscenity laws (see Section 8.48). Justice Holmes once said, in discussing limitations on free speech, that "a man does not have the right to falsely shout 'fire' in a crowded theater and cause a panic" (when there is no fire).

Convictions for violating *criminal syndicalism* laws have been upheld in some cases and reversed in others. Such laws make it illegal to advocate crime, sabotage, or acts of violence against property, other people, or against the government. In some of these cases there is often a difficult factual question as to whether or not the speaker advocated (as opposed to implied or suggested) some sort of violence, and whether or not some violence and property damage or injuries did occur and did in fact result from his speech. The Supreme Court has stated that a person has the right to express unpopular views in public, but he does not have the right to cause a riot or create a disturbance of the peace. Whether or not an arrest of a person delivering a public speech is proper depends upon whether he was arrested for what he was saying or because what he was saying was creating a clear danger of a breach of the peace. However the court also said that the ordinary objections of a hostile audience cannot be used as a basis for silencing a speaker. Before the police can interfere with a person making a public speech, they must first make reasonable efforts to protect him (and his right to speak) from acts of bystanders that may threaten his right to speak. It would be improper for the police to refuse to protect a public speaker's right to talk if, for example, he was physically threatened by bystanders. It would be equally improper for the police to haul a speaker off to jail just to protect him from a hostile audience.

The free speech rights of students in school are subject to some additional legal restrictions that do not apply to citizens in general. Students are free to speak as long as their speech does not materially interfere with the school educational process.

Q. TESTIMONY

[11.25]   1.   Confessions

One of the basic beliefs of our society is that to force a person to confess to a crime is a violation of the most fundamental of laws. Many rights such as the right to counsel (see Section 11.5) and the right against self-incrimination (see Section 11.28) are based upon the fundamental rule against forced confessions.

[11.26]   2.   Confrontation and Witnesses

The Sixth Amendment provides that the accused person must be present when witnesses testify against him. He also has the right to have witnesses testify for him, even if they have to be subpoenaed. *Confrontation* (witnesses present in court) gives the accused the chance to cross-examine his accuser(s) and to challenge his accuracy in court. The accuser(s) can then be observed by the judge or jury and his manner and attitude may be taken into consideration in deciding whether or not he should be believed. Appellate courts and the Supreme Court have reversed convictions based upon testimony of witnesses that were not cross-examined either because their testimony was not given in open court or because it was given under conditions in which the accused did not have an attorney to cross-examine the witness for him.

What about the defendant who disrupts his trial with his unruly conduct? The Supreme Court has held that a defendant who makes the progress of his trial impossible has waived his right to *confrontation.* He can be excluded from the courtroom until he behaves (see Section 8.87).

3. Forced Testimony

[11.27]

The Fourth Amendment provides that the people have a right to be secure in their persons against unreasonable searches and seizures. Forced testimony is not admissible under our law. To force a person to testify, or to use force to obtain evidence is against the dignity of man. The Supreme Court once reversed a conviction based upon evidence in the form of morphine capsules that were pumped from the stomach of the defendant (without his consent) (see Sections 11.18 and 11.23).

4. Self-Incrimination

[11.28]

The Fifth Amendment provides that no one can be made to testify against himself. Every person has the right to remain silent unless he chooses to speak, and should suffer no penalty for maintaining silence. In a criminal trial the jury cannot be told that the fact that the defendant has not taken the stand to testify in his own behalf should be considered by them as some indication of his guilt. When a witness "takes the Fifth" he is invoking the privilege of the Fifth Amendment in refusing to testify.

What if the court offers *immunity* to a witness provided he will testify? In such a case a witness may be required to testify, and if he refuses, he may be found in contempt of court (see Section 8.39). However he must be granted immunity from prosecution by *all* courts, including federal and state courts (see Section 8.106), if he is going to be required to testify in a criminal case. The Supreme Court held in 1972 that a witness can be compelled to testify before a grand jury without a promise of immunity from prosecution as long as the prosecution is barred from using the compelled testimony and any leads developed from it against the witness.

[11.29]   5.   Right to Remain Silent

The Constitution guarantees you the right to remain silent before the questions of police officers. In the *Miranda* case a Mexican-American was arrested for kidnapping and criminal attack. He was questioned for two hours by police, who obtained his signed confession which started off by saying he had confessed of his own free will and with full knowledge of his legal rights. When his case got to the Supreme Court the conviction was reversed because Miranda was not told that he had a right to remain silent. As a result of that case, police officers are now required to give *Miranda warnings* to all persons who have become suspects in the investigation of a crime and all persons who have been arrested for the commission of a crime, before they are interrogated. The Miranda warning includes the statement that a person has the right to remain silent, and that he has the right to an attorney, even if he can't afford one. After getting such a warning one should think carefully before saying anything other than "I want a lawyer" (see Section 8.73).

R. TRIAL

The Constitution contains many guarantees of rights during trial.

1. Indictment

The Fifth Amendment provides that no one can be tried in a federal court for a serious crime unless a *grand jury* has heard evidence and decided that he should be tried. (This does not apply to men in the armed forces in time of war or public danger).

2. Charges

The Sixth Amendment provides that a person has the right to be told what he has been accused of, within a reasonable period of time after his arrest (normally no more than 24 or 48 hours). He then must be given an adequate opportunity to defend himself against those charges.

3. Jury Trial

The Sixth Amendment guarantees the right to a jury trial in a *criminal* case. The Seventh Amendment guarantees the right of trial by jury in *civil* cases where the amount involved is worth more than $20. This applies in federal courts. All states have their own rules providing for jury trials in criminal and civil cases.

4. Fair and Impartial Trial

The Sixth Amendment guarantees an impartial jury trial in criminal cases. The Fifth Amendment guarantees due process of the law. If jurors were selected improperly to insure a conviction, the Constitution would require a reversal and a change in the selection method. If a case had received such advance publicity that an impartial jury could not likely be obtained, then the Constitution would require a trial elsewhere (see Sections 8.85 and 11.8).

[11.35]   5.   Speedy Trial

The Sixth Amendment provides that in all criminal prosecutions the accused has the right to a speedy trial. This means you can't be forced to remain in jail for a long time prior to being brought to trial if you can't get bailed out. It doesn't mean, however, that you have to be tried immediately or else released. The Supreme Court has said that the right to a speedy trial is relative. It depends upon the circumstances, and there may be some unavoidable delays; but, if there isn't a good reason for a delay, it is clear that continual putting off of a trial, without the consent of the defendant violates his constitutional rights.

[11.36]   6.   Public Trial

The Sixth Amendment also guarantees the right to a public trial. This means no *kangaroo courts* or *star chamber* proceedings, behind closed doors. If the court can't try a man in public, he can't be tried at all. However this doesn't mean that the court can't lock him in an adjoining room where he can watch the proceedings by closed-circuit TV if he insists on interrupting the proceedings (see Section 8.87). It also doesn't mean that the whole country has to be in on the trial. If a certain courtroom has a reasonable number of seats and members of the public are admitted without discrimination (except that perhaps newsmen may be given preference over ordinary spectators) then the accused can't claim he was denied the right to a public trial simply because the overflow crowd was turned away.

7.   Presumption of Innocence [11.37]

It has long been a tradition that the accused person is presumed innocent until he is proven guilty. In a criminal trial the prosecution has to prove guilt *beyond a reasonable doubt* (see Section 8.98). Many people make the mistake of thinking that anyone accused of a crime must be guilty, if not of that crime, of something else. If the accused has a past criminal record, things are even tougher. Many times the news media make it almost impossible for a suspect to have a chance of being presumed innocent because by the time he gets to trial everybody in the county not only thinks he committed the crime but also knows exactly how he allegedly did it.

The *right to vote* is guaranteed to all citizens over eighteen years of age. There are certain residency requirements that apply to local elections only. Thirty days' residency qualifies a person to vote in a presidential election (see Section 13.16).

A citizen of the United States is any person born within the fifty states, Puerto Rico, or the Virgin Islands (with certain exceptions such as children of foreign diplomats); any child of American citizens born abroad; and a naturalized citizen. There are certain requirements for registration of birth with a U.S. consulate for children born abroad, and, in the case of a child having only one parent with U.S. citizenship, there are requirements of residency within the U.S. to perfect citizenship.

Every citizen of the U.S. has the right to *travel* within the U.S. and abroad. A *passport* is required for travel outside the U.S. and its Western Hemisphere neighbors. Every citizen is entitled to apply for and obtain a passport.

The right to vote, obtain a passport, travel, etc., can be limited by law. Circumstances where this has been done include emergency wartime regulations, national security matters, and criminal conduct or activities.

XII. Motor Vehicles

A. OWNERSHIP

[12.1]

The term "motor vehicles," as used here, will apply generally to automobiles, trucks, motorcycles, boats, and to a certain extent, airplanes. Because these things were unknown in the early days of the Common Law, the rules that apply are almost entirely statutory. Each state has its own motor vehicle code with extensive regulations pertaining to motor vehicles. In addition there are federal laws that apply to aircraft, boats used in navigable waters, and to trucks and automobiles used in interstate commerce.

Ownership of motor vehicles is based upon certain documents of title which go by various names such as "pink slip," "certificate of title," "owner's certificate," etc. To have title to a motor vehicle transferred to your name, you must obtain the owner's certificate from the present owner, have him endorse it (sign his name in the proper space), and then turn it in to the state so that a new certificate can be issued in your name. When bank financing is involved, the bank's name may appear on the document as legal owner, and the buyer of the motor vehicle will be shown as the registered owner. If you buy such a vehicle, you must assume the balance due (with consent of the bank) or the loan must be paid off.

More than one person can own a motor vehicle. The names

of all the owners should appear upon the certificate. If the names are connected by the word "and," it means that both or all owners must sign in order to legally transfer title. If the words are connected by "and/or," either owner may transfer title. Upon the death of one, the survivor can transfer title without a court order. To transfer title to a vehicle owned by a decedent, a court order is necessary. Such an order is obtained by petitioning the probate court. Minors may own motor vehicles where permitted by the laws of their state. However they must have a valid operator's license in order to be able to use the vehicle.

[12.2] **B.** OPERATION

The operation of motor vehicles is extensively regulated by state statutes. A booklet containing the rules may be obtained from any branch of your state department of motor vehicles. Aside from the many driving rules that apply to everyone, there are one or two rules of recent vintage which a lot of people seem to be unaware of. One of these is a rule passed in many states that makes it a crime to leave your keys in an unattended motor vehicle. Not only is it a punishable offense to do this in some states, but it also subjects the person leaving the keys to liability for harm which results when a thief takes the car because the keys are in it.

Another rule that many people seem to be ignorant of is

the rule that requires you to report any damage you do to another vehicle that is parked. If you put even a small dent in a car in a parking lot, either by carelessly opening your door so that it dents the side of the car next to you or by backing into or scraping another car, the law requires you to leave your name, address, and license number with the other vehicle. You can do this by writing it on a piece of paper and tucking it under the windshield wiper or sticking it through the open window of the car. If you don't do this, but simply drive off, and someone gets your license number, you may find yourself being arrested for the crime of failing to report damage to a parked vehicle. Even if the law didn't require this, it is just good manners to do it anyway. Most people carry insurance that would cover the damage, and by the same token the fellow whose parked car is damaged will have $50 or $100 deductible, so he will have to pay for the damage out of his own pocket if your insurance company does not pay. Contrary to popular belief, your insurance company will not raise your rates if you report such an incident, and they pay the cost of repairing the parked car you may have damaged.

[12.3] C. PARKING LOTS

If you park your car in a parking lot and return to find it stolen or damaged, or find that some things have been stolen from the car, is the parking lot proprietor responsible? Most lots hand you a ticket when you leave your car which you turn in to get your car back when you return. That ticket usually contains a lot of words that are supposed to limit the responsibility of the proprietor. As a practical matter, these provisions are of little effect. The important thing is whether you park the car, lock it, and take the keys, or whether you leave the keys with the car so that the attendant can move your car. If you park your car in an unattended lot, lock it, and take the keys with you, the owner of the lot isn't responsible for damage to your car by other motorists, or for theft of your car or its contents. If you drive up and get out of your car with the motor running, and an attendant parks it for you, you can in most cases collect from the parking lot owner if you find your car was damaged or that the car or its contents was stolen while you were away.

If you park the car yourself, but leave the keys in it at the request of the proprietor, some difficult questions can arise. If the lot is attended and your car is stolen, you can probably recover. However, if something were stolen out of your car, you might have to prove that the lot attendant was negligent in not watching your car. If your car was damaged by another motorist, you might have to prove that the lot owner could have prevented that from happening before you can recover from him (you can recover from the other motorist if you know who did the job)—(see Section 12.2).

D. DRUNK DRIVING

The offense commonly known as *drunk driving* consists of being in control of a motor vehicle while under the influence of alcohol. A similar and related offense is being under the influence of drugs other than alcohol. The treatment of these offenses, and the punishment for a conviction are quite similar.

In order to be convicted, must a person actually be driving the vehicle? It depends on what state you are in, but generally the law requires that the person be driving the vehicle or be in control of it. This doesn't mean the police have to have a witness who saw him drive. It can be established by circumstantial evidence that he was driving the vehicle, for example, when the defendant is found in his vehicle after having run off the road and into a telephone pole.

In some states the offense can only be considered so if it is committed on a public highway; in other states the statutes say that merely driving a vehicle while under the influence of alcohol is a crime, regardless of where it is done.

Being "under the influence" means being in a condition in which there is a lessening of the ability to handle a vehicle because of consumption of alcoholic beverages. The state of lessening varies from *in the slightest degree* to *an appreciable degree.* It is not necessary that the defendant be drunk or that the prosecution prove that he was drunk. The effect of the alcohol may be either on physical coordination or on mental alertness, or both.

It is not necessary to prove that the defendant was driving unsafely. In most cases, merely being under the influence is enough, even though there was nothing wrong with his driving otherwise.

An individual may be convicted of drunk driving even when the amount of alcohol he consumed was very small but when combined with other things, such as cold or hay fever pills, cough medicine, etc., it resulted in a lessening of his ability to handle a vehicle.

Who determines whether or not a person is intoxicated, and how is this done? The arresting officers will put the suspect through a series of tests at the scene if they suspect that he is under the influence of alcohol. They may ask him to close his eyes and touch his index finger to his nose. If he misses his nose on the first try, this is taken as some indication of being under the influence. They may ask him to walk a straight line on the pavement by putting the heel of one foot against the toe of the other foot as each step is made, and then turning around and walking back without losing balance. Another test is for the policemen to drop some small change on the ground and ask the person to pick it up. Still another test consists of repeating after the officer a simple tongue-twister. Some officers shine a flashlight into the eyes of the suspect and note how slowly his pupils contract. If the officer suspects that the driver is intoxicated, based on these tests or upon his observation of the conduct and appearance of the driver, he may ask him to submit to a further test. There are several different types of tests, but the three most common are blood, breath, and urine. A sample of blood or urine may be taken and submitted to a laboratory for analysis. A breath sample is taken by having the driver blow up a balloon, which is then sent to the laboratory for analysis of the air contained. The bood test is the most accurate and the most reliable. The purpose of the tests is to determine the percentage of alcohol contained in the blood. If there is less than 0.05 percent, in most cases the person is not considered to be "under the influence" and no attempt will be made to prosecute him for drunk driving. If the blood contains 0.05 to 0.15 percent, it is possible that the person may have enough alcohol in his system to be under the influence, and in such cases he may or may not be prosecuted, depending upon other factors. If the tests show more than 0.15 percent, the person will be presumed definitely under the influence, and in most cases will be found guilty. The percentage varies from state to state, some of them requiring only 0.10 percent for a presumption of intoxication to apply.

Refusal to take a test can result in immediate revocation of the operator's license. It is possible to avoid a charge of refusal to take a test if there is not a flat refusal, but a conditional request. This could consist of a request that independent witnessess be present at the time the test is administered by the arresting officer. Or a person might request that his personal physician take the blood sample. Another legitimate request would be to contact one's lawyer and get his advice before taking a test.

The concentration of alcohol tends to increase in the urine with time. The urine test, therefore, requires that you first void your bladder and then submit a subsequent urine sample. If this is not possible, the officers will ask you to take another test (breath or blood). If you delay too long, some courts have held that is the same as a refusal to take a test. Unless the officer giving the breath test is alert, it may be possible to cheat by not taking deep breaths before blowing up the balloon. You may have to take the test twice if you are suspected of cheating the first time.

Having been charged, and flunked the test, should you plead *guilty* or ask for a trial? In some jurisdictions it may be possible to plead guilty to the lesser offense of being drunk in public and thus avoid prosecution on the more serious charge of drunk driving. You will need the assistance of an experienced attorney in order to put yourself in a position to be able to do this.

Experts who practice in this area will advise you that you should not go to trial if you are in a situation in which you were arrested by one or more officers, driving alone (and have no witnesses on your behalf), and have come from a place where drinking was going on, and you participated. Even if you only had a few drinks, the deck is stacked against you in such a case. However if all you drank was one or two drinks and you can prove this by independent witnesses, you may have a better case. Or if you have a witness with you, such as your wife or a friend, you might be able to establish a defense. Occasionally a person may have a built-in defense, such as a speech defect or some physical incapacity that causes him to stagger when he walks. In general the question of whether or not to go to trial or plead guilty should be submitted to an experienced attorney.

When a guilty plea is going to be made, in some jurisdictions it is important to enter the plea in front of the right judge. Some statutes give the judges discretion in the area of sentencing for drunk driving offenses, and some judges are notoriously hard on drunk drivers. Here again the advice of an experienced attorney can be invaluable in keeping you out of the hands of a judge who may be very severe in handing out punishment to drunk drivers. Occasionally a situation occurs in which the only judge available is one who is notoriously biased against drunk drivers and hands out very stiff sentences. You may have no choice in that case but to exercise a *peremptory challenge,* if that is permitted by the laws of your state. You have to file an affidavit of prejudice against the judge, and you must do it within the time required by the statute that permits the peremptory challenge to be made.

E. PARENTAL RESPONSIBILITY [12.5]

Most states make parents liable for injuries or damages caused by their children's careless driving. These laws usually limit the liability to a total amount that may vary between $10,000 and $20,000, and in some cases more. The parents can be liable on two different bases: either they signed the application of their child for a driver's license or else they own the vehicle which the child was driving with their permission and consent. Liability of the parent may go beyond the amount set by statute under circumstances in which the parent knew that his child was a negligent driver and nevertheless continued to let him use the automobile.

F. OWNER RESPONSIBILITY [12.6]

Most states have statutes that make the owner of any motor vehicle liable for any injuries or damages resulting from the driving of the vehicle by any person *with permission and consent* of the owner. The total amount of liability is limited, but can be as much as $20,000 or even more.

The following procedures are commonly recommended for anyone involved in an automobile accident (see also Section 5.21).

- Stop immediately, in as safe a place as possible. Even if the damage appears slight, don't drive away (see Section 12.2). Unless the damage is quite minor, notify the police or have someone notify them. It may be helpful to light a flare to warn other vehicles.

- If anyone is injured, call an ambulance. Don't move any injured persons unless absolutely essential for their safety.

- Exchange driver's license information and registration information with the other driver.

- Make a note of the name, address, and telephone number of all persons involved and all witnesses.

- Write your own summary of the accident. Make a diagram to show the number of lanes, any traffic signals present, etc. If you have a camera, take pictures.

- Don't admit responsibility for the accident. Don't engage in an argument with anyone present as to who caused the accident. If you have been injured or are emotionally upset by the accident, try to avoid making any statement except to give your name and address.

- If you are injured, see a doctor as soon as possible.

- Notify your insurance company, and submit evidence of your insurance to the other party, if requested.

- See your lawyer if you or anyone was injured in the accident, or if you were charged with a traffic violation.

- Be sure to leave your name and address on a piece of paper if you damaged a parked car (see Section 12.2).

XIII. Civil Rights

A. CIVIL RIGHTS COMMISSION [13.1]

The Commission on Civil Rights is appointed by the President of the United States. It has the duty to investigate charges that citizens are being deprived of their right to vote, are being denied equal protection of the law, or are being discriminated against in regard to voting, education, housing, employment, use of public facilities, transportation, or the administration of justice. The Commission has the power to subpoena witnesses and to take testimony regarding charges of violations of civil rights that are submitted to it by any citizen. It also acts as a clearing house for information on denial of equal protection of the laws based on discrimination.

B. EQUAL RIGHTS UNDER THE LAW

All persons in the United States have the equal right to make and enforce contracts, and to sue. They have equal rights to the benefit of all laws and are subject to the same punishments, penalties, taxes, etc. Discrimination in any of these matters based upon race, religion, sex, etc. is against the law now (see Section 11.10).

C. PROPERTY RIGHTS

All Citizens have the same right to inherit, purchase, lease, sell, hold, and convey real and personal property.

D. CIVIL ACTION FOR DEPRIVATION OF RIGHTS [13.4]

Any person who is deprived of any of his civil rights has a right to sue the party responsible for the deprivation. A special federal statute creates this right. State laws also exist to protect civil rights. Local or state laws should be consulted first, and state remedies pursued before turning to the federal law and federal law-enforcement agencies. Only if there is no applicable state law, or if it is not enforced, should federal law be turned to for relief.

E. CONSPIRACY TO INTERFERE WITH CIVIL RIGHTS [13.5]

If two or more persons conspire to prevent an official from performing his duties, or if they conspire to prevent a witness from testifying, or if they conspire with intent to deny any citizen the equal protection of the laws or to injure him or his property in order to prevent him from exercising or obtaining his civil rights, those persons can be prosecuted under a federal statute for conspiracy to interfere with civil rights.

[13.6] **F.** PROSECUTION FOR OFFENSE

The United States Attorney General's office, and specifically U.S. Attorneys, marshals, deputy marshals and commissioners appointed by district courts, and other similar officers, are authorized and required, at the expense of the United States government, to prosecute all persons who are alleged to have violated the civil rights of any other persons or to have conspired to violate such rights. That means they have to cause such persons to be arrested and tried for the offense committed. States have similar laws. There are also penalties that apply to persons who willfully make false charges of civil rights violations.

[13.7] **G.** PUBLIC ACCOMMODATIONS

Public accommodations include such things as hotels, motels, lodges, restaurants, cafeterias, lunch counters, soda fountains, or other similar facilities primarily engaged in selling food to be eaten on the premises; also gasoline stations, movie theaters, concert halls, sports arenas, or other places of entertainment, and similar type facilities. Not included are private nonprofit clubs that are not open to the public.

1. No Discrimination [13.8]

All persons are entitled to be free from discrimination or segregation in using public accommodations. Equal enjoyment is guaranteed by special federal statutes, and no coercion or deprivation of the rights to equal access and use is permitted.

2. Civil Action for Injunction [13.9]

If any person is engaging or is about to engage in a practice involving discrimination in the use of public accommodations, the person who is the victim of the discrimination can bring a civil action to enjoin (have the court order a halt to) the discrimination or deprivation of equal rights to use public accommodations. If the person bringing such an action prevails, the court may award him reasonable attorneys' fees as well as costs.

3. Intervention by Attorney General [13.10]

The U.S. Attorney General may intervene in a civil action brought by an individual who claims that his civil right to use public accommodations has been blocked or is going to be blocked.

H. ACTION BY ATTORNEY GENERAL
[13.11]   BASED ON VIOLATION OF CIVIL RIGHTS

If an individual complains to the U.S. Attorney General that he is being deprived of or is being threatened with the loss of civil rights on account of his race, color, religion, sex, etc., by being denied the right to equal use of any public facilities, the Attorney General is authorized to start a civil action against the parties who are allegedly discriminating. If the Attorney General's office has reasonable cause to believe that any person or group of persons is engaging in a practice of resistance to the full enjoyment of any civil rights, the Attorney General may bring a civil action to prevent such resistance and to end such discrimination.

[13.12]   I. PUBLIC EDUCATION

If any parent or group of parents sign a statement that their child or children are being deprived of equal rights to get an education and of equal rights to the use of public schools, the Attorney General can start a suit against the school district or the officials who are alleged to be depriving those children of their rights to equal use of the school facilities. This of course applies only to public schools. An individual can also sue in any court to obtain the right to equal use of public school facilities. He doesn't have to wait for the Attorney General to bring an action for him.

J. FEDERALLY ASSISTED PROGRAMS [13.13]

No qualified person can be excluded from participation in, or be denied the benefits of, any public program that receives federal financial assistance.

K. EQUAL EMPLOYMENT [13.14]

Except in the case of individuals doing work for religious societies (for example priests and nuns), it is unlawful to discriminate against a person with respect to his pay or terms or conditions of employment because of race, color, religion, sex, or national origin. It is also unlawful for any employer or an employment agency to discriminate against an individual, or for a labor organization to discriminate against an applicant for membership on such grounds. There is an exception in cases where religion, sex, or national origin is a bona fide occupational qualification for employment. For example, an airline may advertise openings for female stewardesses, and may limit the applicants who will be considered for the job to females.

An Equal Employment Opportunity Commission has been created which is appointed by the president. The Commission has power to listen to testimony, to subpoena witnesses, and to study and investigate charges of a violation of the right to equal employment. If the Commission can't get the voluntary cooperation of persons charged with such violations, the aggrieved party may file an action and if he prevails he will be entitled to reasonable attorneys' fees and costs. The Attorney General may also bring an action against any persons that he has reason to believe are violating equal employment laws. Each employer, employment agency, and union is required to post notices to employees, applicants, or members setting forth a summary of these equal employment rights and information pertaining to filing of complaints.

[13.15]   1.   Preference of Veterans

The Civil Rights Act did not repeal special laws that create rights or preferences for veterans. Veterans can still be given preference in obtaining jobs, etc.

The right to vote is guaranteed. The application of different standards to different races in determining eligibility to vote is prohibited. In federal elections the age of eligibility is eighteen. In state elections, state law applies in determining voting age (until a constitutional amendment lowering the voting age to eighteen is approved by three-quarters of the states). (See Section 11.38.)

XIV. Miscellaneous Laws

A. CONFLICT OF LAWS [14.1]

Occasionally a case arises in which the laws of two different states may apply, and those laws may be different. If a contract is entered into in Texas, and a suit based upon a breach of the contract is brought in Ohio, what happens if the law of Texas and the law of Ohio are different on some important question? The court would have to decide whether to apply the law of Texas or the law of Ohio. In such a case there is said to be a *conflict of law*. There are complicated legal rules that apply in such cases. Sometimes the law of one state is applied, and sometimes the law of another state is applied. If you ever get involved in a case in which a conflict of law exists, you should have a good attorney on your side. As a general rule, it can be said that the law of the state having the greatest interest in the outcome of the case will be applied.

B. MUNICIPAL ORDINANCES

Every local government passes its own laws, which are usually called *ordinances.* These cover things such as regulation of traffic, disturbing the peace, uses that can be made of real property, etc. If you want to find out whether something is legal or illegal, it is not enough just to look to the state and federal statutes. You must also look to the local ordinances. A copy of these may be obtained (usually for a small fee) from the city clerk's office, or equivalent office. These ordinances may be enforced through the courts and the judicial system the same way state criminal statutes are enforced. In some cases. such as violation of zoning ordinances, the city attorney (or equivalent officer) may prosecute the action instead of the county attorney or district attorney. Some of the things commonly regulated by local ordinances include use and possession of firearms; sale, possession, or use of fireworks; door-to-door selling; burning of trash or leaves; public parades, dances, or demonstrations; and *curfew* (presence of minors on public streets after certain hours).

The laws on lost property vary from state to state. In the frequent case of the lost purse or wallet, if the name of the owner is inside, the finder is obligated to try to notify the owner. If there is no identification, some laws put the burden on the owner to advertise for his lost wallet. Other laws require the finder to file a statement with a court clerk, or to record a description with the county recorder in a lost property book, and in some cases to publish a description of the property. The owner who claims the property must pay the costs of publication.

No reward need be paid by the owner for the return of his lost property unless one has been offered. Unless the amount of the reward offered is definite, the owner can pay whatever he chooses.

If property is lost (left) in a restaurant, theater, bus, taxi, airplane, etc., the owner or operator of such place is the one who should keep the lost article until its owner shows up to claim it (rather than a patron or passenger who finds it). What if you find a wallet containing money but no identification in a theater and turn it over to the manager, but the owner never returns to claim it? Who gets the money? The answer is not always the same. Check the law of your state.

D. PATENTS

It is possible to obtain a *patent* for an invention from the Patent Office in Washington, D.C. The object or design must not have been previously patented, and should not have been on sale or in public use for a certain period of time prior to the application. The application is filed, together with a fee and a drawing or model, with the patent office.

A patent attorney should be retained to do this. He will usually recommend a patent search first, to be certain the invention is patentable. Searches are conducted by specialized firms in the Washington area, and the cost is not usually very much ($100 is average).

Once issued, a patent is good for seventeen years. *Design patents* (a new design for an article) are available for shorter periods. A patent is transferable, like other personal property; it can be sold or given to another. The patent gives the inventor the exclusive right to make, use, and sell the invention. The time required to issue a patent is more than a year, and in some cases more than two years. Special priority is given to inventions that aid in improving the environment—the time may be only six to eight months for antipollution devices.

E. TRADEMARKS

A *trademark* is a distinctive mark, emblem, or word used on goods that are sold in commerce. The mark identifies the goods and the manufacturer.

Trademarks are registered with the Patent Office in Washington, D.C. An applicant files an application form, including the fee, and a drawing (in proper form) of the trademark with the Patent Office. The registration period is twenty years. Registration is renewable. The exclusive use of the trademark is guaranteed by registration.

F. COPYRIGHTS

The author, composer, or artistic creator of a literary work, musical composition, or artistic creation may apply to the Register of Copyrights for a *copyright*. The forms for application are available from the Copyright Office in Washington, D.C.

The work should have a copyright notice on it. The notice consists of the words "copyright 1975 by John Smith" or the letter *c* enclosed in a circle followed by the name or initials of the owner (© John Smith).

The application, together with the fee and copies of the work, are sent to the copyright office. The copyright grants the owner the exclusive right to publish or sell his work for twenty-eight years. A copyright is renewable. It may also be sold or given to another.

Glossary

abortion: an act causing the premature delivery of an undeveloped human embryo to prevent live birth.

abstract of title: a summary of the history of ownership of a parcel of real estate based on deeds and other recorded documents.

accessory: a person who contributes to, or helps in the commission of a crime by participating in its preparation or by later concealing the crime or the criminal.

accomplice: a person who aids the principal offender in the commission of a crime.

accord and satisfaction: the settlement of a disputed claim between two parties by payment or the performance of some act.

acknowledgment: a statement under oath, made before a notary, acknowledging that a legal document has been signed by the person making the statement.

acquittal: the dismissal of a criminal charge against a person by verdict, judgment, or some other legal process.

act of God: an event caused by nature or natural forces rather than by human action.

action: a lawsuit, either civil or criminal, brought by an individual or by the state to protect a civil right or redress a wrong.

actionable: furnishing ground for a lawsuit.

adjudication: the pronouncement of a judgment or decree by a court.

administrative law: a branch of law governing procedures before governmental bodies.

administrator: one appointed by a court to handle a decedent's estate, generally when there is no will. (*administratrix*: a female administrator.)

admissible: evidence or testimony acceptable by a court.

admission: a voluntary concession, or confession of facts by a party to a lawsuit.

adoption: the creation of a relationship of parent and child between two people by judicial proceeding.

adversary system: a system of legal procedure whereby opposing parties present their respective sides to a case and the neutral trier of fact decides which side prevails.

adverse possession: a means of acquiring title to real property through occupancy for a particular period of time.

affidavit: a written and sworn statement witnessed by an authorized official such as a notary public.

agent: a person who acts on behalf of another person, called a principal.

aggravated assault: an attempt to seriously harm another person with a dangerous weapon.

alibi: the claim of an accused person that he was elsewhere when the crime was committed.

alimony: money paid by one spouse for the support of the other spouse pursuant to court order.

allege: to charge, to assert, or to declare.

allegation: an assertion that a party to a suit intends to prove in court.

alter ego doctrine: a rule sometimes applied by courts to hold a stockholder personally liable for corporate debts.

amicus curiae ("friend of the court"): someone who files a brief in a court case in which he is not directly involved.

amortization: the paying off of a loan by a means of periodic payments.

anarchy: the destruction of government by lawlessness.

annulment: the setting aside of a marriage by court order.

answer: a pleading filed in response to a complaint.

appeal: a request by the party who lost a trial that a higher court review the decision.

appellant: the party who appeals to a higher court.

appreciation: an increase in the value of property.

appropriative rights: the right to take water from a stream and store it for later use.

arbitration: the hearing and settlement of a dispute between parties by a third person.

arraignment: calling a suspect before a court to hear the charges against him.

arrears: overdue in payment of a debt.

arrest: the physical detention of a person charged with the commission of a crime.

arson: the deliberate and illegal burning of property.

assault: an unlawful attempt or threat to harm another person.

assembly: the meeting together of a number of people.

assignment: the legal transfer of property, or of some right from one person ("assignor") to another ("assignee").

assumption of risk: the intelligent and voluntary agreement (implied rather than express) of a person to assume responsibility for his personal safety.

attachment: the legal seizure of property by means of a writ or other judicial order.

attainder: (see *bill of attainder*).

attestation of a will: the act of signing one's name as a witness to a will.

attorney-in-fact: a person who is authorized by another to act on behalf of the latter.

bail: a sum of money which can be posted with the court in cash or in the form of a bail bond as security for the release of a prisoner from jail.

bail bond: a document pledging that a certain sum of money will be paid to the court if the prisoner whose release is obtained for the bond fails to appear in court on the date required.

bailee: a person to whom personal property is entrusted.

bailiff: an officer responsible for maintaining order in the courtroom.

bailment: the temporary transfer of personal property from one person to another, with the understanding that it will be returned when the purpose of the bailment is accomplished.

bankruptcy: a person (or entity) whose liabilities exceed his assets and who is unable to pay creditors may distribute his assets among his creditors in accordance with federal rules, thereby going through bankruptcy.

bar: that section of the courtroom used by attorneys and their clients. It also refers to lawyers in general.

barrister: a trial lawyer in England.

battery: unlawful touching or striking of a person.

bearer paper: a negotiable instrument which can be transferred by delivery, without endorsement.

bench warrant: a court order for the arrest of a person.

beneficiary: a person named in a trust or a will to receive something of value.

bequeath: the giving of money or property by will.

bequest: the gift of money or property in a will.

best evidence rule: a rule of trial procedure which requires the introduction of a document as evidence rather than a summary or interpretation of its contents.

bigamy: being married to more than one person at the same time.

bill of attainder: a special law passed for the purpose of punishing someone without a trial.

bill of costs: an itemized statement of expenses which the prevailing party may collect from the losing party in a lawsuit.

bill of particulars: an itemized statement of the basis of a claim for which a suit is brought.

Bill of Rights: the first ten amendments to the Constitution of the United States.

bill of sale: a written document by which title to personal property is transferred.

binder: a written legal document which acts as a temporary contract, such as for the purchase of property or insurance.

blackmail: the extortion of money by threats of exposure.

blue-sky laws: laws regulating the sale of securities in order to prevent fraud.

bona fide: a Latin phrase meaning "in good faith."

bond: a written promise to pay a certain amount of money at a certain time or in a certain event.

booking: the process of entering an official charge against a suspect on a police register.

breach: breaking a law or violating a legal duty.

breach of contract: the unjustified refusal or failure to perform a contractural duty.

breach of promise: the refusal to carry out a promise to marry.

bribery: illegal payment to a public official to influence his action.

brief: a written argument or summary of a case.

broker: an agent who represents a buyer or a seller.

burden of proof: the duty of a litigant to present sufficient evidence to establish a fact or to win his case.

burglary: entering property owned by another person with the intention of committing a crime.

capacity: the legal ability to take certain action.

case law: that part of the law created by court decisions, as opposed to statutes.

cash flow: the net spendable income from an investment.

causa mortis: a Latin phrase meaning "in contemplation of death."

cause of action: the legal basis for a lawsuit.

caveat emptor: a Latin phrase meaning "let the buyer beware."

certiorari: the review by an appellate court of the decision of a lower court.

chain of title: a list of the owners of a parcel of real property, traced from the original owner to the present owner.

challenge: an objection voiced by an attorney to a prospective juror.

challenge for cause: the objection by an attorney to a prospective juror on grounds that the juror is biased.

change of venue: the transfer of a case from one judicial district to another.

charge: a formal legal accusation against a suspected criminal.

chattel: an item of personal property.

chattel mortgage: a security instrument affecting personal property.

child support: the payments that the court requires a divorced or separated parent to make for the costs of raising a child.

circumstantial evidence: evidence that tends to establish other facts that cannot be proven directly.

citation: an order directing a person to appear in a legal proceeding to answer a charge.

citizen's arrest: an arrest made by a person who is not an officer of the law.

civil action: a legal proceeding brought by a plaintiff seeking compensation or relief.

civil disobedience: the deliberate violation of the criminal law by a person who intends to challenge the validity of that law in court.

civil law: the system of law based on written statutes or codes rather than on court decisions. The term is also used to distinguish laws concerned with relationships between people, as distinguished from criminal law.

clemency: the judicial or executive granting of milder punishment to a convicted criminal.

closing: the consummation of a legal transaction, usually involving the purchase of real property.

codicil: a formal legal document used to amend the provisions of an existing will.

collateral: property or money used to secure a promise to pay a debt.

collusion: two or more persons acting secretly together to defraud or deceive another.

comity: the recognition by one state of the judicial decisions of another state.

common law: the body of law based on cases decided by judges, as distinguished from laws contained in codes and statutes.

community property: property acquired by a married couple, during marriage, other than by gift or inheritance, in accordance with the laws of certain Western and Southern states.

commutation: the changing of a criminal punishment to one of a lesser degree of severity.

comparative negligence: a legal system for weighing the relative degree of blame of the parties involved in a civil action based on negligence to determine the amount one party may recover from the other.

competency: the legal ability or fitness of a person to testify.

complaint: in a civil action, a pleading filed by a plaintiff alleging a wrongful act by the defendant and seeking relief or damages; in criminal law, a written charge accusing a person of a crime.

compounding a felony: agreeing not to prosecute or aid the prosecution of a crime in return for a payoff.

conciliation court: a special family law court.

condemn: to sentence a criminal.

condemnation: the taking of private property for public use (see *eminent domain*).

condominum: a multifamily dwelling or group of dwellings in which each person owns his own unit and owns an undivided interest in the rest of the property with the owners of other units.

confession: an admission of guilt made by a person accused of a crime.

conflict of laws: a case in which the laws of two states apply, and the laws are different.

connivance: the consent by one party to the unlawful conduct of another party.

consanguinity: blood relationship.

conscientious objector: one opposed to war because of religious or personal philosophical convictions.

consent decree: settlement of a case by an order of the court approved by both parties.

consideration: giving, promising, or doing something as part of a contract.

consolidation: a union of two or more existing corporations into a new corporation.

consortium: the reciprocal rights of husband and wife for love, affection, companionship, etc.

conspiracy: an agreement by two or more parties to commit a crime.

constitutional law: that body of the law dealing with government and its relationship to the people.

construction: the interpretation of legal documents.

contempt of court: willful disregard of an order of the court; conduct disrespectful of the court.

continuance: the postponement of a court proceeding to a later date.

contract: an agreement by two or more persons which involves a promise to do or refrain from doing something.

contributory negligence: the failure to exercise due care for one's own safety.

conversion: the appropriation of property that belongs to another.

conveyance: the transfer of title to property.

conviction: a finding of "guilty" following a trial.

copyright: the exclusive right to publish, reproduce, or sell a literary or artistic work.

coroner: the official empowered to determine the cause of death.

corpus delicti: a Latin phrase meaning "body of the crime." It means the facts that are essential to prove a crime was committed.

corroboration: the testimony of one witness which supports that of another witness.

co-signer: a person who signs his name to a note along with another person.

count: a single item in a legal document such as a complaint or indictment.

counterclaim: the allegation of a debt or claim by a defendant against a plaintiff.

court martial: the trial of military or naval personnel for violation of service regulations.

covenant: an agreement or promise to do or to refrain from doing something.

credibility: the apparent truthfulness of a witness.

creditor: a person to whom a debt is owed.

cross-examination: the questioning of a witness by the attorney representing the side against whom the witness was called, for the purpose of testing the truthfulness of his testimony.

curfew: a law requiring persons who do not have a good reason to be there to be off the streets.

curtesy: the rights of a husband to the property of his deceased wife at common law.

custody: the care and keeping of property or in family law, of children.

damages: the loss suffered by an injured party; the amount of money awarded to a successful plaintiff.

debenture: a document issued by a corporation in return for a loan, sometimes redeemable for corporate stock.

declaratory judgment: a decision by the court interpreting a written document the meaning of which is in dispute.

decree: the judgment of a court concerning the rights of parties to an action.

deed: a written legal document transferring title to real property.

defacing property: the deliberate damaging or destruction of property.

defamation: the making of false statements (either oral or written) tending to injure a person's reputation.

default: the failure to perform a legal obligation.

default judgment: a judgment entered in favor of a plaintiff where the defendant failed to appear or answer the complaint.

defendant: the person against whom a civil or criminal action is brought.

defraud: to trick or cheat another person.

delinquent: the failure to pay a debt on time; a minor who is unmanageable by his parents or who has committed a crime.

demur: to object to a complaint as being legally insufficient.

demurrer: a pleading filed by one party to an action that admits the allegations of a complaint but says that no case has been stated.

deponent: a person whose deposition is taken.

depose: to take a deposition.

deposition: a written record of the testimony of a witness given under oath.

depreciation: the decline in value of an asset over a period of time which can be written off for tax purposes.

deputy: a person authorized by law to perform some of the functions of an official of the government.

descent: the inheritance of property from a person who died without a will.

desertion: the abandoning of one spouse by the other.

devise: to leave property by means of a will.

devisee: a person who receives property under a will.

direct examination: the questioning of a witness by the attorney who first called him to the stand.

disaffirm: to revoke or repudiate.

disorderly conduct: public behavior that tends to disturb the peace.

disposition: the final termination of a case; the disposing of property by court order.

district courts: federal courts of the United States in which cases involving federal questions are tried.

disturbance of the peace: interruption of the quiet of a neighborhood or community by unreasonable and unnecessary noise.

divorce: the dissolution of marriage by court decree.

docket: a list of cases and the dates they are set for trial.

domicile: the permanent residence of a person.

donor: person making a gift.

double indemnity: a provision in a life insurance policy providing for payment of twice the amount of insurance in the event of accidental death.

double jeopardy: a second prosecution for the same crime in the same jurisdiction.

dower: at common law, that part of a man's estate which his widow was entitled to claim on his death.

drawer: the person who writes a check or otherwise creates a negotiable instrument.

due process of law: the constitutional process that must be followed in order to deprive a person of liberty or property.

duress: use of force or threats.

easement: the right of one or more persons to use the land of another person for a particular purpose.

eleemosynary: charitable.

emancipation: the attainment by a minor of freedom from control of his parents together with the right to keep his earnings and the loss of his right to parental support.

embezzlement: the wrongful taking of another's property by one to whom the property has been entrusted.

eminent domain: the power of the state to acquire private property for public use after compensation to the owner.

encroachment: the intrusion of a structure across the boundary between two properties.

encumbrance: a legal claim against property (usually recorded).

endorsement: a signature on a negotiable instrument, such as a check, which permits the instrument to be transferred.

enticement: coaxing or persuading a person to do an unlawful act.

entrapment: the act by a police officer of inducing a person to commit a crime so he can be arrested.

equal protection of the laws: the constitutional requirement that laws apply uniformly to all citizens.

equity: a supplemental legal system for resolving disputes based on weighing relative merits, fairness, justice, etc.

escrow: the holding of documents or money by a neutral party pursuant to instructions from two or more other parties.

estate: all property a person owns or has an interest in.

estate planning: the application of legal, tax, and financial considerations to enlarge, preserve, and distribute a person's estate.

estoppel: the legal doctrine that prevents a person from taking certain action or taking a certain legal position, because of his previous acts or statements.

eviction: the legal removal of a person (usually a tenant) from real property, pursuant to judgment.

evidence: testimony or documents used at trial for the purpose of proving or disproving facts.

exclusive listing: a contract that gives a real estate broker the sole right to list real property for sale.

execute: to sign a document; to perform the terms of a contract.

executor: the person named in a will to handle the estate during probate period. (*executrix*: a female executor.)

exemplary damages: damages awarded to punish a defendant or make an example of him.

ex parte: a court order issued to one party to an action without the other party being present.

ex post facto: a law passed after an act has occurred which makes that act illegal at the time it was committed.

express contract: a contract the terms of which are spelled out either orally or in writing.

express warranty: a warranty, the terms of which are spelled out either orally or in writing.

extortion: the act of unlawfully depriving a person of something of value by means of threats or blackmail.

extradition: the delivery of a prisoner by one state or nation to the government of another state or nation.

false arrest: the illegal arrest and detention of a person.

false imprisonment: any unlawful detention of a person.

false pretenses: false statements made to defraud a person of money or property.

federal courts: the courts of the United States.

fee simple: full legal title to real property.

felon: one convicted of a felony.

felony: a serious crime that requires a sentence to a federal or state prison for a year or more.

fiduciary: a person holding property in the manner of a trustee such as an executor, guardian, agent, or trustee.

Fifth Amendment rights: those rights guaranteed by the Fifth Amendment to the United States Constitution.

fixtures: equipment, furnishings, or appliances permanently affixed to a building.

foreclosure: the taking over of title to property by the person who holds a mortgage or deed of trust.

foreman: the leader of a jury either appointed by the court or elected by fellow jurors.

forgery: the unauthorized and fraudulent signing of another's name, or alteration of a written legal document.

former jeopardy: a plea entered by an accused in a criminal action who claims he was previously tried for the same crime (see double jeopardy).

franchise: the exclusive right to do business in a certain area, or to operate a specific business.

fraud: the intentional making of a false statement in order to mislead another person to his detriment.

freehold: legal title to land.

garnishment: the seizing or attaching of money or wages of a person.

gift in contemplation of death: under U.S. tax law, a gift given by a donor who believes he is dying.

gift tax: a tax imposed by the federal government and by states on gifts of more than a certain minimum amount.

goodwill: the extra value of a well-run or well-known business.

grand jury: a body of citizens who hear the presentation of evidence by a prosecuting attorney, in secret session, and determine whether or not criminal charges should be brought against someone based on such testimony.

grand larceny: theft of property worth more than a certain value.

grantee: the person to whom property is deeded.

gross negligence: conduct which under the law is reckless or extremely careless.

guarantee (guaranty): a promise to remedy a defect or to pay the obligation of another.

guarantor: the person who makes a guarantee.

guardian: a person appointed by a court to manage and protect the person or estate of another individual.

guardian ad litem: a special or temporary guardian appointed for a particular purpose.

guardianship: the relationship between guardian and ward created by the order of a court.

habeas corpus: ("you have the body"). A court order requiring a prisoner to be brought to court to determine whether or not he is being legally held.

hearsay: testimony by a witness concerning what another person has said who is not present in court and subject to cross-examination, which testimony is offered to prove the truth of what was said out of court.

heir: one who receives the property of a deceased person.

holder in due course: a person who receives a negotiable instrument and is able to pass title to it.

holographic will: a will written, dated, and signed entirely by the testator in his own handwriting.

homestead: a method of protecting one's home from creditors by filing a written legal document.

homicide: the killing of one human being by another.

homosexuality: sexual desire between persons of the same sex.

hypothecate: to pledge personal property.

impanel: to select jurors to try a case.

impeach: to challenge the credibility of a witness.

implied contract: an agreement imposed upon persons by their conduct, or by law.

inadmissible: testimony or documents that cannot be received in evidence.

incest: sexual relations between persons who are so closely related by blood that the law declares the same to be illegal.

incompetency: the lack of legal ability to manage one's own affairs.

indemnity: the agreement of one person to protect another against loss or damage.

indictment: a formal written charge that accuses a person of criminal conduct.

information: a written accusation of criminal conduct presented by a prosecutor.

injunction: a court order prohibiting or requiring certain action

inquest: the inquiry into the cause of death under suspicious circumstances.

insanity: lack of mental capacity to a degree that prevents a person from being legally responsible for his actions.

insolvency: the condition of a person or business having debts that exceed assets.

interlocutory: a temporary or interim ruling by a court, prior to its final decision.

interpleader: the depositing into court by one party of money or property over which two other parties are fighting.

interrogatories: written questions that must be answered in writing, under oath.

intervivos trust: a "living trust," created by the trustor during his lifetime.

intestate: the status of having died without leaving a will.

joint tenants: persons who own an equal interest in the same property. On death the property goes to the survivor.

joint will: a single will executed by two persons together at the same time.

judgment creditor: a person who has won a money judgment in a lawsuit.

judgment lien: a lien on property resulting from judgment after trial.

judicial notice: the acceptance by a court of certain facts without necessity of proof.

jumping bail: the failure of a person who has posted cash bail or bond bail with a court to show up in court at the time required.

jurisdiction: the legal authority of a court to try a case.

jurisprudence: a system of laws; the philosophy of law.

jurist: a person skilled in the law who has served as a judge or written on legal topics.

jury: a group of people selected to hear a civil or criminal case and act as judges.

juvenile court: a court having jurisdiction over minors.

kangaroo court: a court in which a fair trial is impossible either because of the lack of any legal authority to try a case or because of the total absence of due process.

kidnapping: moving or making another person move, against his will, by means of force or threats.

laches: the failure to act within a reasonable time, causing a loss of legal rights.

lapsed policy: an insurance policy terminated for nonpayment of premiums.

larceny: the unlawful taking of another person's property.

last clear chance: the existence of an opportunity to avoid injuring a person who has carelessly placed himself in a perilous position.

lease: a contract giving a "tenant" or "lessee" the right to use the property of another person ("landlord" or "lessor").

legacy: property left to someone in a will.

legatee: the person who receives a legacy under a will.

lessee: a tenant; the person who leases property from the owner.

lessor: a landlord; one who owns and leases property to a tenant.

letters of administration: a document issued by a court giving an administrator the authority to administer the estate of a decedent.

letters testamentary: a document issued by a court giving to the executor named in a will the authority to administer a decedent's estate.

level premium insurance: life insurance, the cost of which is paid evenly over the life of the policy.

leverage: purchase of a large asset using a small amount of capital by borrowing the remainder and using the income to amortize the loan.

liable: responsible under the law.

libel: a defamatory statement or picture that damages a person's reputation.

lien: a claim against property.

life estate: an interest in property which lasts for the lifetime of some person.

life expectancy: the average number of years of life remaining for a person of a given age.

life tenant: a person entitled to enjoy the use of property during his lifetime.

limited partnership: a partnership where in addition to one or more general partners there are limited partners, so called because they contribute cash or property to the partnership, take no part in managing the business, and are not liable for the partnership debts beyond the amount of their contributions.

liquidated damages: a certain amount of money which parties to a contract agree shall be paid in settlement if there is a breach.

lis pendens: ("pending suit"). A notice (recorded) advising everyone that an action affecting property has been filed.

litigant: a party to a lawsuit.

litigation: the carrying on of a lawsuit or legal proceeding.

living trust: a trust that becomes effective during the lifetime of a person creating it.

loitering: lingering or standing around without apparent purpose.

malfeasance: the wrongful performance of a duty.

malice: the intent to do wrong.

malicious mischief: the wrongful and intentional destruction of property.

malicious prosecution: the bringing of civil or criminal charges against a person without reasonable grounds, and with intent to harrass or annoy him.

malpractice: negligent or improper conduct on the part of a professional person.

mandamus action: a suit brought to obtain a court order requiring certain action on the part of a governmental official.

manslaughter: the unlawful killing of a person, without malice.

maturity: the date on which a loan becomes due and must be paid.

mayhem: cutting or otherwise disfiguring a person.

mechanic's lien: a claim against real property for services, labor, or materials.

merger: the bringing together of two corporations where one of them continues in business with the combined assets of the two.

minor: a person below the legal age of an adult.

Miranda warnings: the warnings concerning right to counsel and other rights which must be given by police to a suspect in a criminal case prior to interrogation.

misdemeanor: a violation of law, less serious than a felony, calling for a maximum penalty of one year in jail.

misfeasance: the improper performance of a lawful act.

misprision: failure to act to prevent a crime or to bring a criminal to justice.

mistrial: a trial that is terminated or declared invalid because of some procedural matter.

mortgage: an instrument or process by which property is put up as security for a loan.

municipal: pertaining to a city, town, or village.

murder: the intentional and unlawful killing of a person.

mutuality of remedy: a doctrine in the law of contracts which requires a contract to be enforceable by both parties, not just by one.

necessaries: things such as rent, food, clothing, and medical attention, required to maintain a standard of living.

negligence: the failure, under the law, to use reasonable care to avoid accidents or injuries involving self or others.

negotiable instrument: a written document such as a check which may be transferred by endorsement and delivery.

nolo contendere: ("I do not wish to contest"). A plea in a criminal action by a defendant who will not contest the charge. It has the same legal effect as a plea of guilty.

nonsupport: failure to maintain or provide for spouse or children.

notary public: a public official authorized to administer oaths and witness execution of written documents.

novation: a new contract which takes the place of one previously made.

nuisance: a thing that causes annoyance, disturbance, or damage to adjoining property, to nearby individuals, or to the general public, generally arising from some use of property.

nuncupative will: an oral will by which a person attempts to dispose of his property just before death. It is invalid in most states.

obscene: in the legal sense, something that is vulgar and offensive to ordinary people.

obstruction of justice: any act that tends to interfere with the administration of justice or enforcement of the law.

offense: an illegal act.

offer: a proposal which is the basis of a contract.

option: the right to purchase another's property for a certain price, within a certain time.

O.R.: "own recognizance"; release of a prisoner without bail, based on his promise to return.

ordinary life insurance: life insurance with the policy premiums paid throughout the lifetime of the insured.

pandering: making a profit from the vices of others.

parol evidence: oral statements.

parol evidence rule: a rule of evidence which permits oral testimony to explain apparent ambiguities in a written document.

parole: the shortening of a sentence conditioned upon good behavior.

party-crashing: a form of trespass; entering a residence without an invitation during a party.

party wall: a wall on a property boundary line that separates two ownerships. Ownership of the wall is shared by the two adjoining property owners.

patent: a grant by the government to an inventor of the exclusive right to use an invention.

paternity: a legal proceeding in which an unwed mother accuses a man of fathering her child.

per capita: ("by the head"). A method of distributing property among heirs of a decedent that results in an equal share of the estate going to all those equally related to the decedent.

peremptory challenge: the objection to the serving of a particular juror, without any cause.

perjury: lying under oath.

personal property: movable items such as furniture, clothing, automobiles, etc.

per stirpes: ("by the root"). A method of distributing property of a decedent among his heirs that results in children dividing equally among themselves the share the deceased parent would have received had said parent survived.

petition: a written request for action or relief generally addressed to a court or governmental body.

pimping: soliciting cutomers for a prostitute.

plaintiff: the complaining party in a civil lawsuit.

plea: an answer filed by a defendant to a criminal charge.

plea-bargaining: the process by which the prosecutor and the defense attorney bargain for dismissal of some charge in exchange for a plea of guilty to another charge.

pleading: a written document filed by a plaintiff or defendant in a legal action.

pledge: the delivery of property as security for repayment of a debt.

pornography: literature, art, photographs, or motion pictures which consist of obscene material.

pour-over will: a will designed to distribute the residue of a decedent's estate to a trust created by the decedent during his lifetime.

power of attorney: a written authorization by one person designating another to act in his behalf.

precedent: a court decision that sets an example to be followed in similar cases arising thereafter.

preference: in bankruptcy law the favoring of one creditor over other creditors.

preferred stock: stock that entitles the owners to preference in payment of dividends over owners of common stock.

pretermited heir: an offspring not mentioned in a will.

prima facie: clear; self-evident.

principal: in criminal law, the person most actively and directly involved in commission of a crime.

privileged communication: an exchange of information between two persons where their relationship is such that the information is confidential and neither party can be forced to reveal it. Examples include attorney and client, doctor and patient, husband and wife, etc.

probate: the process by which a court authenticates the last will of a decedent and supervises administration and distribution of his estate.

probation: the release of a crimal with a sentence suspended, conditioned upon good behavior.

503

procedural due process: the conducting of a trial in such a manner that the constitutional rights of the defendant are fully observed.

profanity: the use, in public, of speech that is vulgar and offensive to a normal person.

promissory note: a written document signed by a person who promises to pay a certain sum of money to another person on a certain date, or on demand.

prosecute: to commence and pursue a legal action against a defendant.

prosecutor: a public official whose duty it is to bring criminal actions against those accused of crimes.

prospectus: a document that describes stocks or other investment securities being offered for sale to the public.

prostitution: the exchange or offer to exchange sexual activity for money.

proximate cause: a legal term that describes the relationship between an act and the injury or damage that results from the act.

proxy: the authorization to vote on behalf of another person.

public defender: a public official whose duty it is to defend persons accused of crimes who cannot afford their own lawyer.

punitive damages: damages awarded merely to punish a wrongdoer.

quasi-community property: property that is brought into a community property state and in that state is thereafter treated as community property.

quasi-contract: a contract based on the implied (not expressed) intent of the parties.

quiet title: a legal action to resolve a dispute over title to real property.

quitclaim deed: a written document by which a person transfers whatever interest or title he has in a piece of real property, to another.

quorum: the minimum number of members necessary to constitute a legal meeting.

rape: forcible sexual intercourse with a woman without her consent.

real property: land and structures affixed to the land.

rebuttal: the answer to a charge, evidence, or an argument, by the presentation of evidence or argument to the contrary.

receiver: an official appointed by a court to take over and manage property under supervision of the court.

recess: a short adjournment of the court.

recidivism: repeated relapse into criminal activity.

recrimination: to bring a countercharge against an accuser.

referee: a court official, either permanent or temporary, who acts as a judge in hearing certain legal disputes or in handling certain legal proceedings.

rehabilitation: improvement in the conduct of a convicted criminal.

remainderman: a person designated in a trust to receive the principal or residue of the trust at its termination.

remand: to send a case back to a lower court for correction action.

replevin: a legal action to recover possession of property that was wrongfully taken.

rescission: the cancellation of a contract.

residuary estate: the portion of a decedent's estate that is left after the payment of debts, expenses of administration, and the distribution of specific bequests.

resisting arrest: any act, including "going limp," that obstructs or interferes with the attempt of a law officer or private citizen to make an arrest.

restraint of trade: the practice of restricting competition in order to increase profits.

retainer: the payment of an advance fee by a client to his attorney.

reversionary interest: the right to future enjoyment of property after the present owner's interest terminates.

revocation of will: a formal act by a person which indicates that the will he previously executed is no longer valid.

riot: a massive or violent disturbance of the peace involving many persons.

riparian rights: the rights of an owner of land bordering on a stream to use the water from the stream.

robbery: the taking of money or property from a person by means of force or threats.

sabotage: politically inspired destruction of machinery, goods, or buildings.

satisfaction of judgment: a document stating that a judgment has been paid.

search warrant: a written court order permitting an officer to search specified premises and to seize certain evidence if found there.

second mortgage: a mortgage which is junior in priority, having been recorded later in time than a first mortgage.

security: a written document evidencing ownership of, or an interest in property.

sedition: action promoting discontent, intended to bring about the overthrow of government.

self-defense: the right to use force to protect one's person against attack.

sentence: the judgment of a court awarding punishment.

separate maintenance: legal separation of husband and wife; money paid by one spouse to another where they are living apart.

settlement option: one of the ways the beneficiary of an insurance policy may select to receive the proceeds.

severance damages: damage to the remainder of a parcel of real property where part is taken by condemnation.

shoplifting: stealing items from a store.

slander: oral statements that injure a person's reputation.

solicitation: urging another person to commit a crime.

specific performance: the carrying out of a contract in the agreed manner.

Star Chamber: a court which proceeds by unfair methods, without due process, and which imposes severe sentences.

statute: a written law.

statute of frauds: a written law requiring certain contracts to be in writing.

statute of limitations: a written law setting certain time limits within which certain sections must be brought.

statutory rape: sexual intercourse with a female below a certain age, set by statute in each state.

stipulation: an agreement by both sides to the finding of a certain fact or to the entering of an order.

stock cooperative: a corporation set up to own an apartment house with each stockholder having the right to use a certain apartment.

subornation of perjury: inducing another person to offer false testimony.

subpoena: a court order requiring a witness to appear and testify.

subpoena duces tecum: a court order requiring the production of documents for inspection.

substantive due process: a constitutional requirement of justice, fairness, and reasonableness in the passage of laws.

substantive law: basic legal theory, as opposed to mere legal procedure.

summary judgment: a speedy judgment entered on the basis of undisputed facts, without a trial.

summons: a written document notifying a defendant that he has been sued and that he must appear or answer within a certain time.

surety: guaranteeing the debt of another.

surrogate: in some states, the title of a judge or county officer who presides over probate court.

syndicate: a group of investors who pool their capital to purchase assets.

tenants by the entirety: a method of holding title to real property applicable in certain states.

tenants in common: persons who hold title to the same real property, with the share of each passing to his heirs upon his death.

term insurance: life insurance in which the policy is issued for a particular period of time, and a single premium is paid to cover just the cost of the insurance for that length of time.

term rider: a provision in a life insurance policy which provides special additional coverage for payment of a small additional premium.

testament: a will.

testamentary trust: a trust created by a will and put into effect after death.

testate: the status of a person who left a will when he died.

testator: a person who makes a will.

test case: a case that is brought to test the constitutionality of a particular law.

testify: to give oral evidence under oath.

theft: stealing of property belonging to another.

title search: examination of recorded documents to determine the status of title to real property.

tort: a wrongful act of omission that causes injury to the person or property of another.

tort feasor: a person who commits a tort.

trademark: a design, mark, or label that appears on manufactured goods to distinguish them from other goods.

transcript: a written copy of court proceedings.

treason: betrayal of one's own country.

trespass: the unlawful intrusion upon the property of another.

truancy: unauthorized absence from school.

trust: a legal relationship in which a trustee is given property by a trustor to hold for a beneficiary.

trustee: the person or entity holding property in trust.

trustor: the person who creates a trust.

unconstitutional: contrary to the Constitution of the United States or of any state.

unilateral contract: an agreement in which only one of the two parties promises to do something.

unlawful assembly: the gathering together of a group of people at a time and place that is contrary to a lawful order issued by a proper authority.

unlawful detainer: an action brought by a landlord to dispossess a tenant who continues to hold possession of real property without the right to do so.

use permit: a permit granted by a local government to a property owner, authorizing him to use real property in a manner not otherwise permitted under the zoning laws.

usury: the collection of interest on a loan at a rate higher than that permitted by law.

vagrancy: the conduct of an idle person who is without home, job, or money.

valid: legally proper and effective.

vandalism: the deliberate and malicious damage or destruction of property.

variance: authorization from a local governing body to build a building in a manner otherwise not permitted by local building or zoning laws.

vendee: one who buys.

vendor: one who sells.

venire: a group of citizens called for jury duty.

venireman: a person called for jury duty.

venue: the proper place for a legal proceeding.

verdict: the decision or finding of a jury.

verification: a sworn affidavit confirming the contents of a document.

vest: to become fixed; the creation of a right of ownership.

void: without legal force of effect.

voidable: a document or contract that can be legally set aside.

voir dire: ("to say the truth"). The preliminary questioning of a witness or potential juror to see if he is qualified to testify or to sit on the jury.

voluntary manslaughter: homicide committed by violent action but without intent to kill.

waive: to abandon, repudiate, or surrender a privilege or right.

wanton: extremely reckless.

ward: a person placed under the care of a guardian or a court.

warrant: a written document issued by a judge authorizing the arrest of a person or the seizure of property.

warranty: a promise that title is good or that goods are not defective.

waste: wrongful destruction of property by one in possession, such as a tenant.

whiplash: an injury to neck or spinal column caused by the sudden jerking back and forth of a body involved in an automobile accident.

whole life insurance: life insurance with the premiums paid throughout the lifetime of the insured.

without recourse: an endorsement of a negotiable instrument that limits the liability of the endorser.

will: a legal instrument that provides for the disposition of one's property, after death.

willful: intentional and deliberate conduct.

witness: a person called to testify in a legal proceeding as to events he has seen or has personal knowledge of.

writ: a court order requiring certain action.

Index